INTERPRETING INDONESIAN POLITICS:

THIRTEEN CONTRIBUTIONS TO THE DEBATE

Edited by

Benedict Anderson and Audrey Kahin

INTERIM REPORTS SERIES

(Publication No. 62)

Cornell Modern Indonesia Project
Southeast Asia Program
Cornell University
Ithaca, New York
1982

Price: $9.00

"Democracy in Indonesia" by Harry J. Benda, and "History, Theory, and Indonesian Politics," by Herbert Feith are reprinted from *The Journal of Asian Studies* (May 1964, pp. 449-56; and February 1965, pp. 305-12) by permission of the Association for Asian Studies. © 1964, 1965.

"Ideology and Social Structure in Indonesia" by Joel S. Kahn is reprinted from *Comparative Studies in Society and History* (1978, pp. 103-22) by permission of Cambridge University Press. © 1978 by the Society for the Comparative Study of Society and History.

"Indonesia Since 1945--Problems of Interpretation" by Jamie Mackie first appeared in *Contemporary Indonesia: Political Dimension* (Clayton: Monash University, 1979), and is republished with permission of the Centre of Southeast Asian Studies at Monash University.

© 1982, Cornell Modern Indonesia Project

ISBN 0-87763-028-3

TABLE OF CONTENTS

Introduction
    Daniel S. Lev v

The Birth of the Idea of Bali (1976)
    James A. Boon 1

Democracy in Indonesia (1964)
    Harry J. Benda 13

History, Theory, and Indonesian Politics: A Reply to
Harry J. Benda (1965)
    Herbert Feith 22

History and Social Structure in the Study of Contemporary
Indonesia (1969)
    David Levine 30

The Study of Indonesian Politics: A Survey and an Apologia (1969)
    Herbert Feith 41

Class, Social Cleavage and Indonesian Communism (1969)
    Rex Mortimer 54

Perspective and Method in American Research on Indonesia (1973)
    Benedict O'Gorman Anderson 69

The Beamtenstaat in Indonesia (1977)
    Ruth T. McVey 84

Ideology and Social Structure in Indonesia (1978)
    Joel S. Kahn 92

Indonesia's New Order as a Bureaucratic Polity, a Neopatrimonial
Regime or a Bureaucratic Authoritarian Regime: What Difference
Does It Make? (1979)
    Dwight Y. King 104

Indonesia Since 1945--Problems of Interpretation (1979)
    Jamie Mackie 117

Culture, Politics, and Economy in the Political History of the
New Order (1981)
    Richard Robison 131

Orders of Meaning: Understanding Political Change in a Fishing
Community in Indonesia (1975)
    Donald K. Emmerson 149

EDITORS' NOTE

Over the past two decades there has been a continuing debate among Western scholars concerning the nature of Indonesian politics and the best approaches for understanding them. Several of the most important contributions to this debate were never published and others have gone out of print. Thus, it has been difficult for a new generation of students of Indonesia to be aware of the range of opinions and discussion in Western academic circles concerning the character of postrevolutionary Indonesian politics. For this reason, it appeared to us useful to bring together a series of articles that can provide a framework for understanding the evolution of these perspectives. Clearly, we could not include all the important contributions to the debate, and this selection has been made on the basis of the best representation of differing views over time.

In general the pieces appear in chronological sequence in order to delineate more clearly the evolution of the debate. To maintain this chronological development we have also made no changes in the arguments as originally presented, nor, with one exception, permitted the authors to do so, even when they have altered their opinions since originally writing the essays. Passages, however, have occasionally been cut from published articles where they are too repetitive, or where they are not relevant to the major themes being presented here. All such omissions are indicated by a series of dots (. . .). Because of the continuing nature of the debate, the collection is being published as an Interim Report which we hope will stimulate further reactions and analyses.

In addition to the sources listed on the copyright page, four of the articles initially appeared in *Indonesia*. James Boon's appeared in No. 22 (October 1976); David Levine's in No. 7 (April 1969); Rex Mortimer's in No. 8 (October 1969), and Richard Robison's in No. 31 (April 1981).

Five of the articles were only circulated in mimeographed form to colleagues and have not previously appeared in print. These are the essays by Herbert Feith (1969), Benedict Anderson (1973), Ruth McVey (1977), Dwight King (1979), and Donald Emmerson (1979).

INTRODUCTION

The papers in this collection contain the most seminal theoretical thinking about Indonesian politics to have appeared over the past two decades. Some of them have been published before, some not. They have been brought together here in order to make them conveniently available to any who want to understand the evolution of perspectives on Indonesian politics or to contribute further to it. The volume is presented in the same spirit in which the papers were originally written, not to foreclose argument but to open up new approaches to analysis and explanation. There is no finality, but only an effort to know, more or less, where we are in the study of Indonesia.

In selecting the papers the editors, Benedict Anderson and Audrey Kahin, were less concerned with simple consistency of subject matter than with the variety of interpretations and issues that have emerged. What binds the contributions together is a central core of reflection about how foreign scholars have gone about trying to understand Indonesia. But for the rest, the authors are variously occupied. In the first paper Boon describes the enduring influence over three centuries of views of Balinese culture drawn from the tales of early travelers who saw the island through the cultural filters of Christian Europe and Hindu India. The following papers by Benda, Feith, Levine, Mortimer, and Anderson are concerned with related problems of "interpretive frameworks" in their modern academic form. Each deals critically with conceptual approaches to the study of politics in independent Indonesia and the intellectual and ideological influences that have gone into their making. In the next five papers, however, McVey, Kahn, King, Mackie, and Robison concentrate more on Indonesia than on its observers. They are primarily concerned with the contemporary realities of the New Order and appropriate models for interpreting them. Finally, in the last paper, Emmerson, analyzing an episode of violence in an East Javanese fishing community, combines the main emphases above by contrasting the perceptions of village fishermen, officials, and social scientists.

On the whole, there are few false notes in these papers and little of the opaque conceptualizing that clutters much of modern social science. The basic reason, I suspect, is that all but one of the authors had done extensive field research in Indonesia and knew the country as well as any foreigner can; only Levine, commenting from a distance on the work of others, had not. All were aware, when they wrote, of just how complex and hard to reduce Indonesia is; none was about to play fast and loose with Indonesian realities, as nearly as anyone can understand them, merely for the sake of an elegant theory. Indonesian studies, moreover, have had an advantage in the respectable number of foreign Indonesian scholars who have been seriously engaged long enough to react critically to nonsense, not much of which has survived long in the growing literature.

The selections begin, chronologically, only in 1964, but the analytical issues that arose then and later were quietly adumbrated in earlier research. During the 1950s social science scholarship on Indonesia was dominated intellectually by three figures: the political scientist George McT. Kahin, who developed Indonesian studies in the United States; the Dutch sociologist W. F. Wertheim, whose experience bridged colonial and independent Indonesia; and the North American anthropologist

Clifford Geertz, who began his research in Java during the early 1950s. At the time, too little research had been done on postrevolutionary Indonesia to inspire much of a debate over interpretations. Yet the original empirical work of Kahin, Wertheim, and Geertz did imply different emphases that can be traced in the theoretical arguments that developed later. Kahin, while sensitive to the cultural, economic, and social environment of Indonesian politics, favored careful, detailed, historical analysis. Wertheim's concern was the evolution of Indonesian social structure, with a humane Marxist appreciation of class conflict. Geertz, whose ideas have nourished several generations of Indonesianists, concentrated on the interior meanings of Javanese culture and their connections with economic and social change. Kahin, Wertheim, and Geertz set an example of sound empirical research, unimpressed by artificial disciplinary boundaries and free of gratuitous theorizing in the void, to which Indonesian studies have, by and large, remained faithful. Although none of their writings are included in this volume, they have had influence on most of the papers in it.

These papers are particularly interesting, as a collection, because they are so much a part of the times through which Indonesia and the rest of the world have been living. Turmoil and change, not stability and continuity, make for debates over analytical approaches. The early postrevolutionary period, even apart from the paucity of research to argue about, was not likely to have caused much of a debate. Had the relatively mild times of the 1950s continued, in Indonesia and elsewhere, many of the papers in this volume probably would not have been written. As it was, what happened in Indonesia from the late 1950s on, and nearly everywhere else from the late 1960s on, made divergent interpretations all but inescapable.

The ideological tumult of the Viet-Nam war era alone might have set off some debate about Indonesia, as it did about other countries. Few Indonesianists were ever fully in step with the "development" research that used to dominate much of the scholarship on new states, but the gradual collapse of so many common intellectual and analytical myths, beginning in the late 1960s, did have a noticeable effect on them. It took the form, generally, of growing skepticism, even some cynicism, not only about "development," whatever it might mean, but all the current models of change and the good society, the good faith of political leaders, the purposes of the great powers, and even the inspiration and uses of scholarship. In addition, the unraveling of methodological and ideological understandings led to a revived intellectual interest in Marxism, slightly freed from earlier revolutionary optimism, which began to show up in the work of younger scholars particularly, a growing number of whom were trained in universities outside the United States.

But developments within Indonesia had their own profound influence on the thinking of Indonesianists. Political change was rapid, and ideological change dramatic, as the parliamentary system gave way in 1957-58 to Guided Democracy, which was itself torn apart in bloody cataclysm following the coup of 1965 and replaced by the army's New Order. These transformations made the notion of Indonesianist generations quite real, as different entry points into Indonesian experience gave rise to divergent initial perceptions and perspectives. Whether one began to do research in Indonesia during the early 1950s, the early 1960s, or the early 1970s could not help but color one's understandings, sympathies, and approaches.

Theoretical issues, moreover, arose almost spontaneously out of questions posed, more or less sharply, by the politics of each period. If the papers in this volume are read in chronological order, they follow roughly the progression of regime changes. It is not surprising that the debate began, between Benda and

Feith, over the problematic failure of the parliamentary system, at a time when Guided Democracy was in full swing. Guided Democracy did not inspire new analytical constructs so much as, by its own peculiar involution, it encouraged a turn towards Indonesian perspectives, internal textures, symbols, values, and political detail; failing other stable patterns, the implied theoretical emphasis was on cultural continuity. During this time Geertz's work on Javanese culture had its greatest impact, and Anderson began the research which later produced several influential interpretive essays on values and politics in Indonesia.

The major divide, in interpretations as in Indonesian politics, was between Guided Democracy and the New Order, a decisive break in modern Indonesian history. The parliamentary system and Guided Democracy, for different reasons, had elicited the sympathy of many scholars. But the New Order, perhaps because of its origins in the mayhem of 1965, its military presence, and its evident movement away from a familiar old world towards an equally familiar but in some ways less likeable new one, drew less sympathy, more jaundice, and a great deal more open criticism from many knowledgeable scholars of all analytical persuasions. As New Order leaders themselves were prepared to give up Soekarno's claim to going Indonesia's own way and fall in with the world of "developing" states, the barriers seemed to come down on applying standard comparative social science approaches to Indonesia. Suddenly, it was as if work done on other countries in Asia, Africa, and South America had become more relevant, and concepts such as those dealt with by King showed up more frequently in the literature on Indonesia. The principal innovation, however, borne along mainly by non-American scholars, was Marxist analysis, whose tone, subsequent to Levine's criticism of earlier studies and Mortimer's discussion of Communist difficulties with class structure, became increasingly insistent and full-blown. New Order policies and the kinds of change they promoted logically raised questions about the bases of poverty, peasant and labor disabilities, class interests, economic distribution, the influence of international markets, and much else well suited to Marxist explanations. Unlike almost all other work on Indonesia, with the possible exception of development economics, Marxist analysis came equipped with a whole tradition of theoretical exegesis, evident in the papers by Kahn and Robison, that transcended (though without ignoring) the Indonesian peculiarities which fascinated competing analytical orientations. While less relativist and more dogmatic than earlier interpretive views of Indonesian state and society, Marxist perspectives are proving to be rich sources of insight on problems that other approaches do not address so directly.

Between some of the perspectives, particularly those that emphasize culture on the one hand and political-economy on the other, there is a natural and useful tension. It can easily be exaggerated, however, even by mentioning it. As the footnotes and texts throughout this volume show, there has been more respectful intellectual borrowing and less brittle polemics than one expects from paradigmatic arguments. It was mentioned earlier that the volume does not pretend to be the final word on interpretations of anything Indonesian. With the accumulation of knowledge and experience, we can rely now on a body of literature that allows more leeway of interpretation, and more control over shallow interpretation, than ever before. But if the usual test of a theory is whether it explains significantly more than competing theories do, the views represented in this collection seem so far, paradoxically, to have acquitted themselves reasonably well. On the merits, at least, academic hubris to the contrary notwithstanding, it would be very difficult to argue for a headlong rush to one view or another. In any case, the inherent complexity of Indonesia, and perhaps the inherent limits of social science, make anything of the sort unlikely.

If something is obviously missing among the selected works, it is the writing of Indonesian scholars. Social scientists in Indonesia have not yet written a great deal in the "perspective" mode, partly no doubt because they have had to live through the changes since the revolution and are, of course, more intimately involved in them than foreign scholars. This is not the essential point, however, and several papers from Indonesia might have been considered. But this volume really views Indonesia from outside. Despite the usual myths of science, analytical perspectives inevitably originate in disparate inspirations and serve disparate purposes. The ideas presented here have been influenced by help and criticism from Indonesian colleagues, and they may have had some intellectual influence in Indonesia, but they are essentially part of the history of foreign scholarship on Indonesia.

Daniel S. Lev

THE BIRTH OF THE IDEA OF BALI*

James A. Boon

Cultures are not captured by simple empirical reportage; least of all Bali. Cultures are fabricated by matching available ideas and images against the daily lives and historical conditions of elusive isolates in time and space. For this reason ethnology straddles the history of ideas. And this is as true today as in the sixteenth century.

Any holistic ethnological image is distorted, since it necessarily preselects certain features of a cross-cultural encounter for extra emphasis. To typify an entire culture by glossing its political authority (e.g., "a kingdom") or its general subsistence (e.g., "a peasantry"), or to characterize it as a collection of "village communities" or some alternative abstraction is often to omit important aspects of the self-conceptions of the inhabitants themselves or some sector of them. Moreover, an ethnological blazon, especially if hastily contrived, can lock in general perspectives on a culture which may endure for centuries and confine the questions asked by informed visitors who have inevitably been briefed by the limited accounts available to them. Bali--so rich an ethnographic terrain in matters of religion, subsistence, marriage, and hierarchy--also generated a provocative set of typifying efforts by the earliest European explorers to come in contact with it. Just why the first Dutch observers (and their first English copyist) were obliged to construe Bali as a benevolent monarchy with harmonious subjects is a complex topic for social, political, and colonial history. Our aim here is merely to help prepare the ground for such studies by perusing the vivid stereotypes and conceptual footholds through which the earliest observers generated an ethnological idea to encompass their distinctive contact experience. The "Bali" that emerged, partly as a reflex of sixteenth and seventeenth century expectations and preconceptions, endured for a long time; and it has not been altogether abandoned today.

---

* This study is a somewhat altered version of a section in my forthcoming book, *The Anthropological Romance of Bali, 1597-1972: Dynamic Perspectives in Marriage and Caste, Politics and Religion* (Cambridge: Cambridge University Press, in press). Other field studies that relate to its themes are James A. Boon, "The Progress of the Ancestors in a Balinese Temple Group (pre-1906-1972)," *The Journal of Asian Studies*, 34, 1 (1974), pp. 7-25; and Boon, "The Balinese Marriage Predicament: Individual, Strategical, Cultural," *American Ethnologist*, 3, 2 (1976), pp. 191-214. Many thanks to Ben Anderson for detailed comments on an earlier draft, to Jim Siegel for the opportunity to present the material to Cornell's Southeast Asia Program and Modern Indonesia Project, and to Clifford Geertz for allowing me to discuss it at the Institute for Advanced Study, Princeton. I also acknowledge with gratitude support from the Wenner-Gren Foundation for Anthropological Research.

From the Anecdotal to the Sensational

The first images of Balinese culture were happily inscribed on western consciousness following a stop there in 1597 by Cornelis de Houtman's renowned *eerste schipvaart* to the East Indies. Evidence exists that Magellan's expedition had sighted "Java Minor" some eighty years earlier, that the Portuguese had contacted Bali at mid-century, and that Sir Francis Drake and Thomas Cavendish predated Houtman's arrival by a few years.[1] The island's name was known from a list of the Lesser Sundas obtained in 1521 by Magellan's scribe Pigafetta.[2] But the initial representations of Balinese customs to enter the western record were both fruits of Houtman's final, perhaps least productive, and definitely most appealing stop.

Most twentieth century commentators on the history of Dutch-Balinese relations draw pleasure from the fact that they began not with a shot, but a seduction:

> The island had nothing to offer in the form of trade, but there were other attractions--a carefree way of life and comely women. . . . Two young men found these charms irresistible, and the fleet sailed without them.[3]

Covarrubias exaggerates this point in relating that Houtman and his men "fell in love with the island" and "after a long sojourn . . . [they actually stayed less than a month] returned to Holland to report the discovery of the new 'paradise'; others refused to leave Bali."[4] In fact, we have no clear idea why these sailors abandoned their shipmates. The official report on Bali was not quite ecstatic, merely relatively favorable in light of difficulties experienced by the beleaguered expedition in establishing trade agreements in Java. To the weary explorers, Bali became a pause for recuperation before returning home.

Maps and reports of Bali were completed and published by 1598, even though the island appeared useless for the spice trade. Its size and mountainous profile lent themselves well to sixteenth century guides to navigation; Bali's different volcanoes are immediately identifiable from the first drawings. In 1598 a map appeared which illustrated the *raja* and battling armies mentioned in a verbal account.[5] This

---

1. Willard A. Hanna, *Bali and the West*, Fieldstaff Reports, Southeast Asia Series, 12, 14 (New York: American University, 1971), pp. 1-2.

2. Donald F. Lach, *Asia in the Making of Europe*, vol. 1, *The Century of Discovery*, bks. 1 and 2 (Chicago: University of Chicago Press, 1965), p. 2.

3. George Masselman, *The Cradle of Colonialism* (New Haven: Yale University Press, 1963), p. 96.

4. Miguel Covarrubias, *Island of Bali* (New York: Alfred A. Knopf, 1937), p. 29.

5. In the following discussion I employ three volumes of a twentieth century edition by the Linschoten Vereeniging (vols. 7, 25, and 32 of its works) of the sixteenth century accounts: G. P. Rouffaer and J. W. Ijzerman, eds., *De Eerste Schipvaart der Nederlanders Naar Oost-Indië onder Cornelis de Houtman, 1595-1597* (The Hague: Nijhoff, 1915-29); 1, *D'eerste Boeck van Willem Lodewycksz* (1915); 2, *De Oudste Journalen der Reis* (1925); 3, *Verdere Bescheiden Betreffende de Reis* (1929). The modern commentators referred to below are Rouffaer and Ijzerman, who annotate this edition; the English map is reproduced in vol. 2, pp. 89, 202.

A fourth volume compiled by J. C. Mollema, *De Eerste Schipvaart* (The Hague: Nijhoff, 1935), consolidates a chronological account (*relaas*) with more details of the relations among the Dutchmen. Here we read, for example, a speculation as to the (above-mentioned) obscure motives of those who remained in Bali: "It is not com-

chart is called "crude and sloppy" in a modern commentary, but it is better appreciated as a different sort of illustration--a visual caption to communicate that the name "Baly" stood for a mountainous, many-rivered, war-waging island. Moreover, this conceptual portrait accurately situates the sacred mountain Gunung Agung and reveals the complex river drainage through the southern plains.

In 1625, the first thoroughgoing English summary of Dutch impressions of Bali (which does not forget to mention British claims of prior contact) is included by the Jacobean Samuel Purchas in his edited collection of the discovery literature left unpublished at the death of Richard Hakluyt:

. . . Baly they called Hollandiola, for the fertilitie; there they watered.

> They sent to the King, who accompanied the Messenger to the shoare in a Chariot drawne with Buffals, holding the Whip in his owne hands, having three hundred followers, some with flame-formed Crises and long Speares, Bowes of Canes with poysoned Arrowes. Hee was feasted in Dishes of solid Gold. The Land is an equall and fertile plaine to the West, watered with many little Rivers (some made by hand) and so peopled that the King is able to bring into the field three hundred thousand foot, and one hundred thousand horsemen. Their horse are little like Islanders, their men blacke and using little Merchandize, but with Cotton Cloth in Prawes. The Iland is in compasse about twelve Germane miles. Their Religion is Ethnike, ordered by the Brachmanes or Bramenes, in whose Disciplines the King is trayned up. They have also Banianes which weare about their neckes a stone as bigge as an Egge with a hole in it, whence hang forth three threds; they call it Tambarene, and thinke the Deitie thereby represented: they abstaine from flesh and fish, but not (as the Javan Pythagoreans) from Marriage. Once they may marry, and when they dye their Wives are buried quicke with them. Every seventh day they keepe holy, and many other Holidayes in the yeare besides with solemne Ceremonies. Their Wives burne with their dead Husbands. Here they heard of Captaine Drakes being there eighteene yeares before, and called one Strait by his name. The King observeth state, is spoken to with hands folded, by the best. The Quillon hath power there as the Chancellor in Poland. Two of their companie forsooke them and stayed on the Iland. And of the two hundred fortie nine there were now left but ninetie. In February they began their returne.[6]

Purchas (1625) distilled his overview from the lengthier Dutch logs and journals then published, taking several accompanying plates as guides to the primary features of Balinese life. These early descriptions include William Lodewyckszoon's log of the expedition which appeared in 1598; Steerman Jacob Janszoon Kackerlack's supplementary journal of the same year; and the diary of midshipman Aernout Lintgenszoon, although the availability of the latter's account to the seventeenth century reading public remains obscure.[7]

The most noticeable stylization in Purchas is that the several test stops and hesitating contacts along the Balinese coast described by Lodewycks are condensed into a single grandiose arrival. In Purchas it appears as if the Balinese king and

---

pletely out of the question that the velvet eyes and comely figures of the Balinese maidens made an impression on the two youths" (p. 341).

6. S. Purchas, *Hakluytus Posthumous or Purchas His Pilgrimes* (Glasgow: J. MacLehose and Sons, 1905, reprint of 1625 edition), 5, p. 200.

7. Rouffaer and Ijzerman, *De Eerste Schipvaart*, 1915, 1925, 1929.

his entourage had been awaiting the advent of the worthy West; when actually through the week diverse islanders were leading a depleted crew to water here, an anchorage there, and later asking the sailors if they hailed from the Moluccas.[8] Purchas' sensationalism aimed at evoking a sense of splendiferous trade in commodities in order to revitalize mercantile endeavors under James I and then Charles I. By 1625, Britain's rival was Holland; accordingly Purchas highlighted the glory of Dutch cross-cultural contacts, a glory that by implication could as easily belong to Britain's monarch.

Lodewycks' original lacked such theatrics. For example, to commemorate the initial arrival of Balinese on board a Dutch vessel, he mustered nothing dramatic, merely the simple note that "many inhabitants boarded us."[9] This "first connected description of the island of Bali from the European viewpoint"[10] is relatively straightforward, methodical, and evenhanded. The merchandise-minded sailor mentions the weaving skills of Bali's western province Jembrana; he itemizes fauna, fruit, and metals; he describes weapons and assesses Balinese military strength; and he makes notes on the availability of spices and drugs. Finally we are told that Balinese engage in little or no sea trade and that Chinese come here to exchange swords and porcelain for cloth.

Such pedestrian details aside, Lodewycks' more general views of Bali were limited by the typologies at his disposal. His label of Balinese as "black" may have stemmed from his observation of the Papuan slaves who often boarded the ship *Mauritius*, or it may simply reflect a residual category not directly related to phenotype. Lodewycks knew at least that Balinese were not "Moors"; in fact he alludes to the islanders' religion by deeming them "heathens" who "pray to whatever they first meet in the morning."[11] As the modern commentary explains, "heathen" here means non-Mohammedan, which is the most pertinent observation Lodewycks could have made about Balinese religion, arriving there from coastal Java. Yet his remarks entered the historical record to be repeated, nearly verbatim, a century later in an Englishman's report on Bali: "[the Balinese] are exceeding Brutish People and the Simplest of Heathens. Their God is whatever they first cast their Eye on in the Morning...."[12] Following a century of Protestant reformism, heathen has come

---

8. Such "Demillean" restaging of initial contacts is one of the most tenacious rhetorical devices in the romantic imagery of ethnological literature. It reminds one of the sort of routinized, recurring metaphors called *topoi* by E. R. Curtius in his *European Literature and the Latin Middle Ages* (Princeton: Princeton University Press, 1953), ch. 5. Anthropology's counterpart to topoi such as "the world upside down" or "boy as old man" (*puer senilis*) is "captain greets king" or more recently, "collectivity welcomes fieldworker." The *topos* remains very much with us, as evidenced by a recent television broadcast of a film made of Margaret Mead's return to one of her Pacific islands for a generation-later restudy. Ms. Mead is rowed up in a boat and the jubilant natives run out *en masse* to welcome her (evidently collectively awaited) return. We are not told how she was concealed while the crew got the beach camera into position.

9. Rouffaer and Ijzerman, *De Eerste Schipvaart*, 1915, p. 197.

10. Ibid., p. 197 n.

11. "Zy zijn Heydenen aenbiddende tghene haer des morghens eerst int gomoet comt" (ibid., p. 197). A similar topos appears as early as the writings of Marco Polo. Cf. Harry J. Benda and John A. Larkin, *The World of Southeast Asia, Selected Historical Readings* (New York: Harper and Row, 1967), p. 13.

12. Christopher Frick and Christopher Schweitzer, *Voyages to the East Indies* (London: Cassell, The Seafarers' Library, 1929, first published 1700), p. 109.

to imply "simplest." The same remark that began as a distinction in sectarian types (Christian/Mohammedan/Heathen) has become a proto-evolutionary index of backwardness. Such is the crooked path of "progress" in ethnology.

Kings, not Chiefs

Like his colleagues, Lodewycks found most impressive the office of "king," as observed when the ship's emissaries were conducted to Gelgel. He is most interested in the indigenous royal monopolies of external trade and in policies against the export of rice, to insure that the surplus would be consumed yearly (in elaborate feasts) by the innumerable inhabitants. Apart from this, Lodewycks provides the first simplified, vividly distorted portrait of Bali as an authoritarian maharaja-dom:

> Besides the King is a governor that they call Quillor. He rules over the island as does the great chancellor in Poland. And beneath these stand many other lords, each governing his quarter in the name of the king, which occurs in great harmony (*eendrachticheyt*). . . .[13]

Finally, Lodewycks rounds things off by paraphrasing a royal Balinese chronicle (*babad*), which relates how some years earlier the King's close blood relatives had attempted a conspiracy against him and were subsequently banished to a neighboring island. As we shall see, this native text receives much less attention than the regal splendor of the apparently legitimate King atop his sedan chair, although the chronicle of bloodshed would have served as a more appropriate blazon of Balinese society. Only centuries later, after Berg's work on the sixteenth century Pamancangah texts from Gelgel,[14] did it become completely clear that these first Dutch visitors had stumbled not into a stable realm of an unchallenged divine monarch, but into a generation-long battle between brothers and uncles and nephews for control of the Gelgel palace, marked by disastrous participation in a war in Java:

> When early in 1597 the first Dutchmen arrived at the coast of Blangbangan, the savage war (*woesteoorlog*) between Pasuruhan and Blangbangan was in full swing.[15]

But even as this was recognized, scholars tended to assume this state of affairs was only a temporary lapse in a stable and centralized "golden age" (*glorietijdperk*) rather than the general conditions and mechanics of "statehood" in the Balinese system. The Dutch had skirted in and out and round about a perpetual civil war, only to gain from Bali's ritual surfaces the impression of timeless central authority.

Kackerlack's much briefer piece (1598) goes on explicitly to designate the island of Baly a kingdom (*Coninckrijk*). The regal trappings, complete with scribes and priests, prevented these observers from conceptualizing Bali as tribal chiefdoms such as those known from North America. (Later, however, a chiefly level [*hoofden*] had to be added to handle certain local complexities in the chain of political authority.) Kackerlack dwells on the generosity of the islanders who bear them hogs, ducks, and many fruits and foodstuffs, and the reciprocal Dutch gifts for the King--coral drinking glasses, shoes, mirrors, etc.[16] And he distinguishes what he heard about, such as a king on a buffalo cart, from what he actually observed, such as the lay of the ricefields.

---

13. Rouffaer and Ijzerman, *De Eerste Schipvaart*, 1915, p. 201.

14. C. C. Berg, *Kidung Pamancangah, de Geschiedenis van het Rijk van Gelgel*, 1 (Santpoort: Javaansch-Balische Historische Geschriften, 1929).

15. Rouffaer and Ijzerman, *De Eerste Schipvaart*, 1929, p. xlvi.

16. Ibid., 1925, pp. 169-71.

Aernout Lintgens' story is by contrast a thoroughgoing narrative, complete with vivid scenic details and artfully postponed surprises. He relates his week-long adventure (February 9-16, 1597) in establishing contact with the king's ministers, in instigating correspondence with the Dutch captain, and in arranging for the delivery of the latter's gifts before his own reception at the royal palace in Gelgel. With the help of Jan the Portuguese (apparently coming from Mataram and serving as translator) Lintgens amasses much information that can only be called ethnographic; and more often than not it arose from questions posed by the King of Bali. Here is the West's first report on Balinese marriage:

> Then the King asked us how old we were; I answered "around twenty-five, and Roedenborrich around twenty-three," then if we were all married; to this I answered "no," then I told how in our land the men were not married before twenty years of age, then in great surprise did he communicate that in the island of Baelle the manner was for youths to marry at twelve years and that daughters are betrothed at nine years of age.[17]

Lintgens describes the mode of paying the king homage, the deformed courtiers, a royal procession, the outlying palaces; we learn of the ministers' wives and concubines and impressive material wealth. He obtains a list of important "cities" and assessments of strength of arms and overall population. We also hear of a Balinese view as to why Dutch-Balinese relations are certain to be unusually friendly:

> . . . the minister (*kijlloer*) . . . said that we and they are totally alike, for they saw that we eat pork meat, while no Turks or Moors do this, and that moreover we eat meat also on Friday and Saturday, while no Spaniards or Portuguese do. . . .[18]

(Of special note are the structuralist systematics of this Balinese theory of cultural variation. It employs three oppositions: meat/not-meat, pork/other meat, and sometimes/always; and it combines them differentially to articulate three categories of mankind.)

The most practical information provides additional details of Bali's commercial isolationism: how, whenever foreigners arrived to purchase cotton goods, they were not permitted to travel inland and could only stay as long as their business required, "so that they would not know anything about the Balinese treasures."[19] Lintgens discloses how he exaggerated Dutch military strength to the king's aide and, showing him a map of Europe, claimed Holland was larger than China and included Germany, Scandinavia, and a portion of Russia.[20] There follows a sixteenth century *King and I* where an astounded monarch, after viewing himself in a triptych mirror decorated with the image of a Dutch ship, first hears tell of northern winters and ice, and then suffers a geopolitical Copernican revolution--seeing that by European maps extending to the Philippines, *Baelle* is neither the center of the universe nor even very significant.[21] That, at least, is what Lintgens thought the king suffered.

Lintgens then relates how the Dutch emissaries arrive at the royal seat in Gelgel. There are brief but vivid descriptions of religious processions and ceremonies

---

17. Ibid., 1929, p. 77.
18. Ibid., p. 81.
19. Ibid., p. 87.
20. Ibid., p. 90.
21. Ibid., p. 93.

("some praying to the sun, some the moon, and some an ox"[22]); of pleasure gardens graced with turtledoves and many other birds; and finally of the palace itself, with its steps, distinct sections, and slave quarters. At last among the "nobles" (*edelliede*) in attendance at the court, Lintgens is dumbfounded to encounter a Portuguese-speaking Moluccan who inquires whether the monarch of Portugal is well and has been received in friendship by his counterpart in England. Bali was truly a culture of kinds.

In short, Lintgens goes furthest in commending to his readers this Balinese court without understanding anything of the nature of rivalry among the island's many royal and noble houses (and to judge by later evidence, insurgent commoners as well). Moreover, none of these briefs by sixteenth century partially educated sailors displays that Puritanical, Calvinistic reaction to Indonesian customs so evident in later reports. Indeed, a generation would elapse before the official attitude of the Dutch East India Company was consolidated--that "proud burgher's revulsion of the ostentation and royal arbitrariness evident in Indonesia [which] speaks from many of the earlier records in the Company era."[23] However misunderstood, Bali's regal trappings were initially admired as such. For complex historical reasons, empathy antedated disdain.[24]

Like a Polder chez nous

Apart from his delight over the island's benevolent royalty, Lintgens sensed in Bali a familiar quality, most evident from his descriptions of village domestic quarters and irrigation works that assure a "surabundance of eatables." It is also proclaimed a "jonck Hollandt" with its little towns and cities so cut across by water that it is "amazing to see."[25] This feeling of familiarity is transformed at one point into a delusion of identity, when in his closing pages Lintgens describes a massive fortified wall along a section of Bali's southern coast. (His text was the source of a mystification that confused maps for generations to come. On the basis of no firm evidence, it has been attributed either to intoxication or to a mirage brought on by

---

22. Ibid., p. 86.

23. Justus M. van der Kroef, *The Dialectic of Colonial Indonesian History* (Amsterdam: Van der Peet, 1963), p. 7.

24. Some of these reasons can be glimpsed in Pieter Geyl's succinct account of the political and religious complexities of late sixteenth century Netherlands. Unlike their seventeenth century successors, the voyagers who first confronted Balinese ritual and hierarchy lacked a firm, dogmatic Calvinist base from which to react against Indonesian "idolatries" and "profanations." Geyl describes for our period the slow "Protestantization" from the top down and the tenacity of local Catholic officialdom; for example: "In 1593 a [Reformed] commission appointed by the States of Utrecht . . . made a tour of the province, questioning the newly installed ministers as well as the former priests. Their report gives a vivid picture of the motley and sometimes extraordinary conditions prevailing. In the large majority of villages the old priests were still functioning. . . . Several priests refused to submit, and continued to distribute 'the popish sacrament' at Easter, or at least showed a suspicious reluctance to marry their 'housekeeper'. . . . so, at this moment, were the Reformed Synods in all the seven provinces to which the Union had been reduced admonishing States assemblies and town governments to deal more severely with 'superstitions, idolatries, abuses and profanations.'" Pieter Geyl, *History of the Low Countries* (New York: St. Martin's, 1964), pp. 39-40.

25. Rouffaer and Ijzerman, *De Eerste Schipvaart*, 1929, p. 85.

Lintgens' homesickness for the inner wall that stood in Amsterdam in the late sixteenth century.[26] The kernel of truth behind the delusion is Lintgens' reassured sense of *gemakkelijkheid* amidst his Balinese surroundings. We wonder today what reinforced this cross-cultural coziness, and a totally speculative answer beckons. That barren North Sea bog called in the Odyssey "a land of fog and gloom where there is no sun" had devised a delicate ecological balance somewhat reminiscent of the one found in this tropical land of volcanic fertility where the danger is paddies parched from too much sun. In the Netherlands "diking produced its own code of law. When a break occurred, drums sounded for all men to pick up their spades and rush to the scene."[27] The windmills, the network of canals, and the continuous repair work and silting duties related to the Dutch landscape very much as the river dams, the irrigation channels and tunnels, and their upkeep related to the Balinese landscape, where irrigation also produced its own code of law. One subsistence technology protected fertile fields from an intrusive sea; the other protected rice paddies from the ever-threatening failure of water tapped up the mountains through lands of antagonists to irrigate one's own fields before flowing on. Both ecosystems have the quality of meticulous surplus-yielding games of survival in the face of pending disaster. At least a James Michener might assume this was why the descendants of commoner Frisian-Viking dog-lovers (the legendary founders of Amsterdam), who made profits in spite of the fog and gloom, felt in harmony with descendants of Javanese ancestral gods (the founders of Hindu-Bali) who worshipped the tropical sun. It is difficult to surmise a better reason. While we shall, alas, probably never know exactly why the Dutch and the Balinese saw eye to eye, it is safe to say that in terms of domestic scale and elaborate hydrotechnology, they were made for each other. Even in 1921 Lekkerkerker was still insisting this was so in his sweeping portrait of "De Baliërs" and in particular of their irrigation unit: "A *subak* is somewhat comparable to a plot of reclaimed land at home" (*Een subak is eenigszins te vergelijken met een polder ten onzent*).[28]

Pictorial Emblems

While Lintgens' work is a tantalizing narrative of an original attraction between different worlds, the visual record from the Houtman expedition better suggests the nature of Balinese ethnology, and perhaps of any ethnology. Three illustrations were printed with the log in 1598: (1) slaves (*slaven*) shouldering a noble's (*Edelluyd*) palanquin, (2) a king being drawn by white "buffalos" (*witte Buffels*) in a cart, sheltered by an umbrella, and (3) a wife following her dead (presumed) husband into his cremation flames to a musical accompaniment by several musicians. There are accurate aspects in the sedan chair, but the cart is a Dutch *bolderwagen*, the instrumentalists are Indian and no one in the expedition had witnessed a cremation.[29] In fact, the group of musicians is a near copy of an illustration of South

---

26. Ibid., pp. xlvii, 1.

27. Masselman, *The Cradle*, pp. 3-5.

28. C. Lekkerkerker, "De Baliërs" (1921), in *De Volken van Nederlandsch Indië in Monographieen*, 2 (Amsterdam: J. C. van Eerde, 1943), p. 149.

29. Rouffaer and Ijzerman, *De Eerste Schipvaart*, 1915, pp. 196, 202; plates 40, 41, 42. The composite version discussed below is from L. Hulsius, ed., *Eerste Shiffart an die Orientalische Indien, so die Hollandisch Schiff, im Martio 1595 aussgefahren, und in Augusto 1597 wiederkommen, verzicht* . . . (Nuremberg, 1598, 1st ed.; Frankfurt am Main, 1625, 5th ed.). The plate in question appears on p. 54 of vol. 1 of the 1606 edition (Franckfurt am Mayn: Wolfgang Richter, in Verlegung Leuini Hulsii Erben).

Asian cremations in Portuguese Goa that appeared in the remarkably influential *Itinerario* [*Voyage or Passage by Jan Huyghen van Linschoten to East or Portugal's India (1579-1592)*] by the seasoned traveler Linschoten and the collector Paludamus. A copy of this major impetus to Dutch investment in exploration accompanied the Houtman expedition. Its illustrations were presumed adequate to depict things Balinese, since, according to sixteenth century concepts of cultural geography passed down from medieval cosmographies and the great Iberian chronicles, Bali was an extension of India:

> With Goa as its focal point (according to the Itinerary) India stretched westward as far as Prester John's Land (Ethiopia). It included all of Southeast Asia, and it was only grudgingly admitted that China (Cathay) and Japan might have to be excluded. All of the East India archipelago fell within its boundaries: Sumatra, Java, and the Spice Islands.[30]

Contrary to the view of some modern commentators, it was not "fantasy" to use an engraving of Goanese widow-burning to represent a reputed Balinese custom; it was simply a matter of applying the nearest known equivalent. In western eyes there was never a Bali per se, but only a Bali derived. The original ethnological idea of Bali sprang full-grown from the records of Portuguese Goa, as in some ways it should have.

The three engravings in the Houtman account were subsequently redrawn into a composite emblem of "A King on the Island Bally," published with a summary of the Dutch reports in the famous translations of travel literature by Levin Hulsius. The Dutch bolderwagen remains the vehicle of an umbrella-shaded king, but the suttee scene has been reduced to a background embellishment-in-miniature along with a sun worshipper and another "Ethnike Brahmane," here praying before a cow. The illustration of regal Bali as followers of Surya (the sun), foregoers of beef, and prohibitors of widows surviving has been improved for the wrong reasons. By reducing the size of the suttee scene, the musical instruments have been obscured so that they cannot be recognized as Indian, Balinese, or anything else. However, this was not for the sake of ethnographic accuracy, but to produce a pleasing, balanced illustration to adorn this first of many remarkable cocktail-table books (*prachtwerk*) on Bali. The Dutch published exhaustive travel literature to compile practical information for navigation and commercial strategies; the Elizabethan-Jacobean British followed suit to stimulate interest in entering the world trade system at all. But the more compendious German collections of voyages begun in the late sixteenth century "were primarily designed as entertaining and eye-catching examples of literature" in order to "appeal to the popular taste for the remote and exotic."[31] Thus, the first popularized portrait of Bali was in some ways less misleading than the first efforts at reportage; and the Hulsius emblem remained the most elaborate overview of Balinese practices for the next two centuries.[32]

---

30. Masselman, *The Cradle*, pp. 71-72.

31. Lach, *Asia*, 1, pp. 215, 217.

32. We might note that German book editors, always enthusiastic illustrators, were here doing with the new literature of discovery (incipient ethnology) what they had done a century earlier with popular handbooks on philosophy and morals; ". . . the ubiquitous books of emblems and devices presented the Renaissance reader with verbal pictures of an exemplary moral nature. Initially these were intended to consist only of words; the first emblem writer, Andrea Alciate, defined an emblem as a pictorial epigram, a verbal image, and the first edition of his famous *Emblemata* (1931) was not designed to include illustrations. The pictures were added by Alciati's German publisher, and though they were a logical enough development of the

The original engravings from Bali are worth considering in light of E. H. Gombrich's notion of "adapted stereotypes."[33] It so happens that these first western visual images were adapted from India, but this would be what Gombrich calls a "pathological representation" only if the aim were to distinguish carefully South Asian practices from Balinese ones. More than two hundred years were to pass before Westerners would attempt this. For the purposes of the sixteenth to the eighteenth centuries, this pictorial record adequately emblazoned Bali as sun-worshipping, woman-immolating, and king-honoring. Little matter to the pre-Baconian of 1597 that the musical instruments were not quite that way; little matter the particular circumstances in which women were really burned, the sun really (if ever) bowed to, etc. A major interest in the art of ethnology is to convey a sense of the *whole* society, to typify it in some compelling manner. Like any essentially metaphorical procedure, ethnology resembles the arts of visual illusionism, if one realizes there is no such thing as simple "realism" and no possible one-to-one correspondence between that which is "illusioned to" and the perceptual or conceptual apparatus by which the illusion is perpetrated. Rather in both visual representation and ethnology (distinguished explicitly from ethnography, insofar as ethnology hopes to "capture the whole"):

> Copying . . . proceeds through the rhythms of schema and correction. The schema is not the product of a process of "abstraction," of a tendency to "simplify"; it represents the first approximate, loose category which is gradually tightened to fit the form it is to reproduce.[34]

The first South Asianized loose images of Bali sufficiently distinguished its culture from Holland or Portugal or anything else western readers were likely to measure it against. The representations were "tightened" only when they became ambiguous, when they appeared to reproduce two forms--Bali and South Asia--that according to other criteria were perceived to be different.

This process of gradually tightening inadequate stereotypes continues. Nor are the stereotypes applied to a constant referent, but to an ever-changing social life that has itself meanwhile been altered by incorporating new stereotypes. For example, Bali had been rearranging its death rites according to its own images of Indian cremation, which Balinese literati probably understood no better than western literati later understood Balinese cremation. Thus, the West's first caption of Balinese cremation was a *visual* stereotype of a *socio-ritual* stereotype (whether the latter was actually "brought" to Bali from India, or modeled on texts, or both). And Balinese ethnology--like all ethnology--continues to compound stereotypes, eventually producing (hopefully) tighter captions, but inevitably to the exclusion of certain cultural and social data perceived as critical from other vantages.

---

original idea, they remained very much an addition: the pictorial part of the emblem is a function of the verbal part, and to interpret the picture correctly, one must know how to read it." Stephen Orgel and Roy Strong, *Inigo Jones: The Theatre of the Stuart Court* (London: Southeby Parke Bernet; Berkeley: University of California Press, 1973), p. 3. It is perhaps best to think of seventeenth century pictures, such as Hulsius', as cross-cultural blazons, with a suitable one to adorn each of the word's worthy cultures. For Elizabethan-Jacobean stereotypes and topoi on "East Indies" worship, color (e.g., tawny, sunburnt, swarthy), etc., see R. R. Cawley, *The Voyagers and Elizabethan Drama* (Boston: Heath, 1938), pp. 154 ff.

33. E. H. Gombrich, *Art and Illusion* (Princeton: Princeton University Press, 1969), p. 71.

34. Ibid., p. 74.

Hindu Spectacles and Their Consequences

The original cross-cultural captions of Bali--"absolute monarchy," "happy irrigationists"--proved particularly indelible and they long impeded investigations into the legitimacy of authority and the participation of commoners in caste categories--two complex aspects of Balinese social life. The longevity of this initial idea of Bali can be partially and indirectly attributed to the paucity of research over the next two centuries. Spiceless Bali lacked commodities save for a furtive slave trade--furtive at least from the vantage of European images of the East Indies, since slavery never entered as a component into Dutch emblems of and for Bali. Thus, the *general* idea of its culture as epitomized at the close of the sixteenth century went largely unrevised (although Bali became a major supplier of slaves) until the early nineteenth century, when its proximity to Java assumed great importance for British occupiers of the East Indies during the Napoleonic Wars. Observers began again to ask not merely how to handle Bali, but what it *was*.

Finally, during the latter part of the century, with the development of passenger steamers and an overseas tourist industry, those most conspicuous "productions" of Bali--its splendid temples and pervasive religious ceremonies--themselves became commodities of sorts, now that the customers could be shipped to them. The whole culture was "packaged." Lintgens' original vision of cozy domesticity got dusted off, and it has been successfully reinstated and propagated anew in popular descriptions after every notorious exception that has marred twentieth century Balinese history: the mass court suicides of 1906-8, the continuing years of Balinese violence bemoaned by Sukarno after the Indonesian Revolution, and the terroristic insurrections and marauding murder squads of 1965. Bali remains today in tourist stereotypes Asia's happy isle of homey *joie de vivre* and day-to-day artistic self-fulfillment: an appealing part-truth.

But it was in particular the other caption of Bali--"Hindu kingship"--that distorted scholarly work. Sixteenth century accounts influenced the questions asked by Sir Stamford Raffles and later H. A. van den Borek in their seminal descriptions of Bali in the early nineteenth century. Moreover the "hinduized" view of the island was reinforced by the remarkable work of two early Sanskritists, J. Crawfurd and then R. Friedrich. Subsequent missionaries (e.g., Van Eck) and civil servants (e.g., F. A. Liefrinck) began to emphasize irrigation techniques and commoner rituals in localities apparently less influenced by the Hindu courts of the plains. Finally, V. E. Korn and other *adat* scholars in the 1920s to 1930s also tried to counter the elitist distortions. Perhaps bending too far the other way, they left us with an unlikely polarization: on the one hand, voluntarism and democratic control of subsistence and domestic and civic affairs; on the other hand, extreme status pride in statecraft and religion, decorum, language, etiquette, etc.[35] Moreover, throughout these approaches to Bali, when it came to holistic images of its culture, prominence was given to the Hindu-Javanese literate traditions and to what philologists could disclose of their notions of rank, ritual, and the nature of society and cosmos. Comparativist scholars, even the most populist ones, tended without exception to see the *whole* of Balinese experience through, as Swellengrebel has put it, "Hindu spectacles, and so had a distorted view."[36] And these spectacles, in both senses of the term, dated from 1597.

---

35. These developments in the history of Balinese studies, primarily by Dutchmen, are discussed and documented in Boon, *Anthropological Romance*. The subject of Balinese statecraft is reviewed and interpreted in the work under preparation by C. Geertz, *Negara, the Theater State in Nineteenth Century Bali*.

36. J. L. Swellengrebel, "Bali: Some General Information," in *Bali, Studies in*

Thus, from the very start Bali appeared South Asian, kingly, and stable. Subsequently little comparative study was made of continuities between Balinese social and ecological forms and those of less Hinduized islands in the Lesser Sundas; and almost no attention has been paid to the distinctly Oceanic quality of its culture. Yet, outside its hinduized rites and Sanskritic texts, Bali looks as much Polynesian as Indic. Moreover, while its wet-rice irrigation recalls Southeast Asia, its utilization of surplus production and its fine status gradations even within family lines suggest points further east as well. Indeed, it is provocative to reflect that, coming from the other direction, Houtman's voyagers might have emphasized not the Indic umbrella of Bali's "kings," but the physical elevation of its "chiefs"; not the Brahmana legists, but the conspicuous expenditure in mass rites of an "untradeable" surplus; and not the worship of cows, but the tournament-like competition among leaders to maintain devoted subjects--all traits of the Pacific. If those first ethnologists had arrived in Bali two centuries later, bringing their adaptable stereotypes not from Goa but from the hierarchies of the Maori or even Hawaii, what a different picture might have resulted!

Life, Thought, Ritual (The Hague: W. van Hoeve, 1960), p. 25.

DEMOCRACY IN INDONESIA

Harry J. Benda

The Decline of Constitutional Democracy in Indonesia. By Herbert Feith. Ithaca: Cornell University Press, 1962. xx, 618. $8.75.

No country in Southeast Asia has in postwar years received greater attention, institutional support, and dedicated individual scholarship than Indonesia. Only a decade has elapsed since the beginning of this new chapter in Indonesian studies, yet the progress achieved in these few years is impressive, thanks in no small measure to Cornell University's unique Modern Indonesia Program, sponsor of the book under review, and to which Dr. Feith has so handsomely acknowledged his indebtedness.

The author of *The Decline of Constitutional Democracy in Indonesia*, a lecturer in Government at Monash Uniiversity (Melbourne, Australia), knows Indonesia far more intimately than most other students, having lived and worked there for several years. His mastery of Indonesian (and Dutch), his seemingly indefatigable research, his acquantance with a complex political scene observed from within, his friendships with countless Indonesians--all of these would suffice to establish expertise of a kind rarely encountered. But Feith combines these advantages with catholicity of academic training in Australia and the United States, far-ranging reading in his own discipline as well as in other social sciences, and with a compelling and lucid style that demands respect for this book as a notable addition to the many-faceted literature on the new states.

The book deals with the political history of the Indonesian Republic from the transfer of sovereignty in December 1949 until the eclipse of the parliamentary system in March 1957. Seven of its eleven chapters are devoted to the seven cabinets that straddled the period, but they contain much more than a detailed narrative of the outstanding events that led to the formation, functioning (or malfunctioning), and demise of each cabinet. Feith has, in addition, illumined these accounts with a conceptual analysis that lends coherence to the dynamics of Indonesian politics in those eventful years. Two chapters (VII and XI) survey the broad trends of what Feith calls the decline of constitutional democracy, the first at the half-way mark of the Wilopo cabinet, the second at the end of the book. Social scientists will find much to ponder in the third chapter, "The Elements of Politics," where the author formulates his major analytic tools for the interpretation of the political process in Indonesia and, by implication, in transitional societies generally. Feith has to all intents and purposes accomplished a *tour de force*. His modesty notwithstanding, it is hard to imagine that we will soon encounter a more definitive and better-informed volume on modern Indonesian political history.

If I proceed to some critical comments, I am not moved to do so by the canons of reviewmanship, let alone by allegations of superior knowledge. I may appear to be doing less than justice to Dr. Feith by singling out what to me appears a basic flaw in his frame of reference and in the way in which he approaches and presents the problems he discusses. I am, then, arbitrarily selecting a generic argument, propelled by a sense of misgiving about the direction in which much of our research on Indonesia (and on many other developing countries, certainly in Southeast Asia) has been moving. Though Feith in many respects stands head and shoulders above most of his peers, he has by his very excellence made me once again conscious of this growing intellectual discomfort. Much as I admire his skillful anatomy of the decline of constitutionalism in Indonesia,[1] I feel that he is essentially presenting us highly sophisticated and persuasive answers to an intrinsically mistaken, or irrelevant, question.

I rather suspect that we have been accumulating a whole string of such questions with distressing persistence for at least well over a decade now; and I use the "we" quite advisedly, including myself among the mistaken questioners. Perhaps our basic error all along has been to examine Indonesia with Western eyes; or, to be more precise and more generous, with eyes that, though increasingly trained to see things Indonesian, have continued to look at them selectively, in accordance with preconceived Western models. Most of our questions, so it seems to me, have hitherto resolved around a singularly simple, continuing theme, perhaps best caricatured by the adage, "What's wrong with Indonesia?" The answers given to this all-pervasive, if usually unstated, question vary from author to author, from discipline to discipline; but basically they have led--with greater or lesser ingenuity--to the discovery of a *diabolus ex machina*. What was wrong with Indonesia until 1942? An old and simple question, though answering it apparently causes continuing delight: It was the Dutch.[2] Why, to take another typical example, is there no indigenous middle class in Indonesia? Again, there were the Dutch, if not already the Portuguese before them, and certainly the ubiquitous Chinese to this very day.[3] And why, now asks Dr. Feith, did Indonesia's short-lived democracy die? Because-- I hope he and his readers will forgive me an almost unpardonable oversimplification --in the struggle between good and evil, between "problem-solvers" and "solidarity-makers," the latter have, at least temporarily, won a victory.

My quarrel is not with some undeniable--or for that matter some unpleasant-- facts of Indonesian history and politics that are contained in anticolonial and, *mutatis mutandis*, in anti-Soekarno writings.[4] And to clear the deck of value judg-

---

1. In a more recent study, "The Dynamics of Guided Democracy," in Ruth T. McVey, ed., *Indonesia* (New Haven, 1963), Ch. 8, Dr. Feith has dealt with Indonesian political developments since 1957.

2. Among the most recent and extreme examples may be cited Dorothy Woodman, *The Republic of Indonesia* (New York, 1955) and Jeanne S. Mintz, *Indonesia: A Profile* (Princeton, 1961). I myself have been far from free of this aprioristic approach in *The Crescent and the Rising Sun: Indonesian Islam under the Japanese Occupation, 1942-1945* (Bandung and The Hague, 1958), Part I. For a more balanced interpretation of Indonesia under Dutch rule, see Robert Van Niel, *The Emergence of the Modern Indonesian Elite* (Bandung and The Hague, 1960).

3. See esp. Benjamin and Jean Higgins, *Indonesia: The Crisis of the Millstones* (Princeton, 1963), and Higgins' introductory essay in Benjamin Higgins and Others, *Entrepreneurship and Labor Skills in Indonesian Economic Development: A Symposium* (New Haven, 1961).

4. See in particular Willard A. Hanna, *Bung Karno's Indonesia* (New York, 1961).

ments, let me candidly say that, having lived in colonial Indonesia for several years, I do not yield to most postwar commentators in my sense of selective moral outrage; again, it is very likely that Guided Democracy (which incidentally may have quite a few, though often neglected, roots in the Greater East Asia Co-Prosperity Sphere) makes a difficult abode for many decent people. But even if we *a priori* want to condemn colonialism, any colonialism, on moral grounds, even if we are convinced that unguided democracy is morally preferable to its counterpart, we should beware of poor logic and pseudo-history. At the root of the question, "What's wrong?" lies the unwarranted belief that all societies are essentially similar and that, allowed to develop "normally" they will (tautologically) follow a standard norm, that of "the West." Even if we were to overlook the stubborn facts of diversity in Western history, facts which make it hazardous to generalize about the West as such, by what logic must we deduce that any alleged patterns of Western development must apply to other cultures?

I am not saying that it is not possible or for that matter not desirable to seek out similarities, especially structural similarities, for purposes of comparing and contrasting societies and politics either within the West or on a wider scale. We can certainly endeavor to isolate meaningful categories from the bewildering diversity of historical experience; indeed, we almost always do so, even if unconsciously. But we must not superimpose these categories on historical diversity to the extent of relegating reality to insignificance. Nothing bids us divide the world on an *a priori* basis into "Western" and "non-Western" components; but nothing bids us either to adopt a methodological approach which we might call automatic historical parallelism.[5] Its assumptions, shared i.e., by unsophisticated Liberalism and Marxism (especially post-Marxian Marxism[6]), are unsupportable articles of faith. Once we commit ourselves to look for categorical parallels, especially developmental, chronological parallels, we are in danger of distorting history and reality, albeit unconsciously and guided by the noblest of motivations.

There are three ways in which automatic historical parallelism beclouds a proper understanding of historical and political diversity. First, it leads us too willingly to transfer familiar categories to unfamiliar terrain; it is due to this tendency that we have tended too easily and uncritically to identify "states," "empires," "revolu-

---

5. I am purposely coining this rather clumsy term instead of using the more obvious "historicism," to avoid confusion. See K. R. Popper, *The Poverty of Historicism* (London, 1957) and F. A. Hayek, *The Counter-Revolution of Science: Studies on the Abuse of Reason* (Glencoe, 1952), Ch. III. To the extent that historicism stresses universal historical "laws," it is of course identical with what I here call historical parallelism. Historicism is, in addition, identified with organic theories of historical development, often conceived in terms of the uniqueness of a given society or group. Though I am not an "organicist," I am in fact stressing the importance of certain specific (not necessarily unique) aspects of Indonesian, especially Hindu-Javanese, history. Edward Shils, "On the Comparative Study of the New States," in Clifford Geertz, ed., *Old Societies and New States: The Quest for Modernity in Asia and Africa* (New York and London, 1963), pp. 14-20, warns against the dangers of this approach.

6. See Karl A. Wittfogel, *Oriental Despotism: A Comparative Study of Total Power* (New Haven, 1957), Ch. 9, "The Rise and Fall of the Theory of the Asiatic Mode of Production." This is a detailed discussion of an important and all too often neglected topic in Marxist thought, viz. the dispute between an "Asiatic" model of historical development and global "historical parallelism." Without entering into a discussion of Wittfogel's own controversial theories, one may at least grant the desirability of asking pertinent, generic questions about Asian (or rather, *some* Asian) societies.

tion," "feudalism," and of course "nationalism" and "socialism" in Southeast Asia.[7] In the second place, there has been a similar tendency to argue away what look like unpleasant parallels; one very instructive example is the fairly general treatment of the era of the Japanese occupation in Southeast Asia.[8] And finally, we find that, confronted with the absence of phenomena which "ought" to be present in "normal" societies, the believer in parallelism accusingly turns to the *diabolus* responsible for such absences; it is this latter motive which is responsible for the agonizing search for Southeast Asian entrepreneurial middle classes and for "problem-solvers" in general.

The composite picture of Indonesian history and politics that emerges from these approaches might be summarized in one sentence, viz. that, had Indonesia been left free to develop "normally," it would have more or less "naturally" developed not only into a wealthy and just nation state, but also into a bourgeois democracy. This, for sure, is a caricature, a *reductio ad absurdum*, but I do not think that it is essentially very far off the mark as far as the basic assumptions of very many writers are concerned. Most of these assumptions will not stand up to scrutiny and can, in fact, be easily refuted. But let me narrow my discussion to Dr. Feith's *Decline*. Though I readily admit that he is not guilty of all the unhistorical sins contained in the above caricature, he has, so it seems to me, substituted the search for the domestic devil, so to speak, for the earlier search for the foreign devil. Granting that his careful delineation of the élite struggle immeasurably enriches our understanding of postwar Indonesian political history, I doubt that this kind of élite-centered analysis really can come to grips with the substance of Indonesia's troubled decade.

I believe that it takes an unhistorical starting point or, to put it more precisely, that it sees postwar Indonesia primarily as a continuation of the country's most recent history, while it largely ignores what has gone before. In point of fact, however, the modern colonial era (including the Japanese occupation) was a brief interlude in Indonesian history, a "deviation" we might almost say, from that history in that it subjected the country to alien dictation.[9] No conscientious historian of modern Indonesia can deny that the colonial interlude brought with it some extremely important changes, including lasting structural changes, in Indonesian society;[10] but I am increasingly led to believe that, whatever its impact, alien overlordship did not erase Indonesian history, or divert it from its course. Hence any discus-

---

7. The treatment of nationalism in Southeast Asia has often been unsophisticated. It is usually assumed to be a "natural" phenomenon inherent in the area; it is also presumed to be "good." For a recent critique, see Elie Kedouri, *Nationalism* (New York, 1960). Cf. also Clifford Geertz's searching essay, "The Integrative Revolution: Primordial Sentiments and Civil Politics in the New States," in *Old Societies and New States*, pp. 105-157.

8. Southeast Asian leaders appear in most books as highly sophisticated and courageous, some *pro forma* collaborating with, others openly resisting, the Japanese. See e.g. D. E. G. Hall, *A History of South-East Asia* (London, 1955), pp. 687-699, and George McT. Kahin's *Nationalism and Revolution in Indonesia* (Ithaca, 1952), Ch. IV.

9. The idea of "colonial deviation" is interestingly raised in Justus M. van der Kroef, "The Colonial Deviation in Indonesian History," *East and West* VII (1956), 251-261.

10. I have discussed some of these questions in my article "The Structure of Southeast Asian History: Some Preliminary Observations," *Journal of Southeast Asian History* III (1962), 106-138.

sion of modern Indonesia that takes the colonial *status quo* as its starting point is bound to result in significant interpretational error, and this is where I myself plead guilty,[11] and where I now find fault with Feith.

Let me illustrate. What Feith calls "problem-solvers" (the protagonists of rational administration and "nation building") are, for the greater part, the truly Westernized members of the Indonesian élite or, perhaps more accurately, those in whom Westernization has gone more than skin-deep; they also include, we might add, some conscious Muslims. Many, though certainly not all, of them are non-Javanese. Feith calls them problem-solvers because they see problems the way the Westerner sees them, and attempt solutions along Western, rational lines. Opposed to them, in the political drama unfolding in the pages of the *Decline*, are the "solidarity-makers," to whom *élan*, revolution, and ideological incantations are far more important than the rational solution of economic, administrative, and other problems. This group also includes outstanding Westernized leaders (predominantly, though of course not exclusively, Javanese) but their attachment to Western values appears far less profound. Few modernistic Muslims belong to this segment of the élite, which is depicted as the destroyer of rational politics and the gravedigger of constitutional democracy in Indonesia.

Before I proceed with my main argument, two observations are in order. First, Feith's definition of problem-solving implies that the problems seen and tackled by the group he favors are, in fact, the prime (if not the sole) problems demanding solution, and that its ways of solving them are the most (if not the only) appropriate ones. Although there are ample objective criteria that suggest that rational problem-solving is essential to nation building, this surely does not mean that the solidarity-makers do not perceive problems, or attempt to solve them in their own, not necessarily irrational, way.[12] It is, I think, a moot point whether the problem of forging national unity (including the "return" of West Irian) deserved priority over the problem of, say, economic planning. And this leads to my second observation. The fact that so few Western observers, most notably economists, have been willing to concede that the matter of priorities is *disputandum* has, paradoxically, gotten us pretty close to the standard conservative, colonial argument according to which the "Netherlands Indies" above all needed good administration (i.e., continued Western tutelage), but least of all "demagogues" and "rabble rousers." The Western disenchantment with Indonesia in recent years may, I suspect, be paralleled by Indonesian impatience at a return to "typically Western, colonial" attitudes.

Returning to my major point--the problem of historical perspective--I am suggesting that the contestants in Feith's battle for constitutional democracy appear deceptively evenly matched, their tug of war becoming in the final analysis a matter of *virtù* and *fortuna*. Might it not be more illuminating to argue that the problem-solvers' efforts to continue a rational administration and to maintain a modern economic system, both born of and identified with the apolitical colonial *status quo*, were doomed once Indonesia started to overcome the colonial "deviation" and once

---

11. Harry J. Benda, *The Crescent and the Rising Sun*. Professor Anthony Johns' thoughtful review of my book in *Australian Journal of Politics and History* V (1959), 251-252, first confronted me with these basic interpretational problems. For my more recent appraisals, see "Tradition und Wandel in Indonesien," *Geschichte in Wissenschaft und Unterricht*, XIV (1963), 46-53. Another article, "Tradition and Change in Indonesian Islam," will shortly be published in the *Journal* of the Israel Oriental Society.

12. On the dual meaning of rationality cf. Karl Mannheim, *Man and Society in an Age of Reconstruction*, tr. E. Shils (London, 1940), Part I, Chs. V and VI.

Indonesian (especially Javanese) history found a way back to its own moorings? Indeed, since in many ways colonialism, far from only interrupting and deviating from precolonial historical tendencies had here and there also reinforced them, the odds were from the very outset far more heavily weighted against constitutional democracy in Indonesia than more sympathetic students of the postwar era, including Dr. Feith and myself, have so far been willing to admit.

In the context of Indonesian history Feith's problem-solvers, whether thoroughly Westernized or thoroughly Islamized, appear as a small, intrinsically foreign element in the body social of Indonesia; perhaps it would be more accurate to say that they are a foreign element within the social and ideological world of Indianized Indonesia, especially of Java.[13] By contrast, the solidarity-makers, though they may often speak in deceptively modern terminology, seem to represent just that specifically Javanese culture.[14] It is only by taking into account the deep roots, the longevity as well as the remarkable resilience of that Hindu-Javanese world to foreign, e.g. Islamic and Western, influences that we can fully understand modern Indonesian developments.[15] It *was*, after all, a world in which the language of the present-day solidarity-makers was of far greater intrinsic value than that of rational problem-solving; it *was* a world which, though it had to submit to foreign dictation, remained outside the orbit of modern, rational economic life and a great deal else that belonged to the superimposed Western order. It is not insignificant to note that parts of the Outer Islands, only peripherally touched by Indianization, became not only far more profoundly Islamized but also (in spite of far later and less intensive contact with Westernization) posed far fewer obstacles to the domestication of Western-style economic behavior and "problem-solving" attitudes in general than Java.

In a very rough sense, the elections of 1955, so brilliantly analyzed by Feith in an earlier monograph,[16] showed rather well the numerical distribution of the adherents of problem-solvers and solidarity-makers; the verdict of democracy augured ill for its survival. Certainly what happened did not *have* to happen: the decline of constitutional democracy in Indonesia, though highly probable, was not inevitable. But on balance I believe that the fate of an intrinsically alien political framework must be primarily understood in terms of Indonesian historical continuity rather than in terms of a contemporary élite contest. From this point of view the question "Why did democracy fail in Indonesia?" appears less meaningful than its opposite, "Why should it have survived?"

If I have up to now stressed the crucial importance of history, let me hasten to add that I do not believe it to be sacrosanct. I am very far from endowing "History" with an immutable, impermeable mystique, and I am not even arguing that continuity is necessarily more important than change. Let me summarize my argument under three main headings. First, Western-style-modernization in Indonesia, largely because of its recent beginnings under foreign domination and on account of its identification with that domination, has not--not yet--struck deep roots. The proponents of such modernization constitute a small, virtually alienated, minority whose

---

13. See the important study by Robert R. Jay, *Religion and Politics in Rural Central Java* (New Haven, 1963), Ch. I.

14. Cf. Clifford Geertz's modern classic, *The Religion of Java* (Glencoe, 1960), Parts I and III.

15. See Note 11 for reference to my revised appraisal of the role of Islam in Indonesian history.

16. Herbert Feith, *The Indonesian Elections of 1955* (Ithaca, 1957).

integration into the mainstream of post-independence Indonesian history was in fact hindered by the Indonesian Revolution which, with increasing deliberateness, has set out to whittle down if not destroy the "deviation" of Westernization.

Second, it is nonetheless highly probable that Indonesia will modernize and that therefore change will come to loom larger than continuity. "Solidarity-making" will very likely be forced to yield, or at least to make progressively more room for, "problem-solving," for economic modernization, in particular, is bound to follow its peculiar, rational, and indeed iron logic. But (and this to me is crucial) the ways in which this transformation will take place will very likely be Indonesian-derived. Indonesian-style problem-solving need not necessarily be any prettier than so many of us nowadays believe problem-ignoring to be. The precedents of Japan, Russia, and China should in any case warn us that confronting and solving harsh problems may involve, in addition to rational toughmindedness, some rather repressive and to us often repulsive political engineering. While these examples need have little relevance to Indonesia's future, that of the West's "Great Transformation" may have no more.[17] The assumption that modernization can be spectacular, rapid, yet democratic rests, for the time being at least, on hope rather than on inference from historical fact.

My third point concerns the relevance of these by no means original insights to the problems of meaningful research. I believe that our adherence to essentially Western developmental models leads us to concentrate on parallels, *in casu*, on the study of extrinsic elements in Indonesian society, history, and politics. However brilliantly conducted and reported, such research is, as I said at the outset, focusing on irrelevant questions: questions inspired by chronological parallelism or methodological Europocentrism. It is perturbing, though on purely intellectual grounds not surprising, to find strange bedfellows--the liberal historical parallelist and the doctrinaire Marxist--sharing this particular Procrustean bed. Both, to take one illuminating example, are strenuously on the lookout for the bourgeois, the one hoping to find in him the entrepreneurial problem-solver *par excellence*,[18] the other impatient to proclaim the beginning, if not the completion, of the gospel-decreed bourgeois revolution, the ideological green light for the "next stage."[19] It is admit-

---

17. Cf. Karl Polanyi, *The Great Transformation: The Political and Economic Origins of Our Time* (Beacon Paperback ed., Boston, 1957). It is perhaps becoming gradually obvious that there is no standard Communist model for modernization either, in spite of the ideological "ideal-type." Interestingly enough, "parallelists" usually refer only to "Western" or "Communist," but only very rarely to the Japanese, "model."

18. See Note 3, above. A far more sophisticated study is Clifford Geertz, *Peddlers and Princes: Social Change and Economic Modernization in Two Indonesian Towns* (Chicago and London, 1963). Though Geertz can hardly be accused of strenuously looking for the non-existent, the entrepreneurial prototypes he has so carefully studied in Java and Bali are actually "exceptions" in the framework of the national Indonesian economy, directed as it is by non-entrepreneurial, "managerial" civil servants. Interestingly enough, Geertz does deduce from his findings a critique of Indonesian national economic planning (pp. 153-157). I would suggest that research concerning the bureaucracy is of potentially greater significance than an inquiry into marginal entrepreneurial groups in Indonesia. Unfortunately Donald Fagg's doctoral dissertation, "Authority and Social Structure: A Study of Javanese Bureaucracy" (Harvard, 1958) has so far remained unpublished.

19. The possibility that Indonesia, assuming that the notion of the monolithic model continues to have validity, will follow a Communist "model" is not a consequence of

tedly easier to spot the Marxian splinter than the liberal-parallelist beam, but both are unhistorical or historicist, and to that extent prevent us from looking for all the significant facts we need if we are to understand continuity and change, unity and diversity.

Does my insistence on the importance of history mean that we must eschew comparisons? Certainly not, and for two major reasons. First, even though we should beware of automatically projecting patterns derived from dubious generalizations from "Western," or for that matter from Russian developments on Southeast Asia, we cannot avoid proceeding from the better to the less well known, as we cannot avoid using the tools of our Western-based disciplines. Divorced from preconceived, historicist developmental sequences and schemas, our search can yield highly fruitful and suggestive insights.[20] Second, and no less important, there appears ample justification for a careful study of generic similarities in what we have come to call the "new states" of the "developing" world. It is true that historians, congenitally imbued with the uniqueness and peculiarity of historical phenomena, have been hesitant, overly hesitant perhaps, to admit the fruitfulness and validity of such comparisons, let alone to join in the exciting pioneering on this new intellectual frontier. My genuine admiration for Dr. Feith's analytic skill under this heading should, in any case, not be marred by narrow-minded "disciplinary" strictures. The categories he has so skillfully devised are extremely useful for historians and social scientists alike.

Indeed, I believe that the historian is well qualified to discern the rationale, as well as the inherent limitations, of comparative study on such a breathtakingly global scale. Its rationale lies in the fact that striking parallels *do* exist in many parts of the "non-Western" world as a result of the basic similarities inherent in the Western impact, especially in Western colonialism. Its limitations are, by the same token, that many if not most of these very similarities (among them the groups most susceptible to comparison, as typified by Feith's problem-solvers) are so to speak isolated particles in the historical landscape of each society. We can, then, study the Western-educated intellectual, the Western-trained civil servant, the Western-influenced officer, here and there perhaps even the Western-style entrepreneur, as generic and hence comparable phenomena of a brief, recent, and in a sense world-wide historical epoch. But this, however challenging and promising a scholarly enterprise, is ultimately bound to remain a study of the transitional if not the ephemeral. The laws of biology are sure to claim the objects of our study within a generation or two, and it is highly doubtful that the genera will be reproducing in similar fashion. Or, to put it differently, the long dog of history is bound to reassert itself and to make it increasingly difficult for the short generic tail to go on wagging it with impunity, under the convenient, scientific cloak of "traditional society." Diversity will triumph in the long run and render comparative studies far more difficult and complex than they are now. But since, as has been so well observed, we will all be dead in the long run, we should for the present participate to the fullest extent in the quest

---

an allegedly greater validity of Marxian historical parallelism but of the dexterity with which Indonesian Communists may be able to combine the appeals of solidarity-making with the skills (alleged or real) of problem-solving in an Indonesian historical context. This, rather than "Kremlinology" or even the Sino-Soviet split, is one of the most significant aspects of Communism to be studied. On the relevance of Indonesian Communism to the Javanese social and ideological setting, see the monograph by Jay referred to in Note 13 above.

20. The comparative study of peasant movements may be one example. See Sylvia L. Thrupp, ed., *Millenial Dreams in Action: Essays in Comparative Study* (The Hague, 1962).

for geographic parallelism while guarding against the pitfalls of historical chronological parallelism.

To all intents and purposes, Dr. Feith has contributed an outstandingly important work to this quest. I hope it is not too late for me to say in all sincerity that I wish I could equal his achievement and give as many thoughtful, incisive, and brilliant answers, even to what I have so ungraciously labelled irrelevant questions.

HISTORY, THEORY, AND INDONESIAN POLITICS:
A REPLY TO HARRY J. BENDA

Herbert Feith

There is a lot to be said against authors coming back at their reviewers. Having had many hundreds of pages to make one's points, one should not properly ask for more. But Professor Harry J. Benda's review of my book, *The Decline of Constitutional Democracy in Indonesia* ("Democracy in Indonesia," *Journal of Asian Studies,* XXII, No. 3, May 1964, pp. 449-456), is much more than a review. It is the vigorous and highly stimulating statement of a thesis on the central questions to be asked about society and politics in the Third World. As such, I believe it deserves an answer.

After making a number of exceedingly kind comments on my book, Professor Benda goes on to speak of what he sees as a "basic flaw" in my frame of reference. I have, he says, presented "persuasive answers to an intrinsically mistaken or irrelevant question." He links this with his own "sense of misgiving about the direction in which much of our research on Indonesia (and on many other developing countries, certainly in Southeast Asia) has been moving." "Perhaps our basic error all along," he says, explicitly including his own earlier writings in the condemnation, "has been to examine Indonesia with Western eyes; or to be more precise and more generous, with eyes that, though increasingly trained to see things Indonesian, have continued to look at them selectively in accordance with preconceived Western models."

"Most of our questions," he goes on, "have hitherto revolved around a singularly simple continuing theme, perhaps best caricatured by the adage 'What's wrong with Indonesia?.' The answers given . . . vary from author to author, from discipline to discipline; but basically they have led . . . to the discovery of a *diabolus ex machina*," a person or group on whom blame can be cast for the absence of phenomena which 'ought' to be present. In the case of much writing on Indonesia, it is the Dutch who are cast in this *diabolus* role, and occasionally it is the Chinese. In my case, says Benda, it is the 'solidarity makers' or wielders of integrative symbols.

"At the root of the question 'What's wrong?,'" he argues, "lies the unwarranted belief that all societies are essentially similar and that, allowed to develop 'normally,' they will (tautologically) follow a standard norm, that of 'the West.'" This, he says, is 'automatic historical parallelism'. Its basic assumptions are rooted in unsophisticated Liberalism and Marxism (especially of the post-Marxian variety which ignores Marx's theory of the Asiatic mode of production). Its fruits include an excessive willingness to transfer familiar categories to unfamiliar terrain, to identify non-Western phenomena uncritically as 'states,' 'feudalism,' 'nationalism,' 'collaboration,' and so on. And they also include excessive enthusiasm for comparisons between different societies. Not that Benda is against comparative studies as such. But comparisons, he says, should be tentative, and of structures rather than sequences. It is certainly useful to compare peasant protest movements in different societies, but, he seems to be adding, let us not venture to compare processes of industrialization or modernization, or our Europecentrism is likely to get the better of us. "Once we commit ourselves to looking for categorical parallels, especially developmental, chronological parallels, we are in danger of distorting history and reality" by concentrating undue attention on "extrinsic elements."

In dealing with my own argument, Benda makes three main points. Two of them can be dealt with fairly briefly. In the first place my discussion of Indonesian politics in terms of "administrators" and "solidarity makers" is "elite-centered," he says, in a way which does not enable us to "come to grips with the substance of Indonesia's troubled decade." My reply here would be merely to say that I see the power of "solidarity makers" (of all political colors) as resulting from expressive politics, which arises in turn from the revolutionary transition to independence, from social disturbance and radical dissatisfaction with existing conditions. Most of my story is indeed about the doings of elite factions, but I would argue that I suggested the fate of these factions was determined by deeper social forces.

Secondly Benda suggests that my terminology is value-laden, that I use "problem-solvers" ("administrators") to refer to political leaders who "see problems the way the Westerner sees them, and attempt solutions along Western rational lines." Here I can do little more than enter a straight denial. As I defined the term "administrators"--and I can only hope that my readers have found me to be consistent in its use--it refers to a group of leaders with the administrative, technical, and other skills required to run the distinctively modern apparatus of a modern state. I suggested that these men had an interest in, and an affective commitment to, a type of government which accorded high value to economic and administrative achievement. Now this is a characteristically Western orientation, but only in a peculiar sense, or rather in two peculiar senses: in that it was fostered by an apolitical (or quasi-apolitical) colonialism as part of its rationale, and in that it is transmitted today through much of the ideology of Western "foreign aid." (It is not "the Westerner" but one type of Westerner who is bent only on prosperity and efficiency.) And it is certainly not a rational orientation. I did not describe it as rational, nor would I agree that it could be described in this way, that is as more rational than the orientation of "solidarity makers" whose principal concern was to provide integrative leadership to the ex-revolutionaires and others who craved it. As far as I can see, there is nothing in my definition which implies that the economic and administrative problems to which the "administrators" thought governments should be giving the bulk of their attention were in fact "the prime . . . problems demanding solution." Focussing attention as I did on the question of congruence between administrative and economic policies on the one hand and legitimacy arrangements on the other, I thought I was treating these two spheres of government activity as of equal importance.

Benda's third and principal point is that my book "takes an unhistorical starting point or, to put it more precisely, . . . sees postwar Indonesia primarily as a continuation of the country's most recent history, while it largely ignores what has gone before." By way of counter-argument here, he avers that "the modern colonial era (including the Japanese occupation) was a brief interlude in Indonesian history, a 'deviation' we might almost say, from that history. . . . Whatever its impact, alien overlordship did not erase Indonesian history or divert it from its course (sic)."

He follows this up by suggesting that "the contestants in Feith's battle for constitutional democracy appear deceptively evenly matched." "Might it not be more illuminating," he says, "to argue that the problem-solvers' efforts to continue a rational administration and to maintain a modern economic system, both born of and identified with the apolitical colonial status quo, were doomed once Indonesia started to overcome the colonial 'deviation' and once Indonesian (especially Javanese) history found a way back to its own moorings? . . . . In the context of Indonesian history, Feith's problem-solvers, whether thoroughly Westernized or thoroughly Islamized, appear as a small, intrinsically foreign element in the body social of Indonesia; perhaps it would be more accurate to say that they are a foreign element within the social and ideological world of Indianized Indonesia, especially of Java. By contrast, the solidarity makers, though they may often speak in deceptively modern terminology, seem to represent just that specifically Javanese culture. It is only by taking into account the deep roots, the longevity as well as the remarkable resilience of that Hindu-Javanese world to foreign, e.g. Islamic and Western, influences that we can fully understand modern Indonesian developments. It *was*, after all, a world in which the language of the present-day solidarity makers was of far greater intrinsic value than that of rational problem solving."

I must first admit the justice of much of this criticism. I readily agree that I gave far too little attention in my book to traditional notions of legitimacy, to traditional values and perceptions generally, and more broadly to culture. I agree that there are some remarkable similarities between the language of the "solidarity makers" of the present period and that of their predecessors of pre-colonial Java (or Java of the days before colonialism took its distinctively modern forms). There is indeed a sense in which Guided Democracy is a genuine "Return to our National Identity," accompanied as it is by the reemergence of older and deeply rooted norms, styles and ways of thinking which were eclipsed between 1945 and 1958.

But I cannot agree that "the problem-solvers' efforts to continue a rational administration and to maintain a modern economic system . . . were doomed once Indonesia started to overcome the colonial 'deviation' and once Indonesian (especially Javanese) history found a way back to its own moorings." In the first place the phrase "Indonesian (especially Javanese) history" contains a large element of ambiguity. Indonesian history is not the history of Java and it is certainly not the history of the ethnic Javanese (or the inland and non-*santri*, not strongly Islamic, Javanese) who are the bearers of Hindu-Javanese culture. So for Indonesian history to find its "way back to its own moorings" there was no need for its values or styles to become those of this culture. The fact that *prijaji* Javanese have emerged in a position of political preponderance under Guided Democracy can hardly be seen as a natural consequence of "decolonization," or of the resilience of their culture. (And indeed they would not now be in so strong a position in the readily conceivable situation, given a few changes of circumstance, in which the transition from a pluralistic to an authoritarian political order had been achieved at the expense of the Communists, rather than the Masjumi-Socialist-regionalist group.)

But a second point is more important. How useful is it to speak of a country's history finding ways back to its moorings if that country has in fact been irreversibly transformed in much of its economic and social organization by the events of the period of "deviation"? The 120 or so years of modern colonialism did after all introduce a host of new phenomena which are not easily removed: railways and telegraph lines, cities, large-scale export production and heavy reliance on imports, economic interdependence between different parts of the country, a large bureaucracy discharging a wide range of functions at all levels of society, the monetization of much of village life, an eight-fold increase in population, landlessness, and so on.

It was possible for cultural values to remain largely unaffected by such changes, or for that matter norms and perceptions about political authority. But it was quite impossible for the actual processes of governing to remain unaffected. For keeping a regime in power in a situation of partial modernization requires, *inter alia*, that attention be devoted to the solution of economic and administrative problems, to the operation and maintenance of complex modern facilities if not to their expansion; and devoting attention to these problems requires giving power and resources to those with the skills needed to attend to them. So, while it is undeniable that there were strong cultural and historical factors which favored the "solidarity makers" in the struggles of the 1950's (or rather those "solidarity makers" like President Soekarno who were identified with the cultural traditions of Hindu Java), there were also other politically relevant factors which favored the "administrator" group.

Moreover the eventual victory of the Soekarno group of "solidarity makers" cannot be explained simply in terms of the strength of the Javanese tradition. It must be seen also in relation to the factors which led to the prominence of "solidarity makers" as such, of would-be builders of organic states of all political hues, Muslims as well as traditionalists, nationalists, and Communists. And here we come back to social disruption, to the political ferment and inchoate general dissatisfaction which had developed out of the eight-and-a-half years of war, occupation, and revolution, and whose deeper roots are to be found in a century of capitalist penetration. Yearnings for organic political solutions have after all been a common consequence of social disorganization, in societies of greatly varying historical backgrounds.

On the question of how favorable the prospects of constitutional democracy ever were, the disagreement between Professor Benda and myself seems to be rather narrower. He concedes that "what happened did not *have* to happen: the decline of constitutional democracy, though highly probable, was not inevitable." I for my part would admit that the cards were stacked against the system from the start, what with social disruption and messianic expectations on the one hand, and a poorly integrated army and few indigenous propertied groups of any size on the other. And I readily agree that value attachments to constitutional democracy were never sufficiently intense or widespread within the political elite to make it a stable element of consensus on the purposes of government. (There are clearly important contrasts here with circumstances in India and the Philippines.) Indeed, far from treating the Western-modelled system as something "natural," I devoted a good deal of space to answering why it kept going as long as it did.

But the difference between us is still one worth arguing out. For I would insist that constitutional democracy, perhaps more safely termed the "reconciliation system"[1] --let Professor Benda answer to his fellow historians for driving me further in the direction of sociological jargon!--did have a certain durability, a durability which cannot be explained merely in terms of the power resources of its principal upholders. The choice of this pluralistic political order undoubtedly had much to do with the values and interests of a group of Westernized leaders (though I would argue that Westernization as a cultural attribute was less important than the fact that these men had skills disposing them to promote rule-based government and fear "demogocracy). In addition it was clearly connected with the choice of a compromise settlement with the Dutch (the Round Table Conference agreement of 1949) and with the international fashionability of Western-style democracy in the late 1940's. But one cannot explain why pluralist arrangements survived as long as they did without also

---

1. The term comes from David A. Apter's three-part set of developmental types, reconciliation system (e.g. Nigeria), mobilization system (e.g. Ghana), and modernizing autocracy (e.g. Buganda)--see his "System, Process and the Politics of Economic Development," in Bert F. Hoselitz and Wilbert E. Moore, ed., *Industrialization and Society* (UNESCO-Mouton) 1963, pp. 135-158.

referring to a system factor, one which relates to interaction patterns rather than the purposes and interests of actors, namely the fragmentation of national leadership.

Thanks partly to socio-historical variety in the country as a whole and partly to the conditions in which nationalism had developed in the pre-war period--too much repression and too few governmental opportunities for the equivalent of an Indian National Congress to develop, not enough repression and too many governmental opportunities to give the Communists a chance of capturing the nationalist movement and imposing cohesion on it as in Vietnam--no single party of national integration was in existence at the time of independence. Indeed no party was in anything approaching this position. Moreover the army was deeply divided and weak in its central leadership. Power was in fact widely dispersed; the existence of twenty-two parties and other groups in the parliament of 1950 was a fact of more than surface significance.

The survival of the "reconciliation system" was partly a reflection of this dispersal. For each of the major political groups was willing to tolerate a good deal of hamstrung and charismatically unsatisfying government while the alternative was to concur in changes towards a more authoritarian regime in which the risk was that one's opponents would come out on top. In particular, President Soekarno and the leaders of the army, the two major repositories of power outside the party and parliamentary system, were watchfully checking on each other, lest one of them should be able to effect a Caesarian breakthrough at the expense of the other. The problem was eventually resolved, as we know, by the President and the army leaders making common cause to bring the pluralistic order to an end. But this was only after five or six years of checking and balancing, after two years of intensely bitter election campaigning, in which communal cleavages were so aggravated by ideological antagonisms as to destroy virtually all consensus on the purposes of the state, and after a year or so of blatant and alarmingly successful defiance of Djakarta's authority by the leaders of a number of exporting areas outside Java.

All this does not mean that there was anything fortuitous about the defeat, abandonment, and disintegration of the "reconciliation system." But it suggests that the question of why the system failed to maintain itself is neither irrelevant nor intrinsically mistaken, that it is just as important and meaningful as the question of why it should have remained in operation. And it suggests that these two questions are fruitfully looked at in relation to one another. As I see it, it is an advantage of the kind of systems analysis I was attempting to employ that it enables one to do just this, to set system-sustaining factors (and persons and groups) alongside system-destroying or -transforming factors (and persons and groups). For this provides us with a single framework within which to examine a very wide range of variables: interaction patterns (like the fragmentation of national political leadership or the "shared poverty" of Javanese villages)[2] and linear processes (like population growth, urbanization, the expansion of mass communications, the Indonesianization of the foreign stake in the economy, or the rise and spread of mutually antagonistic ideologies), as well as the values and perceptions of different communities and groups and the commitments and strategies of different leaders.

Does the use of system analysis make one an "automatic historical parallelist"? Does this type of analysis assume "the unwarranted belief that all societies are essentially similar and that, allowed to develop 'normally' they will (tautologically)

---

2. See Clifford Geertz, "Religious Belief and Economic Behavior in a Central Javanese Town: Some Preliminary Consideration," *Economic Development and Cultural Change* IV, No. 2 (January 1956), pp. 134-158.

follow a standard norm, that of the West?" I do not believe it does, although it obviously assumes that societies which have developed separately from one another can nevertheless be sufficiently similar to be worth comparing.

There is no denying that system analysis can produce the most gruesome of ethnocentric and other misconceptions if it is unimaginatively applied. Those who employ it may happily ignore the variety of the world's social and political arrangements and assume that all systems of legitimacy, stratification, administration, and so on work in the same way as their Western equivalents. Pushed to its crudest forms, this means that the question "Why is that political system not working?" becomes "Why don't those people do things the way we and all other sensible people do?" Alternatively, a lack of imagination can mean that the formula is "X, Y, and Z need to be done or else the system will not work" rather than "X, Y, and Z *or their functional equivalents* need to be done or else . . ." If this is automatic historical parallelism, then I am with Professor Benda in throwing up my hands in horror at it.

Finally, system analysis requires that one draw a clear line between change which can be accommodated within an existing set of arrangements and change which tends towards the transformation or destruction of the pattern. This can be done with relatively little forcing of reality in relation to politics in some societies, usually ones where the word "regime" is applied, but it may well be seriously misleading in relation to others. And this leads to the central point that system analysis is no more than a set of heuristic devices and should not be treated as having intrinsic value. It can be most useful in relation to some situations. But one must not allow oneself to become its prisoner to the extent of ignoring either empirical reality--history, if that is what we should call it--or alternative theoretical formulations. Let us be cautious by all means, but not to the point of throwing out the baby with the bathwater!

Finally, what is one to make of Professor Benda's minimalist position on the value of comparative studies of non-Western societies? Such studies can be useful, he says, because "striking parallels do exist in many parts of the 'non-Western' world as a result of the basic similarities inherent in the Western impact, especially in Western colonialism". The limitations of this formula are clear, for "many if not most of these very similarities . . . are so to speak isolated particles in the historical landscape of each society. We can . . . study the Western-educated intellectual, the Western-trained civil servant, the Western-influenced officer, here and there perhaps even the Western-style entrepreneur, as generic and hence comparable phenomena of a brief, recent, and in a sense world-wide historical epoch. But this . . . is ultimately bound to remain a study of the transitional if not the ephemeral. . . . The long dog of history is bound to reassert itself and to make it increasingly difficult for the short generic tail to go on wagging it with impunity under the convenient scientific cloak of 'traditional society.' Diversity will triumph in the long run."

It is at this point that I find myself in strongest disagreement with Professor Benda. This is partly because he seems to be denying that societies whose historical development has been separate can be usually compared. But, more important, he seems to be so intent on looking at the Western impact on the non-Western world in cultural terms that technology is left virtually out of account. Yet the West came to the rest of the world as the bearer of a technology which was not only different but superior (as well as as the bearer of a culture which was merely different). It was of course possible for non-Western governments to reject this technology as the Chinese government did for much of the nineteenth century, but this was invariably at considerable long-term cost to their regimes. For they were forced to operate in an international environment in which the technologically advanced states had preponderant power. This was an environment in which strong rewards were offered to regimes which were flexible enough to adopt the more highly developed technology and allowed their social structures and cultures to be transformed to the extent that this was required. And I would argue that very much the same rewards are offered to the governments of technologically backward countries today--notwithstanding the fact that some of them have succeeded, on the basis of diplomatic virtuosity and only fairly limited technological advancement, to acquire positions of considerable power and prestige in the international community.

It is true that independence has been followed in some of the ex-colonial countries by a tendency for the economy and certain other spheres of the society to be organized on the basis of less structural differentiation than before. But this is quite insufficient basis for the inference that the ex-colonial world is growing ever more diverse as the period of Western dominance recedes further into the past.

Professor Benda does concede that it is "highly probable that Indonesia will modernize and that therefore change will come to loom larger than continuity . . . for economic modernization, in particular, is bound to follow its peculiar, rational, and indeed iron logic;" he qualifies this only by the sentence: "But (and this to me is crucial) the ways in which this transformation will take place will very likely be Indonesian-derived." Yet it is surely not true, as his discussion implies, that the logic of economic modernization will only begin to come into effect when a government starts being as determined about modernization as Stalin, Mao, or the Japanese leaders of the late nineteenth century. I would insist that this logic is operative in some measure today; for any government of a complex partly modernized state, as Indonesia undoubtedly is, must concern itself with the efficient discharging of economic functions, and so sponsor various activities which it sees as culturally alien and *a priori* undesirable. And indeed it is never merely a matter of operating the modern technical facilities one has inherited from the days of colonial control, for all of the governments of the ex-colonial world are introducing new facilities of this kind--even if they are only new weapons or new computers for government departments.

In my view it is here, in the need to continue to operate a variety of modern technical facilities, and in the manifold pressures to expand these, that comparative studies finds its principal *raison d'être*, here rather than in particular groups of Western-trained or Western-influenced intellectuals, civil servants, army officers or entrepreneurs. The existence of much modern technology and economic organization in all of the new states, and the effective or ineffective integration into the patterns of social organization and political culture which have evolved from particular historical legacies, provides an enormously fertile field for comparisons, both among the new states of today and between them and the countries which have already passed through something like a "Great Transformation," in either a slow and messy way or a dramatic and fast one.

I would concede that a lot of recent research on non-Western societies, inspired by sociological theory and by the passion for macro-sociological comparisons, has taken far too little account of the history of these societies, particularly their pre-colonial history. There has no doubt been too little research, and too much generalizing based on it (or *not* based on it); the number of rigorous and systematic studies comparing phenomena in different non-Western societies is in fact still tiny. Furthermore many of the theoretical formulations which are being advanced in the whole area of non-Western studies are taken up for ideological utility, and so gain currency to an extent quite unjustified by their analytical value. The notion of "traditional society" is probably one of these. Attractive to liberal internationalists because of its suggestion that "Asians are basically very much like ourselves"--we used to speak of "feudalism" till the historians caught up to us--it has probably done more harm than good by obscuring the great variety of history and historical legacy in different parts of the world. Finally one can see why Professor Benda should be particularly apprehensive about comparative studies concerned with the sequential or developmental dimension. For this brings one inevitably to "modernization." And the present state of modernization theory is not happy. The word is wrapped in ambiguity and confusion.[3]

Altogether there is a good deal to be criticized about the comparative and theoretical approach to non-Western societies. Its very fashionability is a considerable source of danger. And it is proper and desirable that historians should be waiting to pounce on any of its practitioners whose scholarship is poor.

But it has also drawn our attention to an exciting range of new questions worth asking, to a whole series of new ways of moving from the known to the unknown.

---

3. For some of the many efforts currently being made to clear up the confusion, see the contributions of Wilbert E. Moore and Neil J. Smelser in Hoselitz and Moore, *op. cit.* pp. 32-54, 299-370; S. N. Eisenstadt, "Modernization: Growth and Diversity," *India Quarterly* Vol. 20, No. 1, Jan.-March 1953; Robert N. Bellah, "Reflections on the Protestant Ethic Analogy in Asia," *Journal of Social Issues*, XIX No. 1, Jan. 1963; and Fred W. Riggs, *Reflections on Development*, unpublished paper, University of Hawaii, 1963.

HISTORY AND SOCIAL STRUCTURE IN THE STUDY OF CONTEMPORARY INDONESIA

David Levine

Harry Benda has characterized theorizing about postindependence Indonesia as "essentially presenting us highly sophisticated and persuasive answers to an intrinsically mistaken, or irrelevant, question."[1] Although, as we shall see, his own analysis shares the same basic failings found in those he criticizes, his complaint is well taken. Those who have attempted solutions to the problem of making sense of the last twenty years of Indonesian history have failed, by and large, to see beyond the surface phenomena. They find themselves so absorbed by the intricacies of parliamentary politics that most of their time is spent in the sorting out of month-to-month maneuvers in cabinet and parliament. This failure to penetrate to the essentials of a problem, it must be emphasized, cannot be attributed to lack of intelligence, integrity, or scholarship. Rather the source of the difficulty must be located in the basic perspective from which such analysts operate. The specific approach which a theorist adopts defines not only the character of his analysis but the questions which he poses and, equally, the questions he does not pose. If the questions are posed incorrectly, the analysis will be incapable of explaining the phenomena under study.

All attempts to analyze the Indonesian political system *from within*, by accepting the social structure which forms its underpinning as given, must share in the irrationality of that system. In other words, if the social groups, and classes, which hold political and economic power use that power to obstruct rather than to facilitate progress, then the social system which they dominate is irrational. History has its own internal logic in the sense that it displays objective laws of development. Mental processes should reflect this objective logic. By rejecting the laws of historic development, analytic theory ties itself down to the "present," becomes incapable of envisioning revolutionary social change, and, in essence, denies the possibility of progress. With respect to Indonesia, such theorizing becomes totally bound up in what is an essentially retrogressive social system. When thinking about the problems generated by such a system accepts that system as "given," then that thinking can neither understand the social system as an historically rooted and transitory phenomenon nor allow that solutions to the society's problems must be sought in the transformations of the system itself.

The unsatisfactory nature of the available analyses of modern Indonesia is particularly discouraging because of the immediacy and the seriousness of her problems. The future seems (on the surface at least) to hold no solutions to the problems of unemployment, poverty, inflation, and political instability. The "Constitutional

---

1. "Democracy in Indonesia," *Journal of Asian Studies*, 23, 3 (May 1964), p. 449. (See above, p. 14.)

Democracy" of the 1950s has been gradually transformed into a military dictatorship more in line with underlying social realities. The need for a theory which can be used to help solve these problems has barely begun to be met.

One of the more impressive attempts to explain Indonesian politics is that of Herbert Feith.[2] His work is concerned with accounting for the political instability that plagues the entire period since the Revolution. Feith attempts to explain these events in terms of a cleavage within the Indonesian elite. On the one hand was a group of men (associated with Hatta) whom he designates as an "administrative" elite. These men were particularly involved with the day-to-day concerns of running the country and stabilizing the economy. Opposed to this group was one designated as "solidarity-makers," led by Sukarno. This latter group was more concerned with the symbols of the Revolution and the continuing of the Revolution than with the administration of the government. The first group is seen by Feith as more conservative and Western-oriented as well as more efficient and capable than the second. For Feith "the history of the period is the story of the political failure of the Hatta group of leaders."[3] Within Indonesia the ties of this group were to "nonbureaucratic business"; it wanted to conserve what it could of the "modern administrative and economic structure" left from the colonial period.

It is in the intraelite battle between these two groups that Feith finds the source of the political instability of the period. Yet in accounting for the failure of constitutional democracy, he is forced to focus on "factors related to political unrest." The source of this unrest lay in the Revolution, and the groups with which it was associated were outside of the elite. The very problems with which the elite was forced to deal were (and still are) problems of "how this unrest would be handled."[4]

So far as the true source of the failure of constitutional democracy lies in the unrest of groups outside of the elite, it lies in a factor external to Feith's entire theoretical structure. The problem becomes one of accounting for the existence of this unrest and then accounting for its influence on Indonesian politics. We make little progress by pointing to the rise of a "solidarity-maker" group which exploits this unrest if we do not turn our analysis to the historical, social, and economic relationships between the ruling groups and the masses. The "solidarity-maker" group is still a part of the ruling elite and is in no basic sense representative of the people.

The uneasiness inherent in an analysis such as the above is even more apparent in Daniel Lev's discussion in his *Transition to Guided Democracy*. In basic structure, the work is quite comparable to Feith's. Again Lev is concerned with a month-by-month cataloguing of the events in Indonesian political life. Insofar as he holds to this approach, his concern is with developments within the elite. Yet, perhaps because of the nature of the period he has chosen, a new factor, outside of the elite, breaks into the analysis. The increasing unrest of the masses, generally associated with (though not identical to) the rise of the Communist Party (PKI), forces its way into the political life of the elite-run constitutional democracy. It is in large measure the accessibility of the parliamentary structures to mass demands through the electoral mechanism that is responsible for their dissolution. The confrontation between the ruling classes and the more conscious elements of the masses which forms a central theme of Indonesian politics, undermines the whole analytical

---

2. *Decline of Constitutional Democracy in Indonesia* (Ithaca: Cornell University, Press, 1962).

3. Ibid., p. 604.

4. Ibid., p. 606.

basis of the elite-centered history of Feith and Lev. The latter is somewhat more aware of this than is the former. Although he fails to dissect the relationship between his elite and the masses, it is an essential point of his analysis that "Communist success in the parliamentary system contributed to the eventual replacement of that system by Guided Democracy."[5] Lev's insight into the relationship of the PKI to the system of parliamentary democracy is important because it can form both the basis of a more satisfying analysis of Indonesian politics and a critique of his own work. It is therefore worthwhile to quote him at length:

> . . . the PKI threatened not only the other parties, but the entire social and political order. It was not simply that everyone feared that the Communists, once in power, would overthrow the existing political organization, eliminate the old elite, and invoke their own exclusive ideology. That clearly was the crux of the matter, but it cannot be too strongly emphasized that the social force mobilized by the PKI could not be matched by any of the other parties, by the army, or even (in organizational terms) by President Sukarno. . . . By containing the truly radical PKI, the elite whom it challenged, both party and nonparty, was able to maintain its hopes for the future. It is important to point out that this elite did in fact remain in power under Guided Democracy and that it did so by shifting away from a broader electoral basis of politics towards a narrower and more traditional elite basis.[6]

The increasing popularity of the PKI, while by no means identical with the unrest of the masses, is a strong indication and reflection of the strength of that unrest.

At this point, it is important to see that the discussion thus far has brought the approach of Feith and Lev into serious question. If postindependence developments are best understood in terms of an increasing threat to elite power by a disaffected mass, then the key historical problems focus around the nature of Indonesian social structure itself and the sources of unrest in the Indonesian political economy. Yet, the two discussions cited above are more concerned with developments on the purely political level than with the underlying problems of the political economy.

Before elaborating this critique, it will be instructive to turn to some of the economic theory available to students of contemporary Indonesia.

We might begin with the least satisfactory kind of analysis--that which sees political and economic factors as basically independent, though having important influences on each other. Such an analysis allows political questions into its theorizing only in the very crude sense of political instability creating economic instability. Although "economic conditions . . . have had much to do with aggravating deep-seated political tensions," tensions which are "associated with the general social revolution," nonetheless, basically, "Indonesian experience in 1957 and 1958 presents an almost classic example of the economic ramifications of political instability."[7] By ignoring the unity of economics and politics, Douglas Paauw provides a striking example of an analytical theory which partakes of the irrationality of its subject matter. He sees two fundamental solutions to Indonesia's economic difficulties:

---

5. Daniel Lev, *Transition to Guided Democracy: Indonesian Politics, 1957-1959* (Ithaca: Cornell Modern Indonesia Project, 1966), p. 75.

6. Ibid., p. 171.

7. Douglas S. Paauw, "The High Cost of Political Instability in Indonesia," in *Indonesia's Struggle*, ed. B. H. M. Vlekke (The Hague: Netherlands Institute of International Affairs, 1959), p. 23.

reduction of inflation-financed spending and expansion of aggregate supply.[8] The curious fact about these "solutions" is that they are mutually exclusive, given the present structure of the Indonesian political economy. If no change comes about in the "mode of utilization" of Indonesia's economic surplus,[9] there will be no other indigenous source of financing than inflation, and aggregate supply is not likely to increase without government financing. Thus Paauw's solution is no more (and perhaps considerably less) than a statement of the problem.

We are presented with an essentially sterile framework of analysis: inflation results (in large part) from deficit spending; deficit spending, in its turn, results both from the lack of alternative sources of funds and from the need to meet the expenses of political instability itself. Thus, if the unrest of the masses is to be eased, economic development is essential, and yet outside of inflationary deficit spending, the government has no funds from indigenous sources for effective development programs.

Here we seem confronted with an insurmountable theoretical (and practical) question. It is generally conceived of as a "vicious circle."[10] There seem to be no sources for financing economic development which will not result in political instability which is itself a drain on funds potentially available for development. Such funds are used to build armies and civil services rather than tractors and factories. A closer examination, however, should reveal that the knot in which these theorists seem tied is one strictly of their own making. There is no way out in sight because of the restricted vision of those who are looking. To find the source of their problems it is necessary to isolate their generally unstated underlying assumptions.

In his review of Feith's book, Harry Benda criticizes Feith along these lines. He attempts to bring out the underlying assumptions of Feith's approach which render his results sterile and comes upon the following insight:

> Most of our questions . . . have hitherto resolved around a singularly simple, continuing theme best caricatured by the adage, "What's wrong with Indonesia?" The answers given to this all pervasive, if usually unstated, question vary from author to author, from discipline to discipline; but basically they have led--with greater or less ingenuity--to the discovery of a *diabolus ex machina*.[11]

The trouble with this approach, as Benda suggests, is that it is unhistorical. Such theorizing is bounded by Western history. If something has gone wrong then there must be some right way in which Indonesia should have developed. In a certain sense this assertion is undeniable. There must be something radically unsatisfactory in a country in which social disorder, poverty, and violence have been endemic for a good deal longer than the twenty odd years since independence. However the tone in which the question "what went wrong" is generally asked tends to deny any structural disease in favor of a *diabolus ex machina*. The basic structure of social relationships is seen as adequate for the task of pursuing economic development and political democracy; therefore, if these objectives have not been achieved

---

8. Ibid., p. 30.

9. For a discussion of the concept of the economic surplus see: Paul A. Baran, *The Political Economy of Growth* (New York: Monthly Review, 1962), ch. 2.

10. See, for example: Paauw, "High Cost of Political Instability," p. 23; and Herbert Feith, "Dynamics of Guided Democracy," in *Indonesia*, ed. Ruth McVey (New Haven: H.R.A.F., 1963), p. 409.

11. Benda, "Democracy in Indonesia," p. 450.

it is only because the individuals in charge have been incapable or uninterested in such progress. In other words, this approach accepts the social structure as given and finds the major historical dynamic not in social groups and classes, but in individuals.[12]

The alternative Benda presents us for understanding recent Indonesian history is a kind of identity crisis on a grand scale. In the last twenty years we have witnessed "the agonizing, difficult adjustment of Indonesia to its own identity. . . . A selective process of adapting resurgent continuity to a changing reality."[13] He contends that the colonial period in Indonesia has had little influence on the basic continuity of Indonesian history. His argument is that in terms of elite structure,[14] and in terms of economic change,[15] the influence of the West has been, in a basic sense, superficial.

What Benda succeeds in enforcing is, above all, the reorientation of our approach to Indonesian history. In order to evaluate and criticize his approach we must clarify the relationship between Western imperialism and the course of Indonesian history. The connection is much more organic and continuing than Benda realizes. Insofar as the Indonesian Revolution failed to sever Indonesia's future from the structures and laws of development defined by the colonial relationships of the past, analysts who ignore colonial relationships and concentrate on postindependence politics as if they occurred in a vacuum cannot possibly explain what they see. Equally, insofar as the colonial relationship has radically affected the character of Indonesian society, analysts (such as Benda) who look to an Indonesian "identity" in the precolonial past are searching for something of questionable significance.

Recent studies by Pelzer[16] and van der Kroef[17] indicate that, contrary to Benda's thesis, important changes have been going on in the economic and social structure of rural Indonesia. These studies indicate that "in the past century, and in particular in the last four decades, tenancy, along with the rise of a landlord class, has reached alarming proportions in densely populated sections of rural Java."[18] These changes are greatly influencing Javanese social and cultural institutions.[19] Insofar as these are significant developments, Benda's attempt to return to precolonial history is bound to be seriously misleading. The relationship between the colonial period and the present Indonesian situation is much more important than even these discussions indicate. To see this, we now turn to those analysts who have studied present developments from a historical perspective.

---

12. Feith, *Decline of Constitutional Democracy*, p. 108.

13. Harry Benda, "Decolonization in Indonesia: The Problem of Continuity and Change," *American Historical Review*, 70 (July 1965), p. 1072.

14. Ibid., pp. 1065-66.

15. Ibid., p. 1066.

16. Karl J. Pelzer, "The Agricultural Foundation," in *Indonesia*, ed. McVey.

17. J. M. van der Kroef, "Indonesia's Economic Future," *Pacific Affairs*, 32 (March 1959), "Peasant and Land Reform in Indonesian Communism," *Journal of Southeast Asian History*, 4, 1 (March 1963); and "Land Tenure and Social structure in Rural Java," *Rural Sociology*, 25, 4 (December 1960).

18. Van der Kroef, "Land Tenure," p. 422.

19. Van der Kroef, "Indonesia's Economic Future," p. 60.

One of the few efforts to see contemporary Indonesian history as an integral part of a historical development is that of Clifford Geertz.[20] His analysis operates on an entirely different level than those previously discussed. But, not only does his analysis highlight the inadequacies of our first group of theories of "what went wrong"; in addition, by specifying the colonial relationship as the key to the economic development of Indonesia, Geertz brings Benda's theory into further doubt.

According to Geertz:

> The economy functions much less efficiently but (or, more precisely, because) it is the same economy. The threefold thematic structure announced by the Company, developed by the Culture System, and resolved by the Corporate Plantation System--technological dualism, regional imbalance, and ecological involution--persists; and the frustrations of Indonesian aspirations persist with it.[21]

The influence of Dutch colonialism has been to sacrifice the possibilities of Indonesian industrialization in favor of Dutch. The discussion implies very strongly that Dutch economic development and Indonesian underdevelopment are two sides of the same coin. For the Javanese peasant "there was no industrial sector into which to move and, as the returns from cultivation went, in Furnivall's words, to keep the Netherlands from becoming another Portugal, none developed."[22] It is purely hypothetical to speculate on whether Indonesia would have industrialized had the Dutch not been present. It is not hypothetical, however, to point out that the effect of Dutch involvement was to close off any opportunity for development and ensure that the history of the Indonesian economy would be one of underdevelopment.

The point to be emphasized here is that the forces generating underdevelopment did not disappear with the Revolution in 1949. This is precisely the reason why a correct understanding of the entire colonial period is the essential prerequisite for an understanding of present problems. In the words of Paul Baran:

> Indeed the forces that have moulded the fate of the backward world still exercise a powerful impact on the conditions prevailing at the present time. Their forms have changed, their intensities are different today; their origin and direction have remained unaltered. They control now as they have controlled in the past the destinies of the underdeveloped capitalist countries, and it is the speed with which and the processes by which they will be overcome that will determine these countries' future economic and social development.[23]

H. O. Schmitt has suggested a reinterpretation of Indonesian politics which, in some important respects, fits in well with this thesis. Operating on the premise

---

20. See: *Agricultural Involution: The Process of Ecological Change in Indonesia* (Berkeley: University of California, 1966). One other such study is that of J. H. Boeke, *Economics and Economic Policy of Dual Societies as Exemplified by Indonesia* (New York: Institute of Pacific Relations, 1953). I have neither the time nor space to discuss this latter work. For a criticism of the theory as it applies to Indonesia, see Geertz, *Agricultural Involution*, pp. 61-62. For a more general criticism of "dual" theories see Andrew Gunder Frank, "The Development of Underdevelopment," *Monthly Review*, 18, 4 (September 1966).

21. Geertz, *Agricultural Involution*, p. 125.

22. Ibid., p. 80.

23. Baran, *Political Economy of Growth*, p. 163.

that politics and economics must be united, he has succeeded in explaining some important aspects of political instability in terms of the foreign penetration of the Indonesian economy.

By examining the inflation which has plagued Indonesia since independence and by determining its primary victims, Schmitt is able to account for the conflict between Java and the Outer Islands in terms of "the contrary interests of exporters and importers" which "were quickly translated into a conflict between geographic regions."[24] The analysis takes us a step further by associating the exporters and importers with interest groups. In terms of economic groups "a bureaucracy in control of the state exploited inflationary policies at the expense of trading groups."[25] Here we have a cleavage within the Indonesian elite of significantly greater substance than that which forms the basis of Feith's analysis. Not only does it expose the superficiality of the "administrator"–"solidarity-maker" dichotomy but it also connects the divisions in the elite to foreign penetration of the economy and to economic backwardness. Schmitt suggests that taxing importers (who benefited by the inflation) was "politically dangerous because of the central importance the treatment of importers had in the relations between the Indonesian elite and the foreign managerial groups that controlled the bulk of the economy. . . ."[26]

The relation between political instability and the foreign domination of the economy goes much deeper. As long as the property rights of foreigners were guaranteed, the Indonesian political leadership could "not freely dispose of the resources of their own country,"[27] nor could they mobilize funds to finance economic development. An analysis, such as Feith's, which fails to make this fact central will be incapable of answering the challenge implicit in Schmitt's argument and made explicit by Bruce Glassburner:

> Why, aside from the three almost quixotic attempts to deal with financial crises did all cabinets do so little in any direction? If they were all nationalists, why did they not vigorously attack the vested Dutch interests? Since they all called themselves socialists, why was there no vigorous program of building of state enterprise? Why when the more pragmatic intellectual clique was defeated, was there no clear repudiation of their policies and marked swing to reflect the polar political swing which Herbert Feith finds?[28]

The answer, as Glassburner suggests (in part), is that given the colonial nature of economic relations few alternatives were open.

It should be possible now to specify the source of the failings of the theories discussed at the beginning of this paper. As I pointed out earlier, the approach which asks "what went wrong?" is essentially unhistorical in that it denies the unity of the present with the past in Indonesia. By fixing our attention on the most recent years, it obscures the source of today's problems in the broader historical development. In fact, nothing "went wrong" in Indonesia. Given the colonial legacy and the lack of a true social revolution, things could hardly have gone any other way.

---

24. H. O. Schmitt, "Post-colonial Politics: A Suggested Interpretation of the Indonesian Experience, 1950-1958," *Australian Journal of Politics and History*, 9, 2 (November 1963), p. 177.

25. Ibid., p. 178.

26. Ibid., p. 180.

27. Ibid., p. 181.

28. Bruce Glassburner, "Economic Policy-Making in Indonesia," *Economic Development and Cultural Change*, 10, 2, pt. 1 (January 1962), p. 130.

The root failure of these analysts lies in their inability to envision an alternative to economic development as it came about in the West and to social structure as it developed in Indonesia. This inability manifests itself in various ways. One is the view of economic development as a purely technical or "economic" problem, rather than as a key social issue around which opposing social groups muster their forces. In the first view, solutions are arrived at through consultations with experts on the technical problems of building bridges and of input-output analysis. In the second view solutions are arrived at (sometimes violently) through the triumph of one of the antagonistic groups. The former view is the essence of Feith's concern over an "administrative" or "problem-solving" elite.[29] When it comes down to this basic point, we find Benda grouped with those he criticizes most severely. This is the implication of his contention that, if Indonesia is to modernize (as he thinks it will), "'solidarity-making' will be forced to yield--or at least make progressively more room for--'problem-solving.'" The reason for this being that "economic modernization, in particular, is bound to follow its peculiar, rational, and, indeed, iron logic."[30]

A somewhat different instance of the view of economic development as a purely technical factor is the view that it is politically neutral. Thus if we desire to add substance to Douglas Paauw's "solution" to the economic difficulties in Indonesia, we might be tempted to suggest that if it were not for political instability and the resultant drain on funds, resources would be released for the financing of economic development. We might be further tempted to contend that much of this potential capital comes from payments by foreign enterprise. The problem with this approach is that it disunites political and economic development and "even if partaking of the truth with regard to the parts constitutes falsehoods with regard to the whole," by severing an historical phenomenon "from its inevitable outgrowth."[31] Misuse of funds is a result of the character of power relationships in Indonesia. In this sense it is an outgrowth, or manifestation, of social organization (or disorganization) rather than the cause of it.

Justus van der Kroef, who takes a position initially opposed to the above, ultimately shares this inability to see economic development as involving a deep-seated social and political transformation. He argues that local social structure has been a serious impediment to economic development. But rather than realize the necessity of the transformation of social structure as a key aspect of economic development he sees the existing "variety of social structures and cultural tones . . . as a desirable determinant of economic development."[32] Thus economic development plans should be better adapted to existing social structures.

This perspective contrasts sharply with that which realizes the profound social implications of economic development. We can do little better than quote Paul Baran on this point:

> . . . Economic development has historically always meant a far-reaching transformation of societies' economic, social, and political structure, of the dominant organization of production, distribution, and consumption. Economic development has always been propelled by classes and groups interested in a new economic and social order, has always been opposed and

---

29. Feith, "Dynamics of Guided Democracy," particularly pp. 387-88, 395.

30. Benda, "Democracy in Indonesia," p. 455.

31. Baran, *Political Economy of Growth*, p. 218.

32. J. M. van der Kroef, "Social Structure and Economic Development in Indonesia," *Social Research*, 23 (January 1957), p. 417.

obstructed by those interested in the *status quo*, rooted in and deriving innumerable benefits and habits of thought from the existing fabric of society, the prevailing mores, customs, and institutions. It has always been marked by more or less violent clashes, has proceeded by starts and spurts, suffered setbacks and gained new terrain--it has never been a smooth, harmonious process unfolding placidly over time and space.[33]

Here, then, is one striking instance of a theory which cannot transcend the social system it is constructed to explain. Theorists of economic development look hopefully to a Western-oriented, "responsible," administrative group to accomplish development. Just such a group is closest to the interests of Western capital and this capital is always seen as indispensible to development. The trouble is that it has been in close contact with Western capital which has, in Indonesia, resulted in underdevelopment.

This is the relationship traced so well by Geertz. Yet, in terms of connecting political events with the underlying social and economic forces, his analysis also fails us. He, perhaps more than any of the other writers, is unable to suggest an alternative to the continuation of these developments. The involution theme is essentially unhistorical insofar as it fails to encompass possible alternatives to the present "ecosystem"; rather it asks: "given an ecosystem . . . how is it organized?"[34] This approach falls apart if the given system contains, as an integral part of it, forces which both seek and are capable of accomplishing its transformation. In such cases only an analysis which can itself envision the transformation of a social system has achieved a real understanding of that system.

As far as the analysis of Glassburner and Schmitt takes us,[35] it, too, falls down in this one, all important, respect. After having specified foreign economic domination as a major source of the political and economic difficulties of postindependence Indonesia, both fail seriously to propose some way in which an end to this domination can come about as the first step towards economic development and political stability. "Indonesia's present plight" is, indeed, "the logical consequence of a particularly unfortunate social structure"--a social structure dominated by foreign enterprise. Yet, while Schmitt seems capable of realizing that this "unfortunate social structure" results when "an imperial power transfers political authority to a former colony without concurrently ceding economic power as well,"[36] he does not seem ready to suggest an alternative. Writing in 1963, he suggested that the United States buy up and give to Indonesia the various foreign holdings there, but this is obviously beyond the realm of the conceivable. What we must look to is not the American government turning on its own, but social forces in Indonesia capable of taking positive action to regain control over the Indonesian economy. However, the taking of economic power by "Indonesians" will not, by itself, prove sufficient to assure economic growth and social peace. Forceful and effective development programs can be accomplished only by a party with widespread popular support and organization, a party which can, in effect, bring the masses into an active role in the reconstruction of Indonesian society.

---

33. Baran, *Political Economy of Growth*, pp. 3-4.

34. Geertz, *Agricultural Involution*, p. 10.

35. This is not to deny differences in the analyses of these two. See their exchange in *Economic Development and Cultural Change*, vols. 10, 11, and 12. However, they do seem to be in agreement on this point.

36. Schmitt, "Foreign Capital and Social Conflict in Indonesia, 1950-1958," *Economic Development and Cultural Change*, 10, 3 (April 1962), p. 292.

What is required is a study of the basic structure of Indonesian society, of the basic character--the strengths and weaknesses--of those social groups which will support such a plan of reconstruction, and those which will oppose it. The terms employed in many of the foregoing analyses are suggestive of the amount of work yet to be done. Up to this point the term "elite" has been used uncritically--accurately reflecting the use made of the term in most of the literature. It is not at all clear, however, that the concept of "elite" (or the analogous concept of "mass") provides us with the clarity or rigor necessary for an understanding of Indonesian society. On closer examination the concept, which is quite satisfactory for analyzing the outward appearance of power in Indonesia, breaks down if we are interested in the underlying basis of that power.

The elite, roughly speaking, contains those individuals who hold top positions in the official institutions for wielding power--the parliament, cabinet, political parties, and the army. By implication power resides in these institutions, and is the domain of individuals directly associated with these institutions rather than social groups and classes. But the correctness of this conception is not at all clear, particularly in the light of the rapid decline of these institutions (with the exception of the army) after a brief period of predominance. One lesson we can learn from more recent history is that, again with the exception of the army, real power in Indonesia was not exclusively, or even essentially, the domain of the institutions officially viewed as the center of power. Real power is associated with the making of important decisions and, as Feith has shown,[37] the Indonesian parliaments and cabinets have been largely incapable of decision making.

The ambiguity of the term elite is particularly striking when it is applied to the leadership of the Communist Party. While considering this leadership a part of the elite may or may not clarify something about its relationship with the Party's rank and file, it obscures the relationship of the PKI to the other parties and to the political system itself. Insofar as the PKI had a basis of power in the support of significant social groups and classes (e.g., the urban and rural workers) it stood apart from the other parties (see above, p. 31). To group the leadership of the PKI with the leadership of the nationalist or Moslem parties under the category of elite is to obscure basic divisions in Indonesian society, the analysis of which may lead to a better understanding of Indonesian politics.[38] To take the point a step further, even the grouping of non-Communist leaders under a common heading may gloss over important cleavages in this group (such as that suggested by Schmitt) and thus be seriously misleading.

As noted at the beginning of this essay, groups outside of the elite tend to be given a secondary position in discussions of Indonesian politics. These groups may be designated the "mass"--a catch-all phrase for everyone not in the elite and, therefore, only as meaningful as the term elite from which it is derived by exclusion. Here, too, important distinctions are obscured. The mass, so defined, includes at least the following diverse (and in some cases antagonistic) social groups: peasants, tenant farmers, the rural and urban proletariat, the rural and urban unemployed, middle-class merchants and traders, and, in some cases, small-scale landlords.

---

37. Feith, *Decline of Constitutional Democracy*, pp. 309, 312, 557.

38. Jan Pluvier provides the beginnings of such an analysis. See his *Confrontations* (Kuala Lumpur: Oxford University Press, 1965). His analysis suffers from the fact that he goes little deeper into Indonesian social structure than any of the others. His own elite-mass dichotomy is somewhat more useful but not appreciably less ambiguous.

This confusion of terminology may have its source in recent Indonesian history itself. The nationalist movement, by its socially amorphous character, may have encouraged the depreciation of basic social divisions. Nationalism was supported by a variety of diverse social groups and it has taken time for the apparent unity of the movement to dissolve in the face of resurgent divisions.

In order to understand Indonesian society we need theory which operates along two dimensions which are all too often neglected. What theory we have sees largely the apparent, or surface, dimension. With notable exceptions,[39] this theory is concerned with the manifestations of deep-seated social problems rather than with those problems themselves. More viable theory must penetrate first to the basis of political and economic instability in the social structure, and second, to the historical dimension of contemporary Indonesian problems. If we approach present-day Indonesia as a historical phenomenon, then two important consequences follow. First, contemporary Indonesia cannot be understood in isolation, but only as an outgrowth of the accommodation of an indigenous society to Western imperialism which has influenced, and continues deeply to affect it. The second consequence of viewing the present in historical perspective is the necessity of treating Indonesian social and economic structure, not as a given within which solutions of problems must be sought, but as a historically rooted phenomenon the transformation of which will provide the only solution to these problems.

---

39. For example, W. F. Wertheim, *Indonesian Society in Transition: A Study of Social Change* (The Hague: van Hoeve, 1959).

THE STUDY OF INDONESIAN POLITICS:
A SURVEY AND AN APOLOGIA*

Herbert Feith

Five years ago Harry J. Benda, the Yale historian, described theorizing about postindependence Indonesia as "essentially presenting us highly sophisticated and persuasive answers to an intrinsically mistaken, or irrelevant, question."[1] "Perhaps our basic error all along," he said, "has been to examine Indonesia with Western eyes; or, to be more precise and more generous, with eyes that, though increasingly trained to see things Indonesian, have continued to look at them selectively, in accordance with preconceived Western models. Most of our questions ... [have] revolved around a singularly simple, continuing theme, perhaps best caricatured by the adage 'What's wrong with Indonesia?' The answers given to this all-pervasive, if usually unstated, question vary from author to author, from discipline to discipline; but basically they have led--with greater or lesser ingenuity-- to the discovery of a *diabolus ex machina*."

More recently David Levine, an undergraduate radical at Wisconsin, has castigated the students of contemporary Indonesian politics in even more sweeping terms. Quoting Benda's characterization--"highly sophisticated and persuasive answers to an intrinsically mistaken, or irrelevant, question"--he has gone on to say that Benda's own "analysis shares the same basic failings found in those he criticizes." According to Levine, "Those who have attempted solutions to the problems of making sense of the last twenty years of Indonesian history have failed, by and large, to see beyond the surface phenomena. They find themselves so absorbed by the intricacies of parliamentary politics that most of their time is spent in the sorting out of month-to-month maneuvres in cabinet and parliament. . . . Such theorizing becomes totally bound up in what is an essentially retrogressive social system."[2]

---

* Herbert Feith circulated this preliminary mimeographed paper in 1969 for reactions and criticisms from his fellow Indonesianists. Only the first part, dealing with the period up to about 1960, is in the form of an article. The last few pages, where he dealt with more current themes, problems, and disagreements and where he mentioned areas he felt had been neglected, was only sketched out schematically. This original format has been retained.

1. "Democracy in Indonesia," *Journal of Asian Studies*, 23, 3 (May 1964), p. 449. See above, p. 14.

2. "History and Social Structure in the Study of Contemporary Indonesia," *Indonesia*, 7 (April 1969), p. 5. See above, p. 30.

I propose to argue that the study of Indonesian politics is in much healtheir shape than Benda and Levine suggest. I will contend that it has responded and is responding to challenges like Benda's--to look more seriously at traditional Javanese values and take more interest in the historical evolution of distinctive social structures--and Levine's--to focus attention on class conflicts and on "the accommodation of an indigenous society to Western imperialism which . . . continues deeply to affect it."[3] And I will seek to show that it has advanced dialectically as these and other demands for new perspectives, as well as the changes in the political scene itself, and the changing concerns of Indonesian intellectuals, have led to new questions being asked.

Such advances as have been made may seem insignificant to believers in social science as a grand redemptive enterprise, who look forward to the day when political phenomena will be studied in a truly "scientific," wholly nonevaluative way by specialists working with ever better techniques in ever narrower fields. And they will not come near satisfying vulgar Marxists with a monistic concern for "correct" or "essentially correct" questions which are "rational" because they accord with the "objective laws of historical development." But those who see Politics as a critical discipline and one which should serve to link the world of historical, sociological and economic scholarship with that of engagé intellectuals and political and bureaucratic actors, will, I hope, be persuaded that the study of Indonesian politics, for all of the myopia and muddle which continues to characterize it, has come a long way since its beginnings twenty years ago.

The Kahinian Phase

The kind of political analysis which is today the concern of political scientists, rather than historians or sociologists, scarcely existed before 1950. Prewar Dutch scholarship on the archipelago, voluminous, scrupulous and imaginative in so many fields--history, archaeology, philology, ethnography, law and economics, to name the main ones--concerned itself only very marginally with either the politics of the administrative state or the emerging world of indigenous modern politics. There was a great deal of polemical writing on colonial policy in general, and on constitutional development, some of it very well informed; A. D. A. de Kat Angelino's *Colonial Policy*, the main academic defense of the system, has a classic quality about it. In addition the sociologist B. J. O. Schrieke did highly valuable work on the origins of the Communist revolt in West Sumatra in 1927, and other scholars working on Islam and the local Chinese wrote perceptively on the political activities of the communities they were studying. But Dutch writing on mainstream indigenous politics, the nationalist underbelly of political life in Batavia, Bandoeng and Soerabaja, includes little more, for a period of almost four decades, than a scatter of essays, reflective and polemical, and J. Th. Petrus Blumberger's meticulous but analytically shallow volumes (police file data in good part), on nationalist, communist, and Indo-European political organizations.[4] Visitors to the Indies, like the Englishman J. S. Furnivall,[5] the Frenchman G. H. Bousquet,[6] and the Americans

---

3. Ibid., p. 19.

4. *De Nationalistische Beweging in Nederlandsch-Indië* (Haarlem: Tjeenk Willink, 1931), *De Communistische Beweging in Nederlandsch-Indië* (Haarlem: Tjeenk Willink, 1935), *De Indo-Europeaansche Beweging in Nederlandsch-Indië* (Haarlem: Tjeenk Willink, 1939).

5. *Netherlands India: A Study in Plural Economy* (New York: Macmillan, 1944).

6. *A French View of the Netherlands Indies* (New York and London: Oxford University Press, 1940).

Rupert Emerson[7] and Amry Vandenbosch,[8] were more penetrating on the whole, and several of them were brilliantly clear in their perceptions of the colonial power structure. But they too had only a fairly limited understanding of the dynamics of nationalist politics.

The path-breaking postwar work was done by George McT. Kahin. A doctoral candidate at Johns Hopkins University who made his way to Indonesia in the middle of its nationalist revolution, Kahin spent 1948-49 in various parts of the country. For the first half of his visit he was one of five or six Western residents in Jogjakarta, the capital of the beleaguered Indonesian Republic, and became a personal confidant of Sukarno, Vice-President Hatta, former Prime Minister Sjahrir, and a number of other top leaders. On his return to America he helped the Republic's emissaries with their highly successful lobbying with the US Senate. Since 1952 he has taught at Cornell, which he more than anyone else has made into the world's leading center of Southeast Asian studies.

Kahin's principal contribution to Indonesian political studies came out in 1952: *Nationalism and Revolution in Indonesia*. In this volume, a reworked version of his doctoral dissertation, he devotes 100 pages to the prewar nationalist movement, and another 300 to an historical account of the politics of 1945-49. In the latter there is as much emphasis on party conflicts within the Republic, and on the ideological themes associated with these conflicts, as on the fighting and negotiation between the Republicans on the one hand and the Dutch and their allies, of the quasi-puppet "federal" states, on the other.

Clearly a partisan of the Republic, Kahin emphasized the energy and creativeness which its struggle released, especially among the urban and educated young. And he emphasized the Republic's all-Indonesian character, denying the assertion of the Dutch that it was or would soon become a vehicle for Javanese hegemony in the archipelago. Thus he continued to side with the Republican leaders in 1950 when they encouraged the disintegration, overthrow, and dissolution of the Dutch-built federal states and of the Republic of the United States of Indonesia (which had been established to include both the original Republic and these Dutch-sponsored states, and thus allow the Dutch to save face as they finally withdrew their troops).

In Kahin's view "the preponderant majority [of the Republican leadership] . . . were dedicated to political principles and practices which were roughly the same as those aspired to in the Western democracies," and there was "substantial homogeneity of outlook among most Republican leaders with regard to the socioeconomic aims and program of the new state." This and the "relatively high degree of ideological and religious tolerance among the Indonesian population and the vitality of their resurgent and expanding village democracy" augured well for democracy as did the revolution's "strong levelling effect . . . [on] indigenous society."[9]

But Kahin was by no means wholly sanguine about the prospects for democracy. The central tasks to be faced once independence had been secured were "organizing a new and effective state administration . . . [and carrying out] an extensive program of socio-economic change," and the need to attend to these tasks would require strong government. So, as Kahin saw it in 1952, looking back on the situation in 1950, "a basic question was whether it would prove possible to develop

---

7. *Malaysia, A Study in Direct and Indirect Rule* (New York: Macmillan, 1937).

8. *The Dutch East Indies* (Berkeley: University of California Press, 1944).

9. *Nationalism and Revolution in Indonesia* (Ithaca: Cornell University Press, 1952), pp. 476-78.

such strength while at the same time promoting a democratic system of government. Although the Republic's leaders were sincerely devoted to the attainment of both objectives, some of the most prescient of them feared that the temptation might become strong to resort to authoritarian methods." This was the more to be feared because of the "still-surviving authoritarian tradition. . . . Despite its awakened national consciousness and the much increased vigor of its political life at the village level, peasant society was still not effectively linked with the national government in a mutually activated and mutually responsive relationship. The existing relationship was still predominantly a one-sided affair--from the top down. . . . [The] parties floated as vague shapes above the peasant masses. . . . If the scope of the program which the Republic's leaders undertook to carry out were too limited, or the pace too slow, they might forfeit their popular backing, and those more disposed to employ more authoritarian techniques might replace them at the helm of government."[10]

Kahin's perspective was basically liberal. His principal identification was with Sjahrir, Indonesia's first Prime Minister and later the founder and chairman of the Indonesian Socialist Party. Sjahrir combined a revisionist Marxism with liberal humanism, reserving his strongest condemnations for Indonesia's erstwhile Japanese rulers, for the Indonesians who had opportunistically served them, and for those whose thinking continued to reflect the "fascist," "authoritarian," and militantly anti-Western outlook they had spread. In Kahin's eyes, Sjahrir and the young intellectuals around him were as progressive as they were practical and moderate. They were more likely than any other group to be able to marshall the combination of realism and vigor which would be needed to carry out the extensive program of socioeconomic change on which Kahin thought the new state would have to embark.

Most of the American academic writing of the early and middle 1950s, by men like Rupert Emerson, Charles Wolf Jr., and Robert C. Bone, as well as what Kahin himself wrote after 1952, accepted this basic perspective. In general these writers had considerable sympathy for Indonesian nationalism. Like Kahin, they blamed the restrictive and repressive side of prewar Dutch rule for many of the difficulties the new Republic faced, particularly its shortage of trained administrators and its leaders' lack of experience of parliamentary government. And some of them blamed the Dutch for the large group of restless young ex-revolutionaries with whom successive Indonesian governments contended with little success--for was it not postwar Dutch stubbornness which had made it necessary for a revolution to be fought? Several of these American writers even defended the more radical manifestations of nationalism, such as the claim to West Irian.

But their attraction was to Sjahrir and Vice-President Hatta rather than to Sukarno. Hatta's policies, which Sjahrir substantially endorsed, of protecting the large Dutch business establishment--estates, mines, trading companies, and so on--were described as pragmatic, realistic, and evidence of a forward-looking cast of mind. On the other hand Sukarno's concern with West Irian, his talk of national greatness and his frequent appeals for a return to the spirit of the revolution were regarded as expressions of nativism and obscurantism, or as demagogic diversions from the country's real problems. Sjahrir was often described as the Nehru of Indonesia, and analogues were drawn with the division between moderates and xenophobes in twentieth-century Japanese nationalism and the nineteenth-century nationalisms of Germany and Italy.

The speed with which cabinets rose and fell in the years after 1950 attracted much attention to the "problem of political instability," to the fact that the country

---

10. Ibid., pp. 478-80.

was yet to hold its first parliamentary elections, and to the political storms stirred whenever a cabinet sought to implement unpopular policies. It also demonstrated the weakness of Sjahrir's Socialist Party, which, whatever the luster of its intellectual leadership, was evidently doing little to develop mass support.

Partly for this reason more Westerners concerned with Indonesia became interested in Indonesian Islam, and particularly in the reformist-led Muslim party, Masjumi, which was the country's largest party at the time, in numbers of parliamentary seats and perceived electoral prospects, and was under the leadership of Sjahrir's associate, Mohammad Natsir. For men like Boyd R. Compton, whose letters in the *Institute of Current World Affairs* series provide a fascinating insight into the society and politics in the 1952-56 period, Natsir's Masjumi promised to provide both stability and a commitment to rationality in economic and administrative affairs. Compton's writings of the middle 1950s were concerned with the problem of stability and control, and much less with change than Kahin's of 1952. But the basic perspective was little different from Kahin's.

Moreover this perspective was shared by the economist, Benjamin Higgins, who was in Indonesia for much of the 1952-56 period and directed an MIT research project on the Indonesian economy. Higgins and his colleagues worked strongly with Sjahrir's party colleague, the economist Sumitro Djojohadikusumo, and perceived economic rationality in the same terms as he. These writers saw the control of inflation as a prerequisite for development and therefore hoped that governments would prove strong enough to resist the pressures to which they were subjected, for subsidies, protection, and the "Indonesianization" of Dutch and Chinese-controlled areas of business.[11]

The principal counterweight to Kahin's influence in the early postindependence period came in the writings of an Indonesia-born Dutch sociologist teaching at Michigan State College, and later the University of Bridgeport, J. M. van der Kroef. Van der Kroef rarely saw Indonesia's problems from the vantage point of the leaders of the new Republic, and his general approach to politics was conservative and realist. Thus he was far more skeptical than Kahin about the nationalist leaders' avowed concern for representative democracy. Focusing more attention on ethnic loyalties than had Kahin, he raised doubts about the staying power of all-Indonesian nationalism and thus about the nation's capacity to maintain its territorial integrity. And, freed from the concern of Kahin and the Kahinians to make the Indonesian leadership seem attractive to Western eyes, he turned his attention early--attention of a highly unsympathetic kind--onto Sukarno as the central figure of Indonesian nationalism. A strong anti-Communist, van der Kroef saw the Indonesian Communist Party as a likely beneficiary of both the communalism of Javanese villagers and the Selznickian "mass society" phenomena which he observed in the Indonesian cities (and saw as dough in the hands of the Jacobin Sukarno).

Van der Kroef wrote something like twenty articles per year throughout the 1950s, most of them on Indonesia.[12] Only a small proportion of these were on politics, and many of these were marred by inaccuracy and a lack of feel. But he made a major contribution to political understanding by drawing the attention of English-language readers to the huge Dutch literature on Indonesian society, and by

---

11. See B. Higgins, *Indonesia's Economic Stabilization and Development* (New York: Institute of Pacific Relations, 1957) and Douglas S. Paauw, "The High Cost of Political Instability in Indonesia," in *Indonesia's Struggle, 1957-58*, ed. B. H. M. Vlekke (The Hague: Nederlands Genootschap voor Internationale Zaken, 1959).

12. A selection of these were brought together as *Indonesia in the Modern World* (Bandung: Masa Baru, Vol. 1, 1954, Vol. 2, 1956).

showing the relevance of this literature to those of us who were all too inclined--by our willingness to take nationalist aspiration for reality, as well as our laziness about the Dutch language--to think about independent Indonesia in *tabula rasa* terms.

The Impact of Geertz

Clifford Geertz, the central figure of postwar Indonesia scholarship, began to publish in this field in 1956. An anthropologist and a doctoral candidate in the Harvard Department of Social Relations, he had been in Indonesia between 1952 and 1955 as a member of the team of eight Harvard researchers who studied "Modjokuto," a small town in East Java. Geertz's specialty as a member of the team had been religion, and he was later to publish *The Religion of Java*.[13] More recently he has published *Islam Observed*, comparing the Islam of Indonesia with that of Morocco.[14] But religion has been only one of a large number of Geertz's concerns; he is equally interested in economic history, agricultural ecology, and theories of social change and symbolism, and has brought all of these to his study of Indonesia.

It would be futile for me to attempt a sketch of Geertz's work here. Suffice it to say that he has brought an anthropologist's concern with culture and values to the study of economic development, but never allowed his focus on culture, or present-day social structure, to operate at the expense of history. His conclusions have occasionally fitted well with the ideological bent of the MIT establishmentarians who helped finance his work, particularly with their preference for piecemeal approaches to social engineering. He has for instance argued that "The ideologies of modern nationalism . . . arising as they do out of an intense concern with massive social reconstruction, show a strong tendency toward a neglect, even an outright denial, of important variations in domestic cultural patterns and of internal social discontinuities. . . . With regard to national economic planning this leads to a failure to cast proposals in a form which attempts to take maximum advantage of the peculiarities of various local traditions, to an unwillingness even to consider differentiated plans for different cultural and social groups. . . . In the overconcern with national integration, conceived in a wholly monistic sense, the very construction of such integration . . . may be underminded."[15]

But Geertz is no simple meliorist. Indeed he is a sharp critic of the "myopic pragmatic optimism which allows short-run gains to obscure the general trend of events, which isolates purely technical improvements from the historically created cultural, social, and psychological context in which they are set."[16] His volume on *Agricultural Involution* presents Indonesia's economic crisis of the present period as a late manifestation of a very old disease. Its roots, he insists, lie in the colonial period which, "amid the apparent fluctuations of policy . . . consists, from the economic point of view, of one long attempt to bring Indonesia's crops into the modern world, but not her people."[17] Central to the colonial legacy is what he calls the "shared poverty" pattern of today's Javanese villages, a "post-traditional" condition of stagnancy and cultural flaccidity in which a growing population is absorbed

---

13. Glencoe, Ill.: Free Press, 1960.

14. New Haven: Yale University Press, 1968.

15. *Peddlers and Princes* (Chicago: University of Chicago Press, 1963), pp. 155-56.

16. *Agricultural Involution, the Process of Ecological Change in Indonesia* (Berkeley and Los Angeles: University of California Press, 1963), pp. 146-47.

17. Ibid., p. 48.

into an ever more labor-intensive agricultural organization, with basic patterns not changed but made ever more elaborate. From this there is no easy way out.

Geertz has had no particular interest in Indonesia's national politics, but he concerned himself intensively with the role of national parties at the small town and village level, which was particularly great at the time of his field work, because the country was preparing for its (first and only) nationwide elections. His writings on parties gave political scientists concerned with Indonesia a radically new perspective on their field.

When the long-awaited elections were eventually held in September 1955, four parties emerged far ahead of the many others, the PNI (Indonesian Nationalist Party) with 22.3 percent of the vote, the reformist Islamic Masjumi with 20.9 percent, the more traditional Muslim Party, Nahdatul Ulama (NU), with 18.4 percent, and the Indonesian Communist Party, PKI, with 16.4 percent. No other party obtained as much as 3 percent of the vote and the hitherto influential Indonesian Socialist Party of Sjahrir surprised most observers by receiving only 2 percent. Geertz's writings of 1956 accounted for many aspects of this result, at least for the ethnic Javanese heartland of East and Central Java.

Geertz observed that each of the four parties which emerged as successful at the national level had a large number of ancillary organizations in Java's small towns, and sometimes in the surrounding villages as well: women's organizations, youth groups, labor and peasant unions, religious societies, schools, scout groups, and so on. And so a town or even a village might have a PNI peasant organization, a Communist peasant organization, a Masjumi one, and an NU one. Geertz described this as the *aliran* pattern, using the Indonesian word for stream or current. An aliran, in his sense, is a political party surrounded by a cluster of voluntary associations which share its ideological standpoint. In a formulation he was to use a few years later, "an *aliran* is more than a mere political party, certainly more than a mere ideology; it is a comprehensive pattern of social integration. The intensity with which the Javanese peasantry has fastened on to political and quasi-political organizations in the last decade is not simply a reflex of their enthusiasm for freedom, though it is in part that; primarily it is an index of the degree to which new social structures are needed in the reconstruction of vigorous village life."[18]

The cultural dimension of Geertz's aliran analysis was equally important. Aliran, he said, were communities based on a modern associational form, which corresponded to older sociocultural configurations. The reformist Muslim Masjumi had its roots mainly among *santri* (pious or thorough-going Muslims) in urban areas, and the Nahdatul Ulama was the principal aliran of santri-minded villagers, whereas the Nationalist and Communist parties were tied to socially distinct groupings in the religious world of the *abangan*, the ethnic Javanese who were not santri, who often described themselves as "statistical Muslims," and whose religious beliefs and practices owed more to Hinduism and Buddhism and to Javanese religion as it existed before the Hindu-Buddhist impact than to Islam. Each of these parties had a *Weltanschauung* of its own, something far wider than a political program or even a set of political principles, which was a modern schematic version of older beliefs distinctive for the community for which it spoke.

Geertz's aliran concept gave students of politics their first really valuable tool for understanding the ways in which the ideas of the national parties related to cultural patterns at the grassroots level in any part of the country. His later

---

18. "The Javanese Village," in G. William Skinner, *Local, Ethnic and National Loyalties in Village Indonesia* (New Haven: Yale University, Cultural Report Series, 1959), p. 37.

fieldwork in Bali led him to a theory of two contrasting modes by which national cleavage patterns might be integrated into village life. Describing the aliran pattern of East and Central Java as a "constitutive" mode of integration, he contrasted this with the "infusive" pattern of Bali, where traditional institutions have remained resilient, and parties have simply attached themselves to particular clans, castes, and irrigation societies, thus giving local factional conflict a supercharged quality and leading peasants to see party politics as disruptive and a threat to the integrity of their society.[19]

Political scientists henceforth had a means of testing the common view that party leaderships were highly oligarchic and independent of their village followings. And they had new concepts with which to examine the ways in which the values of the past, which had been described in the Dutch literature on ethnography and customary law, were relevant to the orientations of the present. Kahinians, who had become increasingly aware of the need to see national politics in terms of the traditional and quasi-traditional values of particular ethnic and other communal groupings, but unwilling to be instructed by the "colonial-minded" van der Kroef, fastened on to Geertz's formulations with delight.

The Challenge of Guided Democracy

In the late 1950s the attempt at Western-style parliamentary government was abandoned and Sukarno took greatly increased personal power, exercising it in a somewhat uneasy coalition arrangement with the leaders of the army, under the banner of Guided Democracy. The Masjumi and the Socialist Party, hoping to resist the Guided Democracy tide, had associated themselves with the shortlived Sumatra-Sulawesi rebellion of 1958, and so, when this was defeated, both of these parties were severely restricted. In 1960 they were banned. Western scholars in the Kahinian tradition who sympathized with Indonesian nationalism on the one hand and with the Socialist and the reformist Muslims on the other, were thoroughly confused.

For most Indonesian intellectuals the change was both disturbing and threatening. Sukarno's populist nationalism had a distinctly antiintellectual dimension and his argument that the Indonesian revolution had yet to be brought to completion could readily be used to silence the criticisms of those whose commitments to the goals and leadership of the revolution was held to be dubious.

But the intellectuals' reactions varied widely. Among those in the ambience of Sjahrir's Socialist Party, the new development produced a debate whose echoes continue to be heard. One group saw the Guided Democracy regime as not only curbing democratic freedoms but also an irrational and obscurantist attempt to escape from unpleasant realities. The sociologist Moehammad Slamet, in a courageous pamphlet published in 1960, discussed the current concern with "Returning to Our National Identity" in Fromm's categories, describing it as a product of feelings of inferiority and guilt and as reflecting a search for compensations and substitute satisfactions.[20] Similar criticisms, and ones which focused more directly on the person and role of Sukarno, were expressed in the writings of two prominent exiles of the time, the economist Sumitro Djojohadikusumo[21] and the novelist and essayist

---

19. Ibid., pp. 39-41.

20. *Beberapa gagasan mengenai "Kembali Kepribadian Bangsa" di Indonesia* [Some Ideas on "Returning to Our National Identity" in Indonesia] (Bandung: Social Research Center of Padjadjaran State University, 1960).

21. See especially *Searchlight on Indonesia* (Singapore (?), mimeo, 1959).

S. Takdir Alisjahbana.[22]

Other intellectuals, like the sociologist Selo Soemardjan, took the view that Sukarno's new regime had its positive sides. Believing that party conflict had caused great and unproductive disruptions in village society, Soemardjan welcomed the parties' eclipse. Moreover he argued that authoritarian and one-man patterns of government accorded well with Indonesia's cultural traditions and were therefore likely to be more intelligible to the mass of the peasants than the Western political forms of the period before 1958.[23]

Soedjatmoko, the essayist, historian, and publisher who came to Australia two years ago to give the Dyason lectures and is today Indonesia's ambassador to the United States, took a midway position. Believing that decades would pass before Indonesia achieved the social prerequisites for a functioning democracy, he went on to argue that the authoritarian political structure of Guided Democracy was still pluralistic and heterogeneous enough to offer opportunities for intellectuals committed to democracy and modernization. As Soedjatmoko saw it, and his voice was more influential than any other among his fellow intellectuals, Indonesian nationalism would continue to be a progressive, emancipationist force, however successful Sukarno was in jailing his enemies and impressing his xenophobic romanticism on the youth of the nation.[24]

This debate was in fact part of a broader one going on in many parts of Asia and Africa, and in different ways in the West. 1958-59 was a time when military regimes were being established in many countries of Asia and Africa, and multiparty, parliamentary politics were being transformed into charismatically-led "movement regimes" in others. Asian-African intellectuals, or at least the more xenophilic of them, were thrown into anguished debate, and liberal intellectuals in the West, more dismayed than surprised, were anxious to clarify their attitudes to the change. The Congress for Cultural Freedom responded by arranging a series of international seminars on the erosion of democracy in the Third World, inviting prominent intellectuals from many parts of this world, including Sjahrir and Soedjatmoko from Indonesia.

The range of responses by Western social scientists to the overthrow or abandonment of parliamentary institutions in so many non-Western countries is beyond my scope here. Suffice it to say that the pace of social science study of these

---

22. *Indonesia in the Modern World* (New Delhi: Congress for Cultural Freedom, 1961) (republished in revised form as *Indonesia: Social and Cultural Revolution* [London and Kuala Lumpur, 1966]).

23. See "Some Social and Cultural Implications of Indonesia's Unplanned and Planned Development," a paper presented to the August 1961 Pacific Science Congress and later published in the *Review of Politics*, 25 (January 1963), pp. 64-90.

24. See *An Approach to Indonesian History: Towards an Open Future* (Ithaca: Cornell Modern Indonesia Project, Translation Series, 1960); "The Indonesian Historian and his Time," in *An Introduction to Indonesian Historiography*, ed. Soedjatmoko et al. (Ithaca: Cornell University Press, 1963); "Memorandum on Scope and Method of Conference," in *Religion and Progress in Modern Asia*, ed. Robert N. Bellah (Glencoe, Ill.: Free Press, 1963); and the outstanding but unfortunately unpublished and untranslated 1961 paper "Daja Tjipta sebagai Unsur Mutlak didalam Pembangunan" [Creativity as an Essential Element of Development]. A very similar view presented by the newspaper editor Rosihan Anwar in 1961 will appear as "Between Quixotism and Capitulation" in *Indonesian Political Thinking, 1945-1965*, ed. Lance Castles and Herbert Feith (Ithaca: Cornell University Press, 1970).

countries in Western universities, and particularly American ones, accelerated sharply around 1958-60, partly as a result of the new interest and new questions to which these changes had given rise. Prominent political scientists and sociologists like Almond, Deutsch, Shils and Lipset who had worked on American and European politics up to that time, joined a younger band of men who had done fieldwork in Asia and Africa (Apter, Coleman, Riggs, Pye, Weiner, Binder, Rustow, and others) in a rapid spurt of sociologically oriented comparative study of politics in the "developing areas."

My own main work was done in these same years. Kahin, Geertz, and Soedjatmoko had influenced me before I went to Cornell in 1957, and in the next three years I learned a great deal from the new group of American scholars concerned with the comparative politics of the non-West--and from the Israeli sociologist S. N. Eisenstadt. In my thesis, which came out in 1962 as *The Decline of Constitutional Democracy in Indonesia*, I sought to combine a political history of the 1950-57 period with a quasi-functionalist explanation of why Western-type political institutions had worked unsatisfactorily and finally crumbled.

One of my central themes, a Lasswell-cum-Eisenstadt version of an old Kahin dichotomy, was conflict between "administrators"--politicians whose claim to power lay in their modern state-type skills--and "solidarity-makers"--men whose claims rested on their skill in fashioning integrative symbols. The "administrators," of whom Hatta was both prototype and leader, were initially strong in postrevolutionary Indonesia. They were eventually displaced from power because their policies were both harmful and morally irksome to uprooted ex-revolutionaries, who found it hard to obtain acceptable work and resented the change from the heroic atmosphere of the revolutionary period to the lassitude and prosaic concerns of the years after 1950. After the crucial defeat of the "administrators" in 1952-53, cabinets were obliged to take much more notice of "solidarity-maker" political leaders, especially Sukarno, but also militant Muslims, and so allotted few resources to the tasks of economic management. The rate of inflation rose, as did administrative demoralization. And the bureaucracy managed increasingly to pursue its own concerns, unchecked by outside social forces--echoes here of Fred W. Riggs.

National output rose reasonably rapidly in the 1950-57 period. But it did not rise fast enough; for the level of expectations, of demands for consumer goods, jobs, mobility opportunities and the psychological satisfactions which inspiring leadership could provide, was exceedingly high. This was partly a consequence of the revolution. It was also a product of what Karl W. Deutsch calls "social mobilization," the expansion of schooling, newspaper reading, radio listening, traveling, and membership of parties and other voluntary organizations.

Social mobilization had proceeded very rapidly in the Indonesia of the 1950-57 period, but mobilization was not matched by what Deutsch calls assimilation. Many of the newly mobilized had not been adequately assimilated to the national polity, inasmuch as they had developed loyalties to their party and aliran which could not easily be subordinated to loyalty to the state. The sharp ideological conflict between the four main aliran, combined with the economic contradictions between Java as a net import area and the Outer Islands as net exporters (which rose as inflation made the rate of exchange more unreal), produced centrifugal tendencies which threatened the very existence of Indonesia as a single state. By 1957 the structure of legitimacy had become so shaky that the question was no longer whether the pluralistic party-cum-parliamentary system would survive, but rather which groups would come out on top in the more restrictive regime which would somehow replace it. If Hatta, the Masjumi, and the Socialists had had their way, authoritarianization would have been achieved at the expense of the Communists. But, with the Sumatra-Sulawesi rebellion defeated, and the symbolism of Guided Democracy triumphant, it was achieved at the expense of the Masjumi and the Socialists.

Academic Disagreements of the Late Guided Democracy Period, 1963-1965

a. Was Sukarno's Guided Democracy a Kraton state ("neotraditional polity") or a radical Jacobin one? Harry J. Benda, Ben Anderson, G. J. Resink, Ann Ruth Wilner, A. H. Johns versus J. A. C. Mackie, Herbert Feith, Guy J. Pauker, W. F. Wertheim.

b. Did the trend to economic deterioration presage a cataclysmic collapse of the regime?

c. Was it likely that the Communists would come to power? Could they come to power by "acclamation"? Guy J. Pauker, J. M. van der Kroef versus Donald Hindley, Ruth T. McVey, Daniel S. Lev.

d. Was there a major threat of territorial fragmentation?

The Bitter Debates of 1965-66

a. Did the Communist leaders instigate the coup of October 1965, or was this role played by Sukarnoist younger officers? Anderson, McVey, Wertheim versus Nugroho Notosusanto, Pauker, van der Kroef.

b. Did the coup come close to success?

c. How many lost their lives in the massacres of 1965-66? How are the massacres to be explained? A product of years of violent language and mounting unresolved problems? An expression of class conflict over land? A Malthusian answer to extreme population density? The army's determination to remove the threat of an arch-rival.

The Work of Ben Anderson. A New Radical Perspective

The sharpest critic of the comparative non-Western politics approach. New interpretation of the revolution: Kahin stood on his head. "The Languages of Indonesian Politics"--a new sensitivity to style and idiom.

Small-town Javanese populism versus Jakarta cosmopolitanism. Javanese conceptions of power--taking Javanese history and civilization seriously as a determinant of present-day political values.

Focus on aspects of continuity between Sukarno's pattern of leadership and Suharto's.

Disagreements among Indonesian Intellectuals in New Order Indonesia.

a. Hawks and doves on de-Sukarnoization--"development" versus "stability."

b. The "technocratic approach" versus the "cultural forces" one: should intellectuals accept the army's political hegemony or should they encourage a revival of aliran type parties?

c. Should intellectuals commit themselves fully to the government and its economic programs and so protect and improve their access to the generals at the top, or should they concentrate on "social control," building islands of autonomy: universities, the press, the courts, etc.

d. The dangers of excessive reliance on the West.

e. How important is it to combat corruption?

Academic Disagreements on the Politics of the New Order

a. "The army controls everything that matters" versus "The economists and other intellectuals have persuaded Suharto to see his interests as parallel to theirs."

b. Postmassacres political passivity as likely to be transitory or more long-lived.

c. The persistence of aliran cleavage patterns in rural Java versus the growth of peasant class consciousness. Wertheim versus Basuki Gunawan.

d. Can the army leaders maintain the support of the middle-ranking officers?

e. Are the army leaders committed to economic development? Do they have a stake in it?

f. Reliance on foreign private investment: How much can Indonesia hope to get? The dangers of aggravated technological dualism--Hans O. Schmitt's thesis of 1961. The dangers of aggravated centrifugal pressure (as the Outer Islands get the investment and Jakarta the revenue from it).

g. Will "miracle rice" have dramatic effects on rice production: Will it have dramatic effect in increasing the weight of government power on the peasantry and exacerbating absentee landlordism and debt bondage?

Work Currently in Progress

Studies of particular periods of recent political history. (Not to be disparaged even if they are little more than month-to-month chronicles of capital-city developments.)

Studies of the prewar period. These are the more important because many of the key actors of this period will not live much longer. And few of them are writing memoirs.

Studies of particular groups and institutions: the army, the PKI, the PNI, Muslim parties, students, the Chinese.

Foreign policy studies, several of them concerned with the ideological dimension of Sukarno's foreign policy.

A major study of the sociology of law, by a political scientist, Daniel S. Lev.

A political culture study of parliamentarians, civil servants, and university men in three cities--one of the first attempts to apply survey analysis methods in Indonesia--by D. K. Emmerson.

Neglected Areas of Study

a. Provincial studies which look at the post-1942 period as a whole: politics, bureaucracy, social structure, social mobility, ethnic loyalties and antagonisms, the rise and fall of different ethnic groups, etc. A few studies of this type are under way, but conspicuously few if one compares Indonesian field with the Indian one.

b. Bureaucracy: Corruption, smuggling, racketeering. The role of military men in civilian agencies. Suharto's reforms.

c. The workers of the cities and labor organizations.

d. Abangan religion in the villages of East and Central Java. Mystical movements, messianic and quietist. The postcoup expansion of Christianity and Hinduism in the abangan areas and the onset of Muslim-Christian conflict.

e. Work in cooperation with economists. Many of them, Westerners, Japanese and Indonesians are engaged in research at the present. A political economy perspective is badly needed in relation to foreign aid and foreign private investment, and to the triangle of army generals, Chinese businessmen, and indigenous Indonesian businessmen.

f. Work in cooperation with agricultural economists and rural sociologists. Indonesian universities are doing a lot in this field.

g. Comparative work. Many attempts at this in the past have been superficial--though this can certainly not be said of Geertz's comparison of Indonesian Islam with Morocco's, G. William Skinner's of Indonesia's Chinese community with Thailand's, Furnivall's of prewar Dutch colonial policy with that of Britain in Burma, and Benda's work on the changes on social structure in Southeast Asia in the colonial period. A thorough-going comparison of the role of the Indonesian army with that of Thailand, Pakistan, or Burma, could be extraordinarily valuable. Some aspects of post-Sukarno politics can perhaps be compared with similar ones in other post-Jacobin politics, today's Ghana, post-Mossadeq Iraq or even post-Peron Argentina. More ambitious still, one could compare Indonesia's pattern of bureaucracy--peasant relations with that of other preponderantly bureaucratic societies in which inflation has worked to corrode away central controls over local officialdom.

CLASS, SOCIAL CLEAVAGE AND INDONESIAN COMMUNISM*

Rex Mortimer

Interest conflicts among social classes provide the foundation upon which Communist theories of revolution are constructed, and the strategic formulations of Communist parties place heavy reliance upon class factors as motors of their political development. To a greater or lesser degree, however, specific Communist movements have been affected in their strategies by the operation of other social cleavages impinging on the political process. Thus in the Russian revolution, the "war or peace" issue was a vital element in Bolshevik calculations; in China, Vietnam and Yugoslavia, the national struggle played a critical role in shaping lines of division, to some extent cross-cutting class loyalties. The implications of these interactions for the ideologies of the parties concerned is a complex study, but I think it is true to say at least that class issues in each case have always continued to occupy a prominent role.[1]

In the case of the Indonesian Communist Party under the Aidit leadership (1951-1965), on the other hand, we probably have the most outstanding example among major Communist parties of a trend away from class strategy. The strategic concepts of the PKI were cast in terms of class theory, particularly in the early years after the assumption of the Aidit leadership, but the theory was increasingly "bent" to accommodate the influence of other bases of social cleavage upon the PKI's political work. The fundamental reasons for this ideological shift, it will be argued here, are to be found in the specific features of Indonesian social structure and political history and, in particular, the weakness of class "contradictions" in comparison with other bases of social conflict.

Class formation and class differentiation along a property line of demarcation (or, in Marxist terminology, based on opposed relationships to the means of production) are a relatively recent development in Indonesia.[2] In precolonial society, when agricultural activity occupied a role of dominance even more pronounced than

---

* Based on a working paper submitted to a Seminar of the Centre of Southeast Asian Studies, Monash University, Australia.

1. The varying emphases in Mao's thought are discussed in many works, of which mention may be made of Benjamin Schwartz' *Chinese Communism and the Rise of Mao* (Cambridge: Harvard University Press, 1951) and Stuart Schramm's *Mao Tse-tung* (New York: Simon and Schuster, 1966).

2. The following passages on precolonial and colonial society will in fact be confined to Java where PKI strength was concentrated and its political fate largely determined. The analysis is derived from the writings of Schrieke, Van Leur, Geertz, and Furnivall in the main.

is the case today, all land in theory was under the sole disposition of the ruler. The farming population, however, had exclusive use of most of the productive land, either through periodic allocation by the village head acting on the basis of customary rules or through customarily acquired hereditary rights. The peasants' use of the land was subject to the payment of taxes in kind to the ruler and his agents, and the performance of labor and military services for them. The ruling groups--the nobility and the *prijaji* or official class--were urban-dwelling for the most part and derived their incomes from a share of the taxation and services levied upon the peasants. But these rights were not proprietary in nature; they pertained to offices which themselves were not hereditary as a matter of course. The status and authority of the ruling groups, therefore, did not stem from the ownership of the means of production, but from the exercise, in the sovereign's name, of politico-bureaucratic power over the population. In other words, the crucial social division between rulers and ruled was not one based on property, but on the positions each occupied in relation to the king. Needless to say, the sanction of coercion was available as required to buttress legitimacy. While, as Anderson points out,[3] this system was not strictly patrimonial in the Weberian sense, it was much closer to that pole than to the "feudal" system as it developed in Western Europe.

There were differences of landholding among the peasantry, based upon a division between those who were deemed descendants of the village founders and those who derived from later immigrants. So far as can be determined, however, these distinctions were not of sufficient dimensions to produce marked inequalities of wealth or antagonisms of a class character. Village communal values with their strong egalitarian ethos, seem to have kept such distinctions within a narrow compass. Peasant antipathy was mainly directed towards the ruling groups, whose exactions on occasion were keenly felt, and found outlet in rebellions led by dissident nobles and officials, or messianic prophets generally animated by deviant religious beliefs. These "class" struggles, however, produced no stimulus towards basic social change; their aim was limited to local redress of grievances or the support of dynastic usurpers. Consequently, neither the social system nor the value system was significantly affected, and basic changes in the social structure came, when they did, as a result of exogenous pressures.

Dutch colonial occupation, particularly in its later phases, substantially modified the Javanese social structure. The Dutch retained the traditional system of rulership over much of the island, but subjected the sovereigns to the will of their own administrative hierarchy. Early in the nineteenth century, the nobility and the prijaji were debarred from gaining their living directly from the peasantry, and were converted into salaried officials of the colonial administration. This measure could be carried out with minimal economic or social effects because the role of the indigenous ruling groups was not intimately bound up with the productive system. Any peasant antagonism towards the indigenous ruling strata was not concentrated upon their role as political agents carrying out exactions on behalf of and parasitic upon the foreign occupier. Thus the social basis was laid by which the contradictions between the peasantry and their traditional rulers would find their principal ideological expression in nationalism rather than class antagonism. Additionally, the inhibition against entrepreneurial orientations implicit in the social role and value system of the indigenous ruling strata was strengthened by the premium placed on administrative status under the colonial system.

---

3. Benedict R. O'G. Anderson, "The Idea of Power in Javanese Culture," in *Culture and Politics in Indonesia*, ed. Claire Holt et al. [Ithaca: Cornell University Press, 1972].

The impact of a more developed economic system upon the traditional society initiated greater variety and complexity in the Javanese rural structure in some areas, and particularly in West Java. Here social differentiation increased, and a class of landlords emerged, but, while the available data is sparse and often contradictory, their numbers are usually accepted as having been small and the average size of their holdings modest, at least until the last few decades.[4] In much of the island, however, what has been termed agricultural involution was the outcome --an economic and social "retrogression" characterized by the "shared poverty" system described and analyzed by Geertz.[5] In these villages, social differentiation and the development of class cleavages were inhibited.

The ranks of the landless laborers vastly swelled as the population grew. Some of them were absorbed into the foreign estates as permanent or seasonal laborers; others took their way to the burgeoning towns and cities; those who remained in the environs of the village were either employed as day laborers by landlords and richer peasants or engaged as share-croppers--in any case, they were fitted somewhere into the shared poverty system, with its characteristic mechanisms of coping with increasing population pressure by ever more labor-intensive use of the land.

Trading and manufacturing classes (mostly confined to small-scale activity) expanded, occupying a position intermediate between the Dutch companies and the mass of the Indonesian population. Dutch policy directed this activity predominantly into the hands of the ethnic Chinese, however, hindering the development of an indigenous bourgeoisie. Part of the activity of the small entrepreneur was channeled into money lending in the villages, but the resulting relationship did not establish a class nexus between the quasi-capitalist and the peasant; to the extent that antagonisms were produced by money-lending operations, they sometimes took racial forms, and in addition no doubt gave rise to diffuse resentments in the villages against urbanites, "blood-suckers" and nontraditional ways. In many cases, however, the lender-borrower relationship was "traditionalized," the creditor entering upon the role of paternalistic protector or patron of his client.[6]

The Dutch virtually monopolized large-scale manufacture, estate management, mining, and overseas trade and finance. They also introduced and administered modern means of communication. This in turn produced a small proletarian class, the foreign identity of whose masters also overlaid incipient class feeling with nationalism.[7] Around these enterprises and the new or expanded urban complexes, there developed a wide network of petty artisanship, trade and services, upon

---

4. See Karl Pelzer, "The Agricultural Foundation," in *Indonesia*, ed. Ruth T. McVey (New Haven: HRAF, 1963). Useful summaries of the available data, with somewhat divergent interpretations, are also to be found in: Donald Hindley, *The Communist Party of Indonesia 1951-1963: A Decade of the Aidit Leadership* (Canberra: Australian National University, 1961), pp. 4-5; and Justus M. Van der Kroef, *The Communist Party of Indonesia: Its History, Program and Tactics* (Vancouver: University of British Columbia, 1965), pp. 7-9.

5. Clifford Geertz, *Agricultural Involution: The Process of Ecological Change in Indonesia* (Berkeley: University of California, 1963) and other works.

6. Hindley, *Communist Party*, p. 8. But cf. Pelzer, "Agricultural Foundation," p. 126.

7. In 1930, there were some 350,000 workers in industrial enterprises employing more than ten employees. Douglas Paauw, "From Colonial to Guided Economy," in *Indonesia*, ed. McVey, pp. 178-79.

which a large proportion of the urban population was dependent for fringe employment. These latter represent no more than a semiproletariat in Marxist categorization, notoriously difficult to organize and imbue with social or ideological discipline.

Finally, Dutch measures also called into being a modern-style intelligentsia, almost exclusively out of the families of the nobility and the prijaji. This social grouping, aroused by Western-style education to the opportunities that modern lifeways opened up, but denied under the colonial system sufficient outlet for their material expectations and status aspirations, formed the elite core of the nationalist movement in the twentieth century. The intelligentsia were by no means homogeneous in outlook, however, their inability to found a common vehicle for the national struggle largely reflecting the strength of ethnic, religious, and cultural cleavages in the society at large. Notably, too, this "class" failed to elaborate any but the vaguest goals beyond the achievement of national independence, even its most "radical" elements resting content with an anticolonialist, anticapitalist "socialism," and deferring further consideration of social objectives until the attainment of independence.

The later period of Dutch rule, then, virtually created property-based class relationships and interests, and did so then only to a limited extent. In propounding his theory of revolutionary social transformation, Marx had implicitly conceived of class cleavage as encompassing the whole or the greater part of the society, subsuming other lines of social division. This is surely the inference to be attached to that resounding phrase from the Communist Manifesto, "The history of all hitherto existing societies is the history of class struggle." He also stressed the hegemonic role of the ideology of the ruling class in any social system, and in particular the protracted character of the process by which the modern working class acquires class consciousness (that is, evolves from a "class-in-itself" to a "class-for-itself") --a process accompanied by many blind alleys of "false consciousness" before the exploited find the right road to their emancipation.[8] From Marxian premises themselves, then, we would expect to find class cleavages at the time of Indonesian independence occupying a rather low rating in comparison with other, older and more deeply entrenched social divisions, a number of which, for various reasons, were intensified in the late colonial and early independence years.

So far as the workers and peasants are concerned, the available evidence tends to confirm this expectation. Union organization among the industrial and estate workers began as early as 1908, but did not become a significant force until taken in hand and developed by nationalist groups, including the Marxists, in the latter part of the next decade. The "brittle" character of union organization, and the tendency of its leaders and followers to oscillate between messianic enthusiasm and passivity, provided one indication of the rudimentary level of class consciousness prior to independence. Another was the failure of the working class to throw up leaders from among its own ranks, and its reliance instead for guidance upon the urban intelligentsia, whose concerns were related more to nationalist and party goals than to class demands as such.[9] The village laborer and the poor peasant, needless to say, were still further from freeing themselves from the traditional patronage relationships which provided their security and their prevailing frame of social reference.

---

8. See, for example, T. B. Bottomore and M. Rubel, *Karl Marx: Selected Writings in Sociology and Social Philosophy* (London: Penguin, 1965), pp. 93-95, 191-94.

9. See Everett D. Hawkins, "Labor in Transition," in *Indonesia*, ed. McVey, pp. 257-58, and, more generally, Ruth T. McVey, *The Rise of Indonesian Communism* (Ithaca, N.Y.: Cornell University Press, 1965).

The PKI, after a brief period of efflorescence in the twenties, was effectively destroyed as an organization with mass connections following its abortive uprising against the Dutch in 1926, and did not reemerge till after the outbreak of the national revolution in 1945. Then it quickly undertook the organization of the urban and estate workers, and, to a lesser extent, the village laborers and peasantry, mainly in the areas under Republican control. Union and peasant organizations with PKI influence appear to have been first in the field and to have gained a good deal of head start on the other political parties.[10] This was not a time, however, for placing emphasis on class agitation. The PKI, largely made up of urban intelligentsia and *pemuda* (alienated youth), was part of a national coalition facing a desperate struggle to realize common national aspirations, and the accent of the Party's work therefore was upon moderation and cooperation with its revolutionary partners. In any case, only a small part of the industrial undertakings in the country were in Republican hands, and their operations were badly disrupted by the war. A significant change in party alignments and the character of political conflict in the Republican camp took place in 1948 under the stress of Cold War pressures affecting the nationalist struggle. Communist tactics changed accordingly, and the PKI moved towards a more militant oppositional posture. After the adoption of Musso's *New Road* resolution in August, the PKI proceeded to tighten up its organization and to stimulate antigovernmental feeling among its followers. Its main reliance, however, was placed upon armed units whose grievances stemmed from a threatened demobilization.

In contrast to the direct approach which the PKI used in organizing the workers, its access to the peasantry (such as it was) seems predominantly to have been via channels of patronage, kinship, and traditional influence.[11] Such an operational technique was not calculated to bring out latent class tensions in the countryside, but then it was doubtless dictated by the very weakness of class factors in the villages.[12]

The Madiun affair brought this phase of PKI activity to an end, and in itself revealed something about the level of class consciousness among the lower strata. Although the PKI had by now a substantial trade union organization attached to it, the working class in general did not come to the Party's aid in its time of travail.[13] Of equal significance, the conflict in the rural areas developed, not along class lines, but along the line of *santri-abangan* cleavages.[14]

---

10. Selosoemardjan, *Social Changes in Jogjakarta* (Ithaca, N.Y.: Cornell University Press, 1962), pp. 166-68, 172-73.

11. Ibid., pp. 169-71.

12. Selosoemardjan, *Social Changes*, pp. 177-79, refers to a BTI (Barisan Tani Indonesia, Indonesian Peasants Front) initiative in land sharing in the Gunung Kidul region of Central Java, but from his brief description of the incident it appears to have owed more to millenarian traditions than to class consciousness.

13. See George McT. Kahin, *Nationalism and Revolution in Indonesia* (Ithaca, N.Y.: Cornell University Press, 1952), p. 266; Hindley, *Communist Party*, p. 133. Cf. PKI Chairman Aidit: ". . . in the second half of 1948 the counter-revolution succeeded in misleading some Communist supporters, whose numbers were quite considerable at that time." (*World Marxist Review*, 2, 7 [July 1959].)

14. See Robert Jay, *Religion and Politics in Rural Central Java* (New Haven: Yale University, 1963), pp. 96-97. *Santri-abangan* (lit. white-red) schism which rends the ethnic Javanese has its origins in the uneven impact of Islam on Java, as a result of which a minority of Javanese think of their religion as their main point of

In January 1951, the Aidit leadership group took over the shattered PKI and began to construct the elements of the strategy it was to pursue over the next fourteen years. The difficulties facing the young Communist leaders were formidable. For the Russian, Chinese, Vietnamese, and Yugoslav Communists, war and national revolution had provided great opportunities for establishing their leadership of the forces of national salvation. But in the Indonesian case, by contrast, the Communists had profited only temporarily from these conditions, and had been all but destroyed in their contest with opposed political forces. Far from emerging from the independence struggle with strong nationalist credentials, they were, if anything, suspect on this issue. In their comeback, they had to contend with power groups which themselves enjoyed the prestige and legitimacy deriving from their leading role in the national struggle, and in addition now disposed of significant governmental and power resources.

Social unrest and dissatisfaction certainly existed as a possible base for gathering support: the revolution had unsettled the pemuda generation especially, stirring in them diffuse resentments, undermining the hold of traditional repositories of authority, and arousing high expectations for the era that was to follow upon independence. The governmental elite was neither able to satisfy their expectations nor provide them with an integrative frame for their restless energies. This discontented mass was strongly susceptible to ideological appeals, but the conditions for converting their disenchantment into class outlook and action were anything but favorable.

As the PKI leaders read the situation, a strategy of armed agrarian revolution was ruled out by Party weakness and division, its lack of extensive ties with the peasantry, and the nature of rural schisms. Where was the Party to find a sufficiently powerful appeal that would alienate the peasantry from the ruling groups? How could it fend off the attacks of the army in overcrowded Java with its good system of roads, where the overwhelming bulk of its support was concentrated? Where would it set up rural bases, when the few areas suitable for such emplacements were mostly santri strongholds? Where would it find sanctuary, or a ready source of outside aid? Some Party cadres apparently favored abandoning the cities in favor of preparations for peasant armed struggle;[15] but, although there were some areas where they may have found a following among squatters on government lands and estate workers, the long-term potential of such a strategy was hardly encouraging to a Party that had only recently been dealt a shattering blow by military and religio-cultural forces.

The prospects for oppositional activity based on the workers in the cities and towns were no more enticing. The Sukiman Government responded to a wave of union militancy in 1950-51 with a punishing series of raids on PKI and union cadres in August 1951, as a result of which the Party was politically isolated and its organizational efforts set back for one to two years.[16] The workers at this time showed

---

cultural reference, while the majority, although nominally Moslem, derive their values and religious practices from the traditions of pre-Islamic Javanese culture. The lifeways of each are often intensely repugnant to the other, despite the fact that the traditions are in fact intermingled among both. Generally on this subject, see Clifford Geertz, *The Religion of Java* (Glencoe, Illinois: Free Press, 1960), esp. pp. 121-30. Generally the "more Islamic" or santri tended to be anti-PKI.

15. See Aidit's "Report to the Fifth Congress of the PKI (1954)," *Problems of the Indonesian Revolution* (Bandung: Demos, 1963), p. 254.

16. See Herbert Feith, *The Decline of Constitutional Democracy in Indonesia* (Ithaca, N.Y.: Cornell University Press, 1962), pp. 187-91.

little preparedness to defend their arrested leaders.[17] In view of the small size of the proletariat, its undeveloped state of class and political consciousness, and its vulnerability to governmental and army repression, the PKI leaders decided that the Party needed a top political alliance for the purposes of protection, even at the price of modifying drastically its reliance on class issues as a means of attracting support and exerting pressure in the political arena.

The decision was undoubtedly made easier for the PKI leaders by reason of their own radical nationalist orientation, acquired as pemuda leaders in the national revolution, but there was also a persuasive logic to it. On the one hand, the resources for an antielite struggle were demonstrably weak. On the other hand, the nature of intraelite struggle, and the cleavage factors which nourished it, offered the Party possibilities of achieving the protection and opportunities for expansion it required. No doubt the leaders estimated at the time that, once the PKI's initial weakness was overcome, they would be able to revitalize the class struggle.

In the absence of strong class pressures, political parties and mass organizations organized their followings largely along lines of religious and cultural cleavage. The major elite groupings aggregated these cleavage bases, but intraelite conflict also owed a good deal to differences in political values and styles, and to the divergent socioeconomic interests which they encompassed.[18] The latter were a very important source of conflict, particularly between the Masjumi, with its clientele of santri businessmen and Outer Islands export producers, and the PNI, with its base among the Javanese civil bureaucracy and the patronage it extended to a group of predominantly Javanese importers. Governmental and parliamentary disagreement over exchange rate policy and the role of foreign capital in the economy during the fifties expressed this divergence of interests. However, two aspects of this interest conflict need to be noted. In the first place, it ran parallel to, rather than cutting across, *aliran* (ideological and cultural streams) schisms, and thus became enmeshed with the value contestation at the ideological level. In the second place, the nature of the interest conflict was such that it served PKI purposes only within the context of the kind of nationalist alliance it was pursuing, and not in a class struggle context.

Hence, there was nothing "artificial" about the prominence of primordial issues in the political struggle, in the sense that they were merely whipped up by the elite factions as a means of social control. There was no homogeneity among the elite to support such an interpretation, and the issues themselves not only had long historical antecedents, but were aggravated as a result of the traumatic social disruption caused by war and revolution.[19]

While groups among the political elite did manipulate social unrest for purposes of social control and their own advantage, they did so as actors whose values were themselves tied in with those of larger publics. While it is arguable that too low a rating has often been accorded to *economic interest* as a factor in the struggle

---

17. Hindley, *Communist Party*, p. 134.

18. These differences are discussed by Feith, *Decline of Constitutional Democracy*, pp. 129-43.

19. For a discussion of the factors involved in the frequent phenomenon of primordial "backlash" after independence in the third world, see Clifford Geertz, "The Integrative Revolution--Primordial Loyalties and Civil Politics in the New States," in *Old Societies and New States*, ed. Geertz (Berkeley: University of California, 1963).

among competing elite factions, no "single factor" theory of political conflict will suffice to interpret the complex and clouded history of the period.

The political process may be studied substantially in terms of elite group contest because, social unrest notwithstanding, the terms within which these groups set political conflict, and the control they exercised over its manifestations, were not challenged to any significant degree. The major exception--the Darul Islam rebellion (the extraordinary tenacity of which cannot be explained without reference to class-based differences)--nevertheless arose out of the same pattern of primordial and value conflicts which was expressed through the elite divisions. The PKI formed another exception, but only a partial one. On the one hand, the Party's mobilization of the workers and peasants potentially challenged the elite-centered nature of the political struggle, and its ultimate aims, in Lev's words, "threatened the entire social and political order."[20] But, on the other hand, neither the PKI leaders nor their followers were immune to the issues which sundered the elite formations. Specifically, the more that the Sukarnoists expressed their ambitions in radical nationalist slogans emphasizing "national unity" and "the uncompleted revolution," the more they plucked at sentiments shared by the pemuda generation which provided the leadership and cadre core of the Communist Party. The PKI leaders could not have swum against this stream, even if they had wanted to, since there existed no alternative basis upon which their movement could have gained headway against governmental and military hostility. As a result, in return for protection and a measure of freedom at the grassroots level, the PKI was obliged to moderate its class appeals and underwrite the "revolutionary" legitimacy and power claims of the Sukarnoists. PKI intervention in the political struggle thus tended to reinforce rather than transform the character of the elite-dominated contest.

These considerations set problems for any view which sees as *the* central issue in postindependence politics a threat to the elite posed by the social unrest which the PKI in part expressed.[21] This unrest would only have posed a distinct threat to the elite if the dissatisfied (or a substantial portion of their number) had apprehended social circumstances and their own interests in terms significantly different from those in which intraelite conflict was couched. Not only was this not the case, but neither the PKI nor any other prospective counterelite saw the possibility of gaining advantage by attempting to organize social unrest in ways which cut right across the intraelite pattern of conflict.

In particular, such a view must resolve the question of why significant sections of the elite were prepared to ally themselves with the PKI against other competitors and, after these competitors were eliminated from immediate power considerations, continued to sponsor the Party under Guided Democracy. Was it because these groups were convinced that they had the PKI leaders "tamed"? Or was it rather that they were confident that the PKI could not use its following to threaten the elite's position? Or again, were these groups themselves torn between the desire to assure their own dominance, and their attraction to the dynamic vigor of the PKI and the possibilities for national resurgence offered by Communist prescriptions? Once again, the problems hardly seem reducible to a single explanatory factor, any more than the elite can be regarded as homogeneous.[22]

---

20. Daniel S. Lev, *The Transition to Guided Democracy: Indonesian Politics, 1957-1959* (Ithaca, N.Y.: Cornell Modern Indonesia Project, 1964), p. 171.

21. This view is advanced by David Levine, "History and Social Structure in the Study of Contemporary Indonesia," *Indonesia*, 7 (April 1969). See above pp. 30-40.

22. The disposition to regard problems of revolutionary change as explicable in

The three main elements in the PKI's strategy were: (1) *The cultivation of the closest possible relations with the dominant anti-Islamic nationalist groups (in particular, the PNI and President Sukarno).* The original object of this alliance was primarily protection. Later, as other avenues of obtaining power were cut off, the Party came to view it as holding the prospect of bringing it a share in governmental power under the Nasakom formula, from which it could, with the backing of mass pressure, enlarge its position in the political structures and eventually achieve hegemony either by invitation of, or a short sharp struggle with, its partners. (2) *The accumulation of the largest possible membership and organized support.* In part, this massive following was to be used as a "bluff" in order to enhance the Party's value as an ally and to ward off threats to it; additionally, it became an instrument for keeping the momentum of nationalism alive in tune with Sukarno's preoccupations. So long as the parliamentary system subsisted, the large mass following was highly relevant to PKI power concerns, but it is doubtful that the PKI leaders seriously expected to be allowed to obtain power through the ballot-box. In terms of the strategy, the size of the following was more important than its quality or "proletarian" composition, although of course these were also sought as far as was compatible with the more basic considerations. (3) *According ideological primacy to symbols associated with nationalism and national unity.* Concentration on these issues enabled the PKI to appeal to the widest common denominator of mass support and elite sentiment, and it tended to structure situations in such a way as to strengthen the position of all "radical" anti-Western groups as against their opponents.

The strategy was presented as a class alliance, uniting the working class, the peasantry, the petty bourgeoisie and the national bourgeoisie against their common enemies, imperialism and its domestic agents, the compradore bourgeoisie, and feudalism. In reality, however, it was essentially a political alliance between the radical nationalists among the elite and the Communists. Increasingly, PKI formulations began to recognize this fact more obviously, abandoning class concepts in favor of terminologies reflecting the politics of accommodation. The general trend may be represented by the following modes in which the PKI presented its political analyses:

The identification of the Party's political allies and opponents with incongruent social formations. The PNI, for all its bureaucratic, antientrepreneurial orientation, was treated as virtually equivalent to the "national bourgeoisie," while the Masjumi, which approached as closely as was possible in Indonesian conditions to a party of the "national bourgeoisie," was bracketed together with the PSI as "the compradore bourgeoisie."[23]

The adoption, in preference to class categories, of the Maoist formula of "left, right and middle forces," the infinite flexibility of which arises from the fact that each constituent element in the formula is itself capable of being divided in turn into "left, right and middle forces," and so on.[24]

---

terms of one central knot of "contradiction" which, once it is untied, will unravel all the other knots in the social structure, particularly belongs to the Leninist and Maoist variants of Marxism. The success of their revolutionary strategies in their own countries does not oblige us to accept the universal validity of their theorem.

23. Usually the attribution was implicit in the way the PKI described the respective "class" forces. But occasionally it was more explicit, as when Lukman referred to the PNI as "the main representative of the national bourgeoisie." *World Marxist Review*, 2, 8 (August 1959).

24. See Aidit's "Report to the PKI Sixth Congress (1959)," *Problems*, pp. 314-17. Cf. Mao Tse-tung, *Selected Works*, 3 (London: Lawrence & Wishart, 1954), pp. 194-203.

The acceptance of the three aliran of Nasakom as the substantial foundation of the "united national front."[25]

The posing of the political struggle in terms of a conflict between a united people of all social strata, and foreign or foreign-dominated elements.[26]

Class analysis did not disappear altogether, and in specific conditions (such as the land-reform campaign of 1964-65) it regained some prominence. The overall tendency, however, was to jettison it or to attach class labels to nonclass concepts. Likewise, while the Party used class appeals to some extent in mobilizing support, its massive following was mainly built up along other lines--identification of the Party with the cause of national unity and national revolution; association with prestigious organizations and individuals; welfare activities of various kinds; identification with "modernism"; the use of patronage relationships, especially in the villages; propagation of the achievements of the Communist states; the attraction of a "total" philosophy; the prestige of a party free of corruption and demoralization, and knowing where it was going, etc.

Implicit in much of the PKI's appeal was the conformity of its notions to traditional Javanese concepts and values. As Anderson has pointed out, for example, the projection of politics in terms of *rakjat* versus "alien," which infused the Communist approach to the ongoing nationalist crusade, possessed pronounced resonance in a society where "the urge to one-ness" is central to political attitudes.[27] The abangan of central and east Java adopted the PKI as a vehicle for their interests, consequently deepening the rift which lies at the root of Javanese society by giving religious and cultural divisions a politico-ideological dimension.

Persistent attempts were made by PKI leaders, especially in later years, to convert the basis of Party allegiance to one of class by means of ideological education programs, but the effort encountered great obstacles in the multiclass nature of the Party's composition, the influence of traditional categories of thought, the persistence of outlooks conditioned by nonclass cleavages, the Party's own strategy deemphasizing class, and (it would seem) a disposition on the part of its following to show little inclination for prolonged study unconnected with perceived achievement prospects. Generally, it may be suggested that, in the absence of pronounced experiential factors promoting a shift in value orientations, the imparting of new ideas usually results in the selective incorporation of those ideas into the prevailing value structure, rather than to the transformation of the structure itself.

The PKI's strategy brought it substantial gains in the fifties, in that its numbers and support grew prodigiously, the Masjumi and PSI were widely discredited and ousted from formal power positions, the most radically anti-Communist officers were cashiered for their part in the regional rebellion, the Party won wide respect for its nationalist fervor, and the President bestowed upon it his patronage and protection.

---

25. Lukman, *Tentang Front Persatuan Nasional* (Jakarta: Jajasan Pembaruan, 1962), pp. 34-35; Aidit, "Untuk Pelaksanaan Jang Lebih Konsekwen dari Manifesto Politik," *Bintang Merah*, July-August, 1960, p. 308; Aidit, *Revolusi Indonesia, Latarbelakang Sedjarah dan Haridepannja* (Jakarta: Jajasan Pembaruan, 1964), p. 72.

26. Aidit: "The form of the class struggle in Indonesia at the present time . . . is a struggle of all the Indonesian people who are revolutionary against imperialism (monopoly capitalism) and feudal remnants." *Harian Rakjat*, August 20, 1964.

27. Anderson, "Idea of Power."

The line pursued by the PKI leadership aroused some opposition and misgivings within the Party's ranks, but the fact that there took place no significant breakaway inside the Party or among its following, is confirmatory of the view that social unrest was not to any important extent ideologically demarcated from the cleavage issues which formed the basis of elite conflict.[28]

The PKI's advance along the parliamentary road was rudely cut short when, in 1957, Sukarno teamed up with the army to replace the constitutional structure by a more authoritarian political system. To what extent was the transition to Guided Democracy a reaction on the part of the elite to the threat of PKI domination of the parliamentary system? Here again, multiple-factor analysis appears more capable of providing explanations than a single focus. *Defense of the constitutional system by the Communists' most determined foes among the political parties hardly seems consistent with the view that the PKI's challenge was the single dominating factor in the political crisis of the time.* Alongside it, and perhaps overshadowing it, was the bitter conflict between the regional forces and their allies, on the one side, and the central government and its allies, on the other. (This presentation greatly oversimplifies a complex aggregation of cleavage bases on both sides, but it will have to suffice for our purpose.) Among the chief proponents of Guided Democracy, there were undoubtedly some who regarded the blocking of PKI progress as a major calculation; others, including President Sukarno, can I think be considered as viewing the problem more in terms of a threat arising from a number of directions to the integrity of the nation under their leadership.

The destruction of the parliamentary party system, which was serving it so well, came as a heavy blow to the PKI. Once again, however, the relation of forces appeared to the leaders to leave them no alternative but to accept the new dispensation. To have resisted the changes would have left the Party isolated and acutely vulnerable, sandwiched between the bitterly anti-Communist regional forces on one side and the President-army combination on the other.

Could the PKI have distanced itself from the Guided Democracy developments, refusing to go along with the changes but not actively resisting them, and counting on a combination of governmental ineptitude and economic decline to bring about eventually a pattern of conflict that would enable it to overthrow the regime? Assuming that such a posture did not provoke immediate and drastic repression, the very least the Party would have had to contend with would have been the loss of a great part of its popular support, the takeover of its mass organizations by army and/or Presidentially sponsored fronts, and a substantial growth in military power. It is difficult to see that its prospects of success in these circumstances would have been any brighter than they were a few years earlier.

There is little to suggest that the workers and peasants of Java reacted to the changes from a class viewpoint, or could have been persuaded to do so. To judge by their public responses, they were swayed in their appreciation of the issues by the charismatic and traditional appeals of the President, and generally aligned themselves in accordance with aliran cleavages as modified by the political leaderships.

With evident reluctance, but outward enthusiasm, the PKI leaders chose to embrace Guided Democracy, heartened by the promise of Presidential protection, the

---

28. Indications of some restlessness in the PKI with regard to its political line were given from time to time by the Party's leaders. See B. O. Hutapea's "Report to the Seventh Congress (1962)," *Madju Terus! Dokumen-dokumen Kongres Nasional ke-VII (Luarbiasa) PKI* (Jakarta: Jajasan Pembaruan, 1963), pp. 248-49.

persistence of conflict between army and President, and the decline in the power of their party competitors. With the introduction of Guided Democracy, there took place a neo-traditionalist revival on the political plane, with the ruling cliques of prijaji origin reverting more openly to the ceremonial styles and patterns of status politics of old Java, and waging a contest for court favor and perquisites very much as their forebears had done. Politico-bureaucratic roles again became more exclusively the hallmarks of prestige. At the same time, class did move up somewhat on the ladder of social cleavage. The concentration of major industrial and commercial functions in the hands of state officials after 1957, and the tendency for economic undertakings to be viewed as the appanages of those to whom their management was entrusted, now created the potential for direct conflict of interest between the workers and the "bureaucratic capitalists," as the PKI dubbed the new administrators.

In the countryside, too, an important change was effected as a result of the passage in 1960 of the land laws and Communist efforts to get the government to implement them. By proposing the transfer to landless peasants of land in excess of certain sizes, and setting limits upon the amount of the crop payable to landowners under sharing agreements, these laws laid the ground for a struggle between the interests of the rural dispossessed and the wealthier village strata.

The PKI's experience was to demonstrate, however, that class was still too slender a reed to support a major bid to change the political balance of forces. The position of the industrial workers (only about 60 percent of whom were enrolled in PKI-led unions) was still one of acute weakness in the face of a hostile army officer corps now having a direct interest (via the nationalized enterprises) in industrial peace and buttressed by martial law powers. A large part of the industrial labor force was still semirural in character, and a high proportion consisted of female workers.[29] In addition, workers in state enterprises were dependent to a considerable degree upon government allocations of food, while in private undertakings there often existed strong "paternalistic" relations between employer and employee. In conditions of accelerating economic crisis and declining production, the falling living standards of the workers, rather than promoting militancy, strengthened their long-standing preference for security.[30]

The PKI appeared for a time in 1959-60 to be moving towards a more uncompromising antigovernment stance involving the promotion of union industrial action. In this period, its attacks upon the government were the most intransigent that had been expressed since the early fifties and distinct rumblings were heard from the leftwing labor federation SOBSI. The aim appears to have been to force the Party's admission to the Cabinet, but the army clampdown on the Party following its July 8, 1960 critique of the government, put a stop to this militant shift and convinced the PKI leaders that "class interests must be subordinated to national interests."[31] Neither the consciousness of the Party's following, nor the mood of the workers, nor the general political climate and balance of strengths, was conducive to an offensive in the cities. Although primordial cleavages were initially dampened down somewhat by the blow struck at regional and santri interests, the intense nationalist symbolism of the regime obscured and discouraged the expression

---

29. Hawkins, "Labor in Transition," Hindley, *Communist Party*, esp. pp. 154-56, Lance Castles, *Religion, Politics and Economic Behaviour in Java: The Kudus Cigarette Industry* (New Haven: Yale University, 1967).

30. Castles, *Religion, Politics and Economic Behaviour*, esp. pp. 75-84.

31. Aidit, "Madju Terus Menggempur Imperialisme dan Feodalisme," *Harian Rakjat*, January 2, 1961.

of class interests from below. In addition, official "retooling" campaigns and pseudo-radical slogans held out to the workers phantom promises of the remedying of their grievances.

After its early disenchantment with militant oppositional tactics in 1959-60, the Party adopted a new variant of its established strategy. Using nationalism as its major vehicle for mobilizing the masses and cementing political alliances, it sought to impress the President and his entourage with its indispensability in attaining their ends, and so to gain entry to the key power structures. Although by September 1965 the PKI had not succeeded in its prime objective of seizing major levers of bureaucratic power, it nevertheless had proved its versatility and resourcefulness in overcoming many of the disabilities from which it suffered in the early years of Guided Democracy and placing itself in the center of future power considerations. The Party's leaders by this time enjoyed very close personal relations with the President, to the point of arousing great envy among their rivals. It built up an enormous mass following, gained preponderant influence in the official mass vehicle of the regime (the national front), extended its organization on a national basis, and won widespread recognition of its patriotism and political capacity. From 1963 onwards, it was able to have "rightists" removed from many power positions, though not to destroy the structures which sustained and supported them (the army, the bureaucracy, NU, Moslem mass organizations, informal political cliques, etc.). The President was pursuing an increasingly leftward course, culminating in the formation of an "international front" with China and sharp breaks with Western powers headed by the United States.

Meanwhile the PKI had not altogether abandoned its quest for a militant base of support that it could use as an aid in persuading the elite to acknowledge its claims to a more decisive role in the regime. Already by 1959, this quest had begun to shift towards the countryside, where the weight of army power was less pronounced. The Party spent the next four years trying to strengthen the class character of its rural organizations and preparing the peasants to stand up for their rights under the land laws. By late 1963, it judged the time ripe for a class offensive in the villages, the first decisive turn to a struggle hinged on class cleavages. The result was the *aksi sefihak* (unilateral action) campaign of 1964-65. This was a sustained PKI attempt to mobilize the poor peasants and share-croppers to assert their rights under the land reform laws of 1960, the implementation of which had bogged down under the weight of bureaucratic inertia and the resistance of interested persons and groups. The "actions" ranged from holding a deputation, presenting a petition, or staging a demonstration, to the unilateral seizure of land by force and the refusal to pay the landowner more than a certain percentage of the crop.

A thorough study of the aksi sefihak campaign remains to be undertaken, and many aspects of it (including the extent to which the PKI leadership was proceeding on the basis of its own appreciation of political conditions, or was responding to pressures from its rural cadres) are still obscure, but I would hazard the following tentative conclusions about it:

The PKI succeeded in developing a sufficient degree of class solidarity among the village poor, predominantly those of abangan persuasion, to support a fairly extensive campaign on Java, Bali, and, to a lesser extent, parts of Sumatra.

Bitter opposition arose to the aksi sefihak and the PKI among landowners and their clients. The opposition was stimulated and encouraged by *kijaji* (village holy men), Moslem organizations and many PNI local leaders. The religious sentiment of the santri was deliberately and effectively aroused against the "godless" who were threatening the lands of the *pesantren* (the Moslem religious schools, which in some cases did own quite a good deal of land, and in addition frequently served as "dummies" for Moslem landowners). Violent outbursts of Moslem resentment distorted the class character of the campaign and converted it in many areas into one of aliran discord.

Army and civilian authorities in local districts were generally on the side of the opponents of the aksi, either openly or tacitly. Traditions of village harmony and deference to authority also operated against the PKI.

Despite favorable intervention by the President, the anti-PKI forces appear to have gained the upper hand in the struggle; their long, pent-up passion and their solidarism, backed by local authority, made many peasants recoil from the discord which was fomented by the presentation of their demands.

By the PKI's own accounts, its rural organizations were by no means wholly committed to the aksi or disciplined in carrying it out. In 1964, PKI leaders were still obstructing Party decisions.[32] At the same time, critics of the PKI alleged that Moslem and PNI antipathy to the aksi was intensified by the PKI's "hypocrisy" in protecting its own landlord patrons from the effects of the land laws.[33]

On the other hand, the Party's leaders became worried lest they had overplayed their hand. In May 1965, in the aftermath of the campaign, Aidit accused "some Party cadres" of having displayed impatience, adventurism and lack of concern for "national front" considerations.[34]

The extent and violence of the Moslem upsurge seems to have come as something of a surprise to the PKI leaders. Yet it had been building up for some time. Political events from 1957 onwards had represented a major defeat for Moslem parties, business interests, and religious concerns. Resentments rankled, particularly among the younger generation, who, in reaction against the incapacity and compromising attitudes of their elders, developed a now-or-never spirit of uncompromising struggle against the Communist advance, inspired by religious revivalism.[35] Communist and nationalist attacks on the HMI, the Moslem student organization, were one of a number of factors which led the Islamic youth to take to action in defense of their threatened interests, and the land-reform issue, by adding to their insecurity, aroused them to violent attacks upon the PKI and allied organizations.

The PKI leaders, seeing feeling against them welling up in the PNI as well, and so placing their whole alliance strategy in jeopardy, were not altogether unhappy when a Presidentially promoted compromise on the land issue was reached in December 1964. Thereafter, despite verbal offensives on land reform, the emphasis of the PKI's work shifted back to welfare and cultural questions. The aksi sefihak

---

32. PKI leaders expressed these views to me in November 1964. See also Asmu's Report to the National Conference of the BTI in September 1964, *Suara Tani*, 2, 1965.

33. I am indebted to Dr. Ruth McVey and Professor E. Utrecht for discussions which have helped greatly to clarify my understanding of the aksi sefihak campaign. Neither of them, however, is responsible in any way for the interpretation presented here. See also W. F. Wertheim, "Indonesia Before and After the Untung Coup," *Pacific Affairs*, 39, 1 and 2 (Spring and Summer 1966), and "From Aliran Towards Class Struggle in the Countryside of Java" (Paper delivered at the International Conference on Asian History at Kuala Lumpur, August 1968); and (with special reference to Moslem reactions) Lance Castles, "Notes on the Islamic School at Gontor," *Indonesia*, 1 (April 1966).

34. See his report to the CC of the PKI, *Harian Rakjat*, May 12-14, 1965.

35. See Castles, *Religion, Politics and Economic Behaviour*, pp. 67-68.

had stimulated class awareness in the villages, but this had not reacted to the Party's benefit; on the contrary, consciousness of their class interests had driven the landed elements in the Islamic parties and the PNI to mobilize aliran sentiment against the Communists to a point where it posed serious dangers for them.

By early 1965, politics had become sharply polarized between those who were prepared to cooperate with the PKI, even to the point of sharing power with it, and those who were determined to block the Communists' road. To many among the politically influential, there was a strong sense that "the revolution was moving ahead fast," in other words, that the future lay with Sukarno as head of the left-wing camp; additionally, polarization had brought many non-Communist nationalists into a position where they had more to fear from the PKI's defeat than from its victory. Even among the PKI's allies, however, there were not a few who had private reservations about supping with the tiger, especially since they were not unaware of the fact that their way of life differed considerably from the ideals underlying Communist moral discipline and, to a lesser extent, from the actual life-styles of the PKI leaders. As the year wore on, uneasiness about Sukarno's intentions and the country's foreign policy drift, compounded by the rundown in the momentum of Malaysian confrontation and drastic economic decline, manifested especially in a marked acceleration in the rate of inflation, induced a profound crisis in the society. The President, however, still held the political balance, and he avoided or delayed taking those steps--admission of the PKI to administrative power positions, creation of a fifth armed force--which were being urged upon him from the left and which may have tilted the scales one way or the other. As rumors of Sukarno's ill-health gained currency, every faction began to look to their defenses; plot and counterplot proliferated, and the soothsayers (traditional harbingers of dynastic collapse) were consulted with ever greater frequency. Time was running out on the PKI's patient strategy, and a class-based alternative had proved unworkable. The Party had hurdled most of the obstacles placed in the way of its climb to power, but it still had to contend with its longstanding enemies, the army generals, with their formidable machine of violence. The stage was thus set for the denouement of October 1, 1965.

PERSPECTIVE AND METHOD IN AMERICAN
RESEARCH ON INDONESIA*

Benedict O'Gorman Anderson

That academics are not simply specialists in particular fields of knowledge but also members of specific cultures and social orders, is something at once obvious and yet too frequently ignored, not least by academics themselves. The prestige and influence of academics rest so largely on the scarcity value of their specialized knowledge that there is a natural tendency for this aspect of their work to be stressed at the expense of others. Claims to impartiality and objectivity are another means for establishing the corporate autonomy and prestige of the academic world.

Yet in fact academics inevitably share the dominant assumptions and values of their societies, and even when they have reservations or objections to some of these assumptions and values, their opposition is normally framed within the limits of the "stretch" of the culture they have inherited. In a narrower sense, too, academics as a group tend to be bound more or less tightly to the power structures in their society, partly because of their class origins, but also because of the technological and institutional order within which most of their work is carried on. Particularly in America in recent years, academics in many different fields have come to require an increasingly heavily capitalized infrastructure--laboratories, libraries, data banks, computers, research assistants, etc.--which only large and powerful institutions can adequately furnish. These new consumer needs have inevitably created an unprecedented dependence on, and sensitivity to, the interests of the custodians of state and private corporate power.

One would be inclined to expect to find this pattern of conformity to be particularly clear in the social sciences, since research in these fields frequently impinges directly on public policy, and, by comparison with research in the natural sciences, is less "protected" by the rigor of established method. The pattern should be even more obvious in social science research conducted on societies of serious concern to the makers of foreign policy, since here research and "national interest" (as officially conceived) are most explicitly engaged with one another.

---

* There is an unavoidable element of artificiality in such a title. "American research on Indonesia" is not an easily isolable theme. Many non-American specialists on Indonesia have been trained at American universities and/or have published most of their writing in the United States. On the other hand, many American specialists have been influenced in varying degrees by work done on Indonesia in Australia, Holland, England, and other countries. For present purposes, I have decided to confine my discussion largely to the scholarly writing published in America by Americans or non-Americans.

American research on Indonesia serves as a useful case in point. I think it can be shown that the general contours of this research, and its changing foci, can best be understood as the result of the interaction between American culture (including American academic culture) and American interests in Southeast Asia as conceived and pursued over time by the holders of American state power.

*   *   *

The general characteristics of what one might call the American "cultural paradigm" are well known and have not changed markedly since they were first systematically described by Tocqueville. In recent years they have been the focus of the work of Louis Hartz, William Appleman Williams, Gary Wills, and others.[1] It is perhaps enough to say here that the cultural paradigm assumes a natural and inextricable interconnection between private enterprise and property (capitalism), constitutional democracy, personal liberty, and progress. American history represents the unfolding of these ideas and their institutional realization. World progress is measured by the degree to which this paradigm establishes itself around the globe.

In the academic social science context, the importance of the paradigm has been less as a conscious framework of reference for research and analysis, than as an almost unconscious shaper of the very language of academic discourse itself. To put it another way, it is less that liberal democracy has been used as an explicit standard for assessing and judging other societies than that the paradigm makes it very difficult to imagine seriously any other standard, let alone put it to systematic use. Liberalism, in the Hartzian sense, is the language of academic social science politesse, and by that very fact fundamentally shapes the world of American social science research. This alchemy is so powerful that even "dissident" research most often reflects, in style and orientation, the patterns which it conceives itself opposing. This should become clearer when we come to look at some of the best research on Indonesia, a fair portion of which has been "dissident" in intention.[2]

If the paradigm of American liberal culture has shaped the contours of American research on Indonesia in the most basic sense, the foci of interest and the methodologies employed have tended to vary in accord (though with a certain time lag caused by the measured pace of research and publication itself) with America's role and the trajectory of indigenous historical development in the area of Southeast Asia, and in Indonesia in particular. In the history of research on Indonesia in the past 25 years, one can in fact detect the presence of two broad academic "formats," by no means wholly separated from one another either in time or in the work of particular scholars, but nonetheless quite distinct in orientation and methodology, and corresponding to important changes in Indonesian-American relationships. For convenience

---

1. Alexis de Tocqueville, *Democracy in America* (New York: Mentor, 1956); Louis Hartz, *The Liberal Tradition in America* (New York: Harcourt, Brace, 1955); William Appleman Williams, *The Roots of the Modern American Empire* (New York: Random House, 1969); Gary Wills, *Nixon Agonistes* (Boston: Houghton Mifflin, 1970).

2. It should be acknowledged at the start that the field of "Indonesianology" presents unusual difficulties for the type of analysis I am attempting, since a remarkably high proportion of its better-known practitioners in America have not been native Americans, and thus have been as much molded by European as by American culture. (Some examples are: Harry Benda, Lance Castles, Herbert Feith, Donald Hindley, Claire Holt, Guy Pauker, Karl Pelzer, Hans Schmitt, John Smail, J. M. van der Kroef.) Nothing comparable is true for, say, Burmese, Philippine, or Thai studies.

I shall call the first "anticolonial liberalism and the historical method," the second "imperial liberalism and the comparative method."

I. Anticolonial Liberalism and the Historical Method

The utilization of this format for the study of Indonesia was primarily the result of a particular conjuncture of historical forces in Southeast Asia during and after World War II. Prior to the war, American power and influence in the area had essentially been confined to the Philippines, while the European imperial powers dominated the rest of the region. The Europeans emerged from the war with their resources depleted, their military strength reduced and their prestige gravely undermined. The reverse was true of the United States. Accordingly, the years after 1945 witnessed an initial, largely unsuccessful, attempt by the Europeans to restore their prewar domination, and subsequently an uneven and partial withdrawal from the area; at the same time, and with increasing speed, American power and American influence over the direction of indigenous political developments expanded. This forward movement was most marked in territories where the European colonial powers were least able to reassert their prewar hegemony--Thailand, Indonesia, and to a later and lesser degree, Vietnam. The closed doors of the colonies would perhaps have been pried even wider open had not American interests in Western Europe required some sensitivity to the concerns of the imperial nations of that area.

But the weakness of the European powers in Southeast Asia not only permitted the advance of American influence, but also facilitated the rapid growth of local nationalist movements, many of which had been encouraged by the Japanese during the period of wartime occupation. In Indonesia, this growth was rapid and deep enough to make possible an extended, largely successful, politico-military struggle against the Dutch. In effect there was thus a partial and temporary convergence of American and Indonesian policies. On occasion American influence was deployed in such a way as to give considerable support to the Indonesian state leadership. Yet, as early as 1948, the pattern of this assistance, which has persisted up till our time, was set: it was conditional on the exclusion from effective power of the Indonesian left, particularly the Indonesian communists, who embraced a paradigm fundamentally incompatible with the American one.[3]

It was in 1948 that George Kahin came to Indonesia and began the research that was to produce his path-breaking book, *Nationalism and Revolution in Indonesia*.

---

3. Early in 1948 the American representative in Indonesia, Frank Graham, was abruptly recalled and his commitments to the moderately left-wing Amir Sjarifuddin government were effectively repudiated with the result that this government fell from power. When the subsequent Hatta government crushed the left later that year, American support became much more significant than hitherto. For details, see George McT. Kahin, *Nationalism and Revolution in Indonesia* (Ithaca: Cornell University Press, 1952), chapters VII, XI, and XIII; Alistair M. Taylor, *Indonesian Independence and the United Nations* (London: Stevens and Sons, 1960), Parts Two and Three; Roger Vailland, *Boroboudour* (Paris: Correa, 1951), especially the chapter entitled "La Nuit de Sarangan," where Vailland goes so far as to claim that an explicit deal to this effect was made between Hatta and the then U.S. representative in Indonesia, Merle Cochran. For studies showing the basic continuity of U.S. policy through the 1950s and 1960s see, e.g., Howard P. Jones, *Indonesia: The Possible Dream* (New York: Harcourt Brace Jovanovich, 1971); and Frederick P. Bunnell, "The Kennedy Initiatives in Indonesia, 1962-1963" (Ph.D. Thesis, Cornell University, 1969).

The central assumptions of this study were that Indonesian nationalism was a historically determined and progressive force moving Indonesia away from colonial authoritarianism and exploitation towards a liberal constitutional order.[4] There was, therefore, or should be, a natural congruence between the interests of Indonesia and the United States. His book was in part a plea for a wider public understanding of this congruence, and a critique of those in policy-making circles who had argued that American interests in Europe demanded a tactful posture vis-à-vis the Dutch attempt to restore their prewar ascendancy in Indonesia.

The impact of Kahin's work was such that it produced what Herbert Feith has justly termed a "Kahinian" school of Indonesia specialists.[5] In the research of this school, the characteristic features of Format I are quite clear: a strong sympathy for Indonesian nationalism; a primary focus on the "problems" of Indonesia's development in a democratic and constitutional direction, as seen from the perspective of the nationalist leadership which survived the revolution; and the use of the historical method.

These elements were tightly linked to one another, and their interrelationships can perhaps best be seen in the work of Kahin himself. For the historical method, with its strong emphasis on the uniqueness and intrinsic dynamic of historical experience, was ideally suited for Kahin's purposes. Only by a careful and concrete *historical* analysis could the arraignment of Dutch colonial rule be effectively achieved. In Kahin's pages the reader is soberly shown the consequences of colonialism's deepening impact: population disequilibria, bureaucratic cooptation of indigenous elites, political repression, racial stratification, economic exploitation, etc. At the same time, by tracing the emergence of the Indonesian nationalist elite from the inner contradictions of the colonial system, Kahin was able to give it an aura of historic mission. Furthermore, the uniqueness of a specifically Indonesian nationalism, not to be subsumed under any general category of nationalism *qua* ideology, could only be effectively brought out by historical analysis.

While the strengths of the work done within Format I lay in its thorough and meticulous scholarship, its humane concern for civil liberties and social justice, and its recognition of the historic authenticity and autonomy of Indonesian nationalism,[6] these strengths were partially offset by weaknesses inherent in Format I itself.

---

4. Such a judgment is obviously greatly oversimplified. While Kahin expressed his belief that "the preponderant majority [of the nationalist leadership] . . . were devoted to political principles and practices which were roughly the same as those aspired to in the Western democracies" (p. 477), he was also fully aware of the powerful influence exerted by non-Western and anti-Western ideas and sentiments. Nonetheless I think it is fair to say that a "paradigmatic" congruence between (progressive) American and Indonesian political thinking was an important element in the argument of *Nationalism and Revolution*.

5. See Herbert Feith, "The Study of Indonesian Politics: A Survey and an Apologia" (unpublished paper presented to the Conference of the Australian Political Studies Association, August 1969). Feith's stimulating discussion was the first detailed attempt at a critical assessment of Indonesian studies as a whole, and the present essay is deeply influenced by it. The term Kahinians is justified by the fact that a high proportion of the better-known specialists were trained by Kahin himself, including, for example, Benda, Feith, Lev, and McVey.

6. The major work written purely in the Kahinian tradition was Ruth T. McVey's superb *The Rise of Indonesian Communism* (Ithaca: Cornell University Press, 1965). Strictly historical in method, this book was in part intended to demonstrate the "Indonesian-ness" of the fathers of the Indonesian Communist movement, and their

For example, the liberal-democratic concerns of the Kahinians led to a pronounced focus on constitutional politics and parliamentary institutions. In a narrower sense, it was particularly the Westernized political leaders of Sjahrir's Indonesian Socialist Party and Mohammad Natsir's wing of the Islamic Masjumi party whose ideas and programs were treated with the most sympathy and respect. Political groups and forces whose activities did not primarily impinge on parliamentary institutions, or whose ideological orientations were regarded as partly or wholly undemocratic, were often ignored or were analyzed in less than flattering terms. This was true both of the Indonesian Communist Party (PKI) and the Indonesian military.[7]

Secondly, the Kahinians' commitment to Indonesian nationalism, or rather to a certain expression of it, tended to encourage an identification with the *center* (Djakarta, or Java), at one level, and, at another, with the postrevolutionary political and intellectual elite. While sympathy for what were usually defined as "regional" movements was by no means lacking, this sympathy (and scholarly interest) was primarily limited to groups, who, while based in the "regions," hoped to increase their power *within* the framework of a secular, integrated Indonesian state, rather than those who sought to remove themselves from, or radically alter this framework. One can compare, for example, the quite different attitude towards and attention paid to the dissidence of the secular, anti-Communist PRRI-Permesta rebellion of 1958, which aimed at overthrowing the ruling coalition in Djakarta, as opposed to the dissidence exemplified by the breakaway Republic of the South Moluccas or the "theocratic" Darul Islam movement led by Kartosuwirjo. And there was a corollary tendency to focus research on the Djakarta elite (usually regarded as the authentic custodians of Indonesian nationalism) and on the problems posed for this elite by other segments of Indonesian society, rather than on the problems posed for these segments by the elite at the center. Thus racial, ethnic and religious minorities, to say nothing of peasant majorities, were treated primarily as object blocks out of which the subject center would have to construct the full-fledged Indonesian nation of the future.

But it was not basically these problems which, in the middle and late 1950s, undermined the hegemony of Format I. Rather the conditions for its elaboration and coherence were bypassed by events. It became increasingly difficult to conceive of a natural congruence between even the best interests of America and Indonesia, and, at the same time, in Indonesia itself, nationalism and constitutional democracy came to appear less coterminous than antagonistic principles.

II. *Imperial Liberalism and the Comparative Method*

It may well be that, in retrospect, historians will look back on the decade 1955-1965 as the zenith of America's rise to global power. Outside the Communist states, her hegemony expanded triumphantly and virtually without serious opposition. In this period American policy-makers found themselves dealing with scores of national units within the vast American orbit--in Asia, Africa, Latin America, the Middle East and Europe. The speed with which this ascendancy was achieved meant, however, that American power in these areas generally far outran American knowledge of them. The need to fill this knowledge vacuum was felt with growing urgency as the 1950s drew to a close.

---

relative autonomy from the Comintern. (It was thus an implicit critique of the globalist abstractions then fashionable among American writers on communism.)

7. The major exceptions were Donald Hindley's *The Communist Party of Indonesia, 1951-1963* (Berkeley: University of California Press, 1964), and Ruth McVey's various pieces on Indonesian communism since independence.

It was largely in response to this need that there took place a vast expansion of what came to be known as "area studies," symbolized by the National Defense Education Act, and marked by greatly enlarged graduate programs, language training efforts, research grants, and so forth. Area specialists multiplied rapidly, their professional advice was increasingly asked for, and their academic and political prominence was considerably enhanced.[8]

But it was not simply more knowledge that was required. It was also knowledge organized in a particular way, and within a particular framework. Particularistic historically oriented research threatened to generate a snow-balling accumulation of disparate and indigestible information. What was needed was a framework which could reduce this intractable pluralism of particularity to an orderly, structured global ("universal") pattern, on the basis of which "systematic" analysis and policy-formulation could go forward. Reflecting this need in part, a vogue developed for "comparative" analysis and theory, pioneered by men like Gabriel Almond, Lucian Pye, David Apter, Edward Shils, and so forth. The instructive thing about the new "comparative" orientation was not so much, as is often remarked, that it was ethnocentric and worked from basically American and Western European models, but rather that comparativism *qua* comparativism reflected the current global role of the United States.[9]

In the comparative approach developed in the late 1950s and early 1960s two elements deserve particular attention: an addiction to what can be loosely described as functionalism and an ill-concealed hostility to "nationalism."[10] In a sense these were two sides of the same coin. For the assumptions of this functionalism were universalist, ahistorical and mechanistic, and thus admirably adapted, as we shall see, to the social engineering bent of its proponents and the requirements of American policy. Nationalism and history could not be wholly excluded from comparative analysis, but they were typically brought in "to save the phenomena." (Note the popularity of the odd pseudo-concept "political culture" in political science writing of the period.) But since nationalism *in concreto* is an irreducibly *particular* phe-

---

8. In the case of Indonesian studies, the following figures on Ph.D. dissertations completed by students in the United States (other than Indonesian nationals) speak for themselves. (One should bear in mind the time-lag necessarily entailed by the long process of finally completing dissertations):

pre-1941	*1941-45*	*1946-50*	*1951-55*	*1956-60*	*1961-65*	*1966-mid-1968*
4	1	4	10	28	27	28

Even more striking are the following figures on the disciplinary foci of these dissertations. (Figures for Indonesian nationals are included in parentheses.)

Anth/Soc	*Econ*	*Educ*	*Geog*	*Hist*	*Lang/Lit*	*Phil/Rel*	*Pol Sci*	*Other*
20 (2)	10 (6)	7 (8)	3 (1)	11 (-)	5 (4)	1 (3)	41 (12)	3 (-)

In effect 41 percent of the non-Indonesian and 33 percent of the Indonesian students completing dissertations did so in political science. (Figures are drawn from Lian The and Paul W. van der Veur, *Treasures and Trivia* [Ohio University, Center of International Studies, 1968], Tables I and II, pp. 125-26.)

9. As will become clearer below, I am not arguing that *any* comparative approach is hegemonic, but that imperial scholarship in the social sciences will naturally tend toward comparativism, albeit of a particular kind.

10. An interesting exception is the case of China studies after 1950. The reasons for this exception will be suggested below.

nomenon, it made the comparativists no less uneasy than the policy-makers who had to deal with it within the sphere of American hegemony.

Comparativism and functionalism of this type were closely linked to the theory and doctrines of "modernization." For the teleological and technico-administrative character of "modernization" theory hinged on the universalist assumptions of Format II's comparativism and the managerial implications of its functionalism. At the same time, "modernization" theory perfectly filled the need for a new linkage between the American paradigm and the changing character of America's relations with the ex-colonial world. If Format I had highlighted the political aspects of the paradigm (liberal democratic values, for example), Format II's "modernization" doctrines brought into high relief its expansionary economic liberalism. They provided a rationale for the massive export of American capital, as well as educational institutions and styles, administrative practices and conventions, social organization, values and culture. In effect, "modernization" was largely conceived and defined so as to imply the spread of the paradigm.[11]

The larger pattern suggested here was evident in the small worlds of Southeast Asia and Southeast Asian studies. The period 1955-1965 was marked by a vast expansion of American power in the area, signaled by and implemented through the influx of military and aid missions, business corporations, academic teams, agencies of cultural propaganda, assorted missionaries both religious and secular, and so forth.[12] Having successfully supplanted the European colonial powers, America shifted her attention to consolidation and stabilization of her new hegemony.

The spread of her power brought the United States into a new and fundamentally antagonistic relationship with the authentic nationalisms of the area. The parallel trajectories of an earlier period now tended to converge and cross. In the countries of Southeast Asia the euphoria of the immediate postwar years was fading, and the nationalist elites found themselves faced with choices that were difficult to accept but were impossible to avoid. The logic of nationalism, the drive for autonomy, pushed them in the direction of resistance to the spread of American hegemony; successful resistance, however, if possible at all, required nerve, moral discipline, austerity, skill and unchallenged legitimacy, commodities rarely in plentiful supply. In many of the countries, the nationalist elites had also to take very seriously the hegemonic power's capacity to steer against them the discontents of armies, provinces and ethnic or religious groups, if their resistance proved too

---

11. More sophisticated versions of modernization doctrines were based on a generalized "Western" liberal-democratic welfare-capitalist paradigm rather than a narrowly American one. While some scholars talked of the possibility of "different roads" to modernization, it was rare in practice for them to take seriously, let alone advocate any "road" deviating markedly from that of welfare capitalism, certainly not any "road" clearly outside the paradigm, such as that of communism. It is instructive, for example, that Communist states were excluded from the purview of the influential book edited by Gabriel Almond and James S. Coleman, *The Politics of the Developing Areas* (Princeton: Princeton University Press, 1960), essentially for "paradigmatic" reasons.

12. The overall climax of this ascendancy probably came in 1958-59, years marked, *inter alia*, by: the installation of the Sarit Thanarat dictatorship in Bangkok in close collaboration with the United States; the U.S.-engineered overthrow of Souvannaphouma and the rise of Phoumi Nosavan in Laos; the Bangkok- and Saigon-backed Dap Chhuon conspiracy in Cambodia; CIA support for the PRRI-Permesta rebellion in Indonesia; and the consolidation of the Diemist autocracy in South Vietnam signaled by the enactment of the notorious Law 10/1959.

obdurate. The autonomist choice was a difficult and dangerous one, at least in the short run. The easier choice was that of compliance, cooperation and subordination. The rewards were economic and military subventions and the stabilization or preservation of political power; the risks were that, in the long run, the force of nationalism would pass the elites by, generating oppositions that would denounce their collaboration and might eventually supplant them.

In Indonesia, for reasons that are too complex to enter into here, the nationalist elite (or that portion of it which survived the "physical revolution" of 1945-1949) was never fully committed to either choice until it was too late; in the so-called "liberal period" (1950-1957) they oscillated back and forth between relatively autonomist and relatively cooperationist positions. During the era of Guided Democracy (1959-1965) the choice was increasingly made for autonomism, largely because of the growing power of and alliance between President Sukarno and the Indonesian Communist Party (PKI). After the events of October 1, 1965, the old nationalist leadership was largely shoved aside to make room for a new military elite fully committed to cooperationism.

American scholarship on Indonesia was profoundly affected by these developments. With the exception of Vietnam, no country in Southeast Asia caused more annoyance and anxiety to American specialists or more trouble to American policy-makers. In fact, the specialists were divided among themselves, pulled one way by the hegemonic framework of Format II, pulled another by the residual strength of the Kahinian tradition. In general, however, the rise of Guided Democracy and the increasingly antagonistic relationship between Indonesia and the United States put the Kahinians on the defensive, in a position, in fact, where they were not infrequently attacked as apologists for Sukarno and his regime. In retrospect, it is instructive that the "defense" of Guided Democracy by the Kahinians was typically in terms of its contribution to national unity, its expression of authentic Indonesian (Javanese) traditions, and its "normality" as a reaction to CIA intervention on behalf of the PRRI-Permesta rebels. Almost never was it defended on the grounds that it permitted the Indonesian left (particularly the PKI) to make rapid headway: to make such a case would have begun to put the Kahinians outside the paradigm, certainly outside the framework of "serious" academic discourse.[13]

On the other side, in the research carried on more or less within Format II, while the foci were many, the central target was Indonesian nationalism (autonomism) and those who claimed to be its authentic spokesmen.

---

13. Ironically enough, the one Indonesianist to make a case of sorts for the PKI was Guy J. Pauker of the Rand Corporation. See his essay "Indonesia: The PKI's 'Road to Power,'" in *The Communist Revolution in Asia*, ed. Robert A. Scalapino (Englewood Cliffs, N.J.: Prentice-Hall, 1965), pp. 256-89. In this piece, Pauker spoke of the PKI as "a creative Party . . . confident of its ability to fit Marxism-Leninism to the specific conditions of its country" (p. 257). Since he believed that the Indonesian elite had "lost the will to resist a Communist take-over" (p. 259), he thought that "the odds are that under these leaders the PKI will come to power in Indonesia" (p. 285). "The Indonesian political elite is not likely to stomach the harsh measures that would be necessary to destroy the PKI, now that it has millions of followers" (p. 267). This essay was evidently something of an aberration, since earlier (and later) Pauker consistently attacked the regime of Guided Democracy; indeed he had even gone so far as indirectly to accuse the strongly anti-Communist Army Chief of Staff, General Nasution, of selling out to the Russians when he negotiated a large-scale arms deal with Moscow in 1960. See Guy J. Pauker, "General Nasution's Mission to Moscow," *Asian Survey*, I (1961), pp. 13-22.

The *economic* research was, with some important exceptions, typically oriented towards the discrediting of autonomist policies within the framework of capitalist axioms and in the name of modernization and development. A barrage of attacks was launched against the Indonesianization program of the first Ali Cabinet (1953-1955), the nationalization of Dutch enterprises in 1957, and the anti-American policies and *berdikari* (self-reliance) goals of late Guided Democracy. Economic research provided a powerful weapon for the discrediting of nationalist autonomism on the grounds of its economic irrationality, irresponsibility and hostility to modernization/development.[14] Thus, for example, in the view of Benjamin Higgins, doyen of the Indonesianist economists, "On the issue of foreign capital, vital to Indonesia's economic development, Indonesian leaders split into two groups. . . . The 'developmentalist' group, led by the relatively young, often foreign-trained intellectuals, attached a high priority to economic and social development. They believed that this development must follow Western lines in large measure and were willing to cooperate with the West, at least to the extent of seeking technical and capital assistance from the West, to achieve the goal. The 'nationalist' group was a mixture of Communists and of a larger number of PNI nationalists and isolationists. The leaders, among them Sukarno, attached great importance to eliminating the control exerted over Indonesian economic life by foreigners through economic activity."[15] Higgins also frequently referred to what he saw as a confrontation between "rational economics and emotional nationalism" and quoted with approval Clifford Geertz' dictum that without the growth of "some sort of sturdy, indigenous business class the Indonesian government is likely to find the task of inducing rapid economic growth an insuperable one."[16] In a comparable vein Ralph Anspach, a scholar with left-wing views within the American context, could still write that "The important question is which policies consistently and persistently applied would be the most effective for promoting a healthy middle class."[17]

The *political* research carried on under the influence of Format II worked to discredit autonomism from a different perspective. In its more obvious forms, this was evinced in a growing stress on the antiliberal authoritarianism and the implicitly retrogressive traditionalism of Indonesian nationalism as symbolized by Sukarno and Guided Democracy.[18] Sukarno's close relationship with the PKI at the end of Guided Democracy gave nationalism a still more disagreeable aspect, which did not fail to be exploited: this relationship was frequently analyzed in such a way as to

---

14. It is instructive that so little of the economic writing was concerned with the evil effects of Guided Democracy economic policy on the urban and rural poor. More attention was usually given to under-paid officials.

15. Benjamin Higgins, *Indonesia: The Crisis of the Millstones* (New York: Van Nostrand Searchlight Book, 1963), p. 88.

16. Ibid., pp. 87 and 104-5.

17. Ralph Anspach, "Indonesia," in *Under-Development and Economic Nationalism in Southeast Asia*, ed. Frank Golay et al. (Ithaca, N.Y.: Cornell University Press, 1969), p. 125.

18. In this vein, the most sophisticated version was Herbert Feith's "Dynamics of Guided Democracy," in *Indonesia*, ed. Ruth T. McVey (New Haven: HRAF Press, 1963), pp. 309-409. The change was probably accentuated by the fact that Guided Democracy marked the (temporary as it proved) eclipse of the Western-educated intellectuals and politicians, who, because of their ideological orientations and mastery of English, were the main intermediaries between American academics and Indonesian society.

suggest that nationalism was compromised by communism, rather than that communism was enhanced by nationalism.[19]

At a more complex and sophisticated level, the attack was more indirect. It is best seen in Herbert Feith's *The Decline of Constitutional Democracy in Indonesia*, by far the most influential political science study of the period.[20] Feith came out of the Kahinian school but was much attracted by the work of Shils, Pye, Apter, and other Format II comparativists. In an interesting fashion, Feith used elements from both formats to undermine the credentials of nationalism. The democratic liberalism of Format I was expressed in his assessment of the *meaning* of the period he studied (1950-1957), and was epitomized in the very title of his book. For Feith, what happened to Indonesia in those years was precisely "the decline of constitutional democracy," rather than, for example, "the rise of radical autonomism." From this liberal perspective, nationalism was indicted for contributing to the death of democracy or at least to its betrayal. On the other hand, the functionalism of Format II was evinced in his well-known analysis of political conflict in Indonesia in terms of a struggle between "administrators" and "solidarity-makers." By depicting Indonesian leaders as exemplars of skill-groups conforming to general ahistorical ideal-types, Feith came close to abstracting them from their specific and concrete historical role in Indonesian society, in Southeast Asia, in the era of American hegemony. Thus, for example, the fact that most of the "administrators" were cooperationists, and most of the "solidarity-makers" autonomists escaped attention; in the work of many who used Feith's terminology and framework, "the solidarity-makers" tended only too often to figure as mere trouble-makers and vacuous ideologues.

In a different way, the *anthropological* and *sociological* writing of the period also contributed indirectly to the same assault. Two examples may serve to illustrate this point. First, the seminal work of Clifford Geertz on the *aliran* had an enormous impact on virtually all the Indonesia specialists.[21] Geertz had worked out a conceptual framework for analyzing Javanese society which divided it into three politico-cultural communities (*aliran*)--*prijaji*, *santri*, and *abangan*. The political scientists largely adopted Geertz's framework, but utilized it often in a subtly selective way. By treating the three aliran as parallel vertical pyramids, they frequently overlooked or underestimated the power relationships between them. In part this distortion was inherent in Geertz's own formulation: by identifying the prijaji as a separate aliran from, rather than as the power-holders within, the abangan aliran, he encouraged a treatment of the prijaji as just another sector or interest group within a pluralist society, rather than as the core of the Javanese, indeed Indonesian, ruling class. Furthermore, political scientists were inclined, in the vein of Format II, to treat the aliran cleavages as "primordial," as constant givens

---

19. See, e.g., J. M. van der Kroef, *The Communist Party of Indonesia: Its History, Program, and Tactics* (Vancouver: University of Columbia Publication Center, 1965).

20. Herbert Feith, *The Decline of Constitutional Democracy in Indonesia* (Ithaca, N.Y.: Cornell University Press, 1962). I would like to emphasize that the critical comments which follow in no way detract from my admiration for the superb scholarship of this study and for the humane values it embodies. It should also be made clear that I do not mean that Feith deliberately aimed at discrediting nationalism, but that this was the effect of his approach.

21. See Clifford Geertz, "The Javanese Village," in *Local, Ethnic, and National Loyalties in Village Indonesia: A Symposium*, ed. G. William Skinner (New Haven: Yale University Southeast Asia Studies, 1959), pp. 34-41; and, in full elaboration, Clifford Geertz, *The Religion of Java* (Glencoe: The Free Press, 1960).

within Indonesian society, rather than as changing products of the historical process.[22] The emphasis on the primordialness of aliran conflict served to highlight the factitiousness of Sukarnoism and Guided Democracy, and thus of the radical nationalism of that regime. If Java was so irremediably divided, how could Indonesian nationalism be anything but febrile escapist rhetoric? The stress on the communal character of the aliran also permitted political scientists to treat them essentially as interest groups, or minorities, to be used as evidence of the inherent pluralism of Indonesian society (thus as an argument of the need for a liberal constitutional order), as a way of dissolving the popular constituency of Indonesian nationalism, and also for underplaying the real class conflict within the Indonesian (here particularly the Javanese) social system. The abangan were always conceived more as abangan than peasants, the santri more as santri than as businessmen and rural landowners, the prijaji more as prijaji than as aristocrats and officials.

The second example I would offer is the character of the research done on the Chinese in Indonesia, mainly by anthropologists, sociologists and displaced Sinologists. This research consistently treated the Chinese primarily as a *racial minority* rather than as a *commercial bourgeoisie*.[23] The uniformity of this research emphasis can best be explained by reference to the typical features of Format II, and the historical role the Chinese have long played--and continue to play today--as "middlemen" between the imperial powers dominating the international market system and the indigenous Indonesian population. For by treating the Chinese primarily as a racial minority, the specialists were able to characterize attacks on the economic position of the Chinese as revealing the racism latent in Indonesian nationalism. Economists helped to buttress this line by arguing that attacks on the Chinese were antidevelopment, antimodernization and economically irrational, obscuring the fact that Chinese entrepreneurs are major outposts of the international capitalist system in Indonesian society and are exceptionally dependent on outside support and protection for their survival. (Where dependency was remarked on in the literature its locus was situated in mainland China, rather than in the Nippo-American bloc.) In all kinds of ways, the Chinese commercial bourgeoisie were made a "given" of Indonesian society, and then used as a criterion of its satisfactory, or more usually unsatisfactory, progress.[24] Treated as a racial group, they were a measure of its constitutionalism and humanity; as a business interest group, they were a measure of its differentiation and modernity. Nowhere were they treated as, for example, Barrington Moore treats the commercial bourgeoisies of China, India, and Japan, i.e., as classes, whose conflicts and alliances with other classes determine the destinies of civilizations.[25]

---

22. This trend began to change after the events of 1965. See, above all, Ruth T. McVey's introduction to Sukarno, *Nationalism, Islam and Marxism* (Ithaca, N.Y.: Cornell Modern Indonesia Project, Translation Series, 1970), and R. William Liddle, *Ethnicity, Party, and National Integration: An Indonesia Case Study* (New Haven: Yale University Press, 1970).

23. Characteristically, *Indonesia*, ed. Ruth T. McVey (cited above) has a section in it (pp. 97-117) written by G. William Skinner entitled "The Chinese Minority." Cf. also Donald E. Willmott, *The Chinese of Semarang: A Changing Minority Community in Indonesia* (Ithaca, N.Y.: Cornell University Press, 1960), and the essay by Ralph Anspach cited above, especially pp. 129-33, and 181-84.

24. The Ne Win government's destruction of the Indian bourgeoisie in Burma in the early 1960s should have showed how "ungiven" the position of the Chinese bourgeoisie in Indonesia really was and is.

25. Barrington Moore, Jr., *Social Origins of Dictatorship and Democracy* (Boston: Beacon Press, 1966).

This brief survey of the writing characteristic of Format II would be incomplete, however, without some reference to what it neglected as well as to what it focused on. For the omissions, in their own way, are no less significant than the emphases discussed hitherto.

First of all, there was a virtually complete lack of any serious and comprehensive analysis of the evolving relationship between Indonesia and the United States.[26] In the literature of the period this relationship, which impinged directly or indirectly on all important aspects of Indonesian politics, was typically pushed to the margin.[27] In the best and most used textbook of the time, discussion of the relationship was largely confined to a small subsection entitled "Foreign Relations."[28] Given this silence with regard to America's pervasive role, not just in Indonesia, but over most of Southeast Asia, it was all the easier to characterize Indonesia's foreign policy after 1956 as autogenic, the self-generated expansionary thrust of perverted and escapist nationalism. Thus, the omissions of "international relations" research on Indonesia in their own way contributed to Format II's antinationalist perspective.[29]

A second major omission was any serious study of the Indonesian military.[30] This is all the more striking in that during the years after 1955, the Indonesian

---

26. An important exception was the dissertation of Frederick Bunnell cited above.

27. A few examples may be illustrative: The Seventh Fleet was unchallenged in East and Southeast Asian waters. A large portion of the Indonesian Army's officer corps was given training in the United States. American oil companies dominated the Indonesian oil industry, the country's major source of export earnings. The economic "stabilization" program of 1963 was shaped to satisfy conditions imposed by the IMF for the grant of urgently needed loans.

28. George McT. Kahin, ed., *Governments and Politics of Southeast Asia*, second edition (Ithaca, N.Y.: Cornell University Press, 1962). The weakness of this otherwise excellent text is that its structure conforms largely to the conventional political science divorce of "international relations" from "comparative politics" as separate subdisciplinary fields. This is typical of Format II. It encourages the student of "comparative politics" to treat foreign pressures and intrusions as intermittent, extrinsic, and secondary factors, and the student of "international relations" to overlook the profound domestic consequences for a weak state of its "relationship" to a hegemonic one.

29. This was true even for so sophisticated and leftwing an analyst as Donald Hindley. See his "Indonesia's Confrontation with Malaysia: A Search for Motives," *Asian Survey*, 4 (June 1964), pp. 904-13. Perhaps this is the place to say something about the curious case of China as treated by specialists influenced by Format II. To a limited extent nationalism was favorably treated by these specialists. In some cases this can be explained by the close ties between the United States and the "nationalist" regime of Chiang Kai-shek. In other cases, such as Chalmers Johnson's *Peasant Nationalism and Communist Power: The Emergence of Revolutionary China* (Stanford: Stanford University Press, 1962), Chinese nationalism was easier to accept since it was directed against the Japanese in the period under study; furthermore it was part of Johnson's purpose to discredit the Chinese Communist movement by insisting that it had come to power less as a result of class conflict in China, than as a result of the fortuitous outbreak of the Sino-Japanese War, which allowed it to "capture" Chinese nationalism.

30. Only in 1971 did this omission begin to be corrected. See Ruth T. McVey, "The Post-Revolutionary Transformation of the Indonesian Army," *Indonesia*, 11

military, particularly the Army, were not only massively involved in everyday politics but were also undergoing a rapid process of centralization, "capitalization," and professionalization--a process which put them in a position to assume the hegemony they hold in Indonesia today. In part, perhaps, this neglect can be attributed to the relative difficulty of access to the military--though difficulties of access did not deter students of the Indonesian Communist Party. A more basic explanation, I believe, is that this curious omission was analogous to the electoral "apathy" attributed by Berelson and Lazarsfeld to the cross-pressures voters sometimes experience.[31] Virtually all Indonesia specialists were aware that American influence in Indonesia was mediated most powerfully through the Indonesian Army, and that the Army was the most trustworthy and formidable obstacle to the advance of radical nationalism and the PKI. At the same time, they were also aware that the Army had been the single most important agent in the overthrow of the liberal constitutional order, that through most of Guided Democracy it consumed two-thirds of the national budget, that it had bled the nationalized corporations white for its own sustenance, and that it was an improbable guardian of human rights and civil liberties. Caught in this cross-pressure, most specialists avoided dealing squarely with the military and focused their main attention elsewhere.

There was, however, a small minority of specialists who did not take this path. They accepted the demise of the liberal constitutional order without too much fuss and argued that the military, as a modern-style organization, was likely to prove a most satisfactory agent for modernization. The influence and popularity of this view, advanced in the Indonesian case by Guy Pauker, and for other parts of Southeast Asia by Lucian Pye and David Wilson, were temporary and limited--in academic if not in policy-making circles.[32] Partly this was because these specialists' acceptance of the end of constitutional liberal politics unsettled many academics with its air of complaisance, cynicism and *realpolitik*, and its tendency to breach the boundaries of liberal discourse. But it was also clear to many scholars that the "modernized" corporate format of the military was not and could not in the near future be self-sustaining or self-generating; rather it depended on continuing blood-transfusions from the outside in the form of funds, training, technological expertise and heavily capitalized equipment. Moreover, a "modernized" format by no means logically implied a commitment to or capacity for "modernizing" the rest of society. Lastly, the performance of military regimes in virtually all parts of the American orbit in recent years has rendered militaries-as-modernizers theories more ephemeral than most.[33]

(April 1971), pp. 131-76, and 13 (April 1972), pp. 147-82. Two important earlier pieces should not be overlooked, however: Daniel S. Lev, "The Political Role of the Army in Indonesia," *Pacific Affairs*, XXXVI (Winter 1963-64), pp. 349-64; and John R. W. Smail, "The Military Politics of North Sumatra: December 1956-October 1957," *Indonesia*, 6 (October 1968), pp. 128-87.

31. B. R. Berelson, P. F. Lazarsfeld, and W. N. McPhee, *Voting* (Chicago: University of Chicago Press, 1954).

32. See, for example, their contributions to John J. Johnson, ed., *The Role of the Military in Underdeveloped Countries* (Princeton, N.J.: Princeton University Press, 1962).

33. See the devastating statistical evidence presented in Eric Nordlinger, "Soldiers in Mufti: The Impact of Military Rule upon Economic Change in the Non-western States," *American Political Science Review*, LXIV, 4 (December 1970), pp. 1131-48.

What is to be Done?

It seems clear that the present decline of Format II's authority and relevance has been caused both by the impact of the American-Vietnamese war and the evolution of American society itself. The defeats and humiliations endured during a decade of fighting with a small Asian state, the enormous waste and misallocation of national resources involved, and the increase of turmoil and decay in the United States have reinforced each other's effects.

Because the Vietnam War has so directly impinged on all of Southeast Asia, the Southeast Asian specialists, more than other area specialists, have found it difficult to sustain Format II with the old confidence. In the first place, the war has made it much harder than hitherto to ignore the contradictions between American hegemony and national autonomy in the ex-colonial world. American domination, largely concealed in the early 1960s under a flood of amiable rhetoric and a plethora of peaceable trade, educational, military and other missions, has become quite manifest as a result of the war. Secondly, the inescapable fact that tiny Communist North Vietnam has built an intensely nationalist, progressive and stable political organization which has survived for years an onslaught which no other state in Southeast Asia could have endured for more than a few weeks, has made much of the modernizing theory of Format II patently bankrupt.[34]

What will succeed it is by no means clear. Much will depend on the degree to which American culture and consciousness are likely to change, on the pattern of American foreign policy, and, of course, on economic, political and social change in Southeast Asia. Little can be said with confidence on these topics. What does seem likely is that the spread of militarism in the region will continue in the coming decade, that urbanization, population explosions, commercialization of traditional agriculture, etc., will go forward, generating deeper antagonisms between rich and poor, privileged and destitute, ruler and ruled. In Indonesia, at least, the ruling coalition of generals, Chinese bourgeoisie, professionals and bureaucrats seems likely to survive indefinitely provided the present heavy flow of external funds and materiel is sustained.

In such circumstances, it may be that Format II will locally regain something of its earlier persuasiveness. On the other hand, should it happen that, for example, Indonesia increasingly falls under Japanese rather than American hegemony, it may be easier for the specialists as a whole to adopt a more critical stance than at present. One might even find developing a serious literature on militarism, on class conflict (probably outside a classical Marxist framework), and so forth.

Rather than attempting to predict future trends in research on Indonesia, it might be better, certainly more modest, to suggest some areas, topics or themes, which could profitably be explored at the present juncture, and which in a sense grow out of the traditions of Indonesianology as they have been established in America since World War II.

---

34. If it is necessary to use the term "modernization" at all, it might be advisable to define it along somewhat the following lines: a growing capacity to mobilize and utilize endogenous resources for social change. This would permit the attribution of a high degree of modernity to North Vietnam--in view of its highly efficient use of such endogenous resources as peasant manpower, Vietnamese nationalism, traditional symbols, etc. My own belief, however, as suggested earlier, is that "modernization" is a pseudo-concept, masking the real differences between quite different histories, social orders, and cultures under a bogus universalist objectivity.

I. In a period of political and economic subordination, it may be well to study those aspects of Indonesian life where autonomy is likely to prove strongest, i.e., the realm of culture and experience. The seeds of such work were sown in Kahin's and Geertz's writing, and in James T. Siegel's *Rope of God* have grown to magnificent fruit.[35] Such "cultural" studies take as their standpoint the autonomy of culture as an authentic interpretation of unique experience. Explicitly or implicitly, they assume that other cultures are not simply different, but even inaccessible in considerable part, and that cultural interpretations are necessarily subjective, relative and nonconquering.

II. Even if it should prove difficult to create a traditionally Marxist scholarship on Indonesia, a more serious class-analysis type of literature on Indonesia can surely be hoped for. The need for this was signaled (in the United States) as early as 1969 in David Levine's article "History and Social Structure in the Study of Contemporary Indonesia."[36] Work currently underway by younger scholars suggests that Levine's appeal is not being wholly ignored. Along with this one could expect critical studies of American hegemony in Indonesia and of military rule there under its aegis.

III. It should also be possible to return to the Kahinian historical method, combined with a less abstractly universalist and mechanical comparativism than in the past; the work of Barrington Moore is suggestive here. It would be interesting to see, for example, what might come of research which combined Moore's method with the perspectives suggested by Geertz' illuminating *Agricultural Involution*.[37]

All these themes and topics seem to me useful and important, and perhaps more important, "practicable," since they lie within the framework set by contemporary American culture and the institutional structures within which American academic research is carried on. They also suggest the possibility of helping in the larger task of transcending and transforming both framework and institutional structure in the longer run.

---

35. James T. Siegel, *The Rope of God* (Berkeley: University of California Press, 1969). This is easily the most original and provocative book on Indonesia to appear in the last decade.

36. This article is contained in *Indonesia*, 7 (April 1969), pp. 5-19.

37. Clifford Geertz, *Agricultural Involution, the Processes of Ecological Change in Indonesia* (Berkeley: University of California Press, 1968).

THE BEAMTENSTAAT IN INDONESIA

Ruth T. McVey

Historically minded observers of post-Sukarno Indonesia have occasionally noted the stylistic similarity of Suharto's New Order to that of Dutch colonial rule, with their common emphasis on administration rather than politics and their stress on technical expertise and economic development as primary values. That style was epitomized in the last decade of Netherlands rule, the 1930s, when the emphasis on modern, efficient, developmental governance reached its peak and (as Harry Benda pointed out) the Indies approached as near as it ever did to the ideal of the *Beamtenstaat*, the state as efficient bureaucratic machine. What I should like to do here is to consider the implications of this stylistic similarity and the relevance of the Beamtenstaat model to Indonesian rule. As a number of the characteristics of the New Order are shared by other third-world states, it may also have some relevance for regimes elsewhere.

We might start by asking some obvious questions: Is there any real relationship between the New Order and the latter-day colonial one, or is there simply a superficial coincidence of styles? If there is a meaningful connection, does it lie in the particular problems presented by twentieth-century Indonesian economy and society, in common characteristics of the colonial and New Order ruling elites, or in the ideological and/or organizational requirements of the larger world in which they existed? We must also ask whether the emphasis on efficiency, technical expertise, and so forth represents a real commitment or only a mask--and if a mask, what is it meant to hide? How much coincidence and how much tension exists between those who staff the bureaucratic machine, those who control it, and those whose ultimate interests it serves? Finally, since both the late colonial and the New orders stressed legality and the eventual establishment of constitutional democracy, to what extent should the Indonesian Beamtenstaat be seen as a stage on the way to a more open system of rule?

For reasons that will, I hope, become clear below, I do not think it accidental that the colonial and New orders adopted a similar mystique for their rule. Nor does it seem likely that historical familiarity was the sole or even primary reason for this. Certainly there was some inheritance of values, especially through the relative continuity of the Indonesian civil service from colonial to postrevolutionary times; but it has been a full generation since Dutch rule, and in the intervening decades the experience of Japanese occupation, revolution, parliamentary democracy, and Guided Democracy did a great deal to weaken the hold of colonial administrative values. Moreover, it is not the civil service which founded or provided ideological leadership for the New Order. Rather, it was the military, its technocrat civilian advisers, and--at least in the formative years of the regime--the educated younger generation of the urban middle class. These have been heavily influenced by Western ideas, but they are postwar American values and not prewar Dutch. This, however, points us to two other questions: to what extent is there a similarity in the objective situations of the colonial and New Order elites, and to what extent did they participate in a larger international system whose values could not be ignored?

At first blush, the East Indies and the New Order elites appear quite dissimilar: The former was overwhelmingly foreign, the latter indigenous. In the New Order, the military has a hegemonic role, whereas the late colonial regime was indisputably civilian. But this contrast disguises a fundamental similarity, the fact that both military and colonial rule rested openly on force. They were not legitimate in any terms of local understanding, and insofar as they wished to gain more positive acceptance of their rule they needed to adopt some appeal that went beyond their most prominent features. The foreign-ness of the colonial regime severely limited its options in this; a few minority groups could be attracted through religious appeals or favoritism, but clearly the great majority of the population had little in common with the Dutch. The Indonesian military could appeal to nationalist emotions; but, coming into power as a counter to Sukarno and highly dependent on foreign investment and support, the New Order leaders could not utilize this approach very effectively.

Moreover, one of the most obvious differences between the two regimes--the foreignness of the one and the indigenousness of the other--is not as absolute a distinction as it would seem. In third world countries that have not closed their economies and cultures to the outside, urban elites tend to become orientated in a greater or lesser degree towards an international "center" dominated politically, economically, and culturally by the great industrial powers. Often, they are more highly integrated with foreign interests and culture than with the rural population which forms their own hinterland. This has occurred to a marked degree in present-day Indonesia; many upper middle-class Jakartans would find it easier to operate in Tokyo or New York--whether or not they had ever been there--than in a village in their own country. In a modernizing society open to influence from abroad, the cultural gap between city and countryside widens at an accelerating pace, while the rapid enrichment of the top levels of urban society--very notable in Suharto's Indonesia--has led to a striking display of material differences. The resulting attenuation of links between the national political center and rural hinterland has resulted in some approximation of the colonial regime's relationship with its subjects; they are seen as essentially alien, less comprehensible and in many ways less important than the "center" abroad; they are viewed both with suspicion and as a trust. The result was to encourage, on the part of both regimes, a distinctly managerial and tutorial air in their approach to the populace, and at the same time a relative indifference to its problems.

This alienation is an important reason for one striking similarity between the late colonial and New Order regimes. their marked emphasis on political demobilization. The Dutch had experimented gingerly with broader political participation under the Ethical Policy in the first decades of the century; this venture had resulted, from the viewpoint of the Indies regime, in unreasonable expectations and the breakdown of order. The deathblow to the Ethical endeavor was dealt by a Communist-led rebellion which took place in 1926-27; and it is significant that, although earlier Indonesian nationalist historiography portrayed this as a significant moment in the independence struggle, New Order commentators have regarded it, along with the Madiun Affair of 1948 and the September Thirtieth Movement of 1965, as one more example of Communist betrayal. The betrayal was, of course, not of the Dutch but (implicitly) of order. Both the colonial regime that followed the Communist rising and the New Order that toppled Sukarno had as primary initial concerns the need to return the genie of popular agitation to its bottle. For both, people were to be turned toward economic and not political projects; agitators were to be banished to Boven Digul or Buru; and political parties, when not banned, were subjected to the greatest restraint.

Because the New Order leaders overturned Guided Democracy by force, and because Sukarno's charisma and the Indonesian Communists' mass strength were notable features of the latter system, we may be tempted to think that the difference between them on the matter of political mobilization was absolute. However, although Guided Democracy placed great emphasis on the ceremonial display of mass support, it also reversed the policy of moving towards elected rather than bureaucratic rule in territorial government, ended parliamentary rule, sharply reduced the boundaries of permissible political organization and discourse, and used the masses largely as a chorus for what was increasingly a palace-centered politics. Its attitude towards political mobilization was in fact profoundly ambivalent, a hesitation which arose in good part from the fact that, while Sukarno and the left were the most visible elements in Guided Democracy, most of the real keys to power were held by the army and a conservative bureaucratic elite. Even with the restrictions the system imposed, the allowed room for maneuver provided too much scope for demands; the last years of Guided Democracy saw growing political polarization, increasing local violence, and finally a determination to end political mobilization by force.

This continuity of purpose between important elements in Guided Democracy and the New Order is an important reason why, in spite of the dramatic and drastic reversal of Indonesia's political and economic orientation, there has not been a significant change in the bureaucratic, economic, social, and even much of the political elite. The Communists were not really part of Guided Democracy's "Establishment," great though their public prominence was; rather, a national elite that was increasingly conscious of its interests as a ruling class resolutely kept them from positions of critical political, military, and bureaucratic power. At the same time, the civilians who had replaced Dutch rule with their own opened their arms to the military, whose role in the administration and economy expanded rapidly between 1957 and 1965. Though officials of the old school might grumble about the upstart intruders, the growing polarization between left and right made them increasingly appreciative of a close relationship with those who had command over force. In this sense Guided Democracy was a transitional stage between a relatively open parliamentary period and a thoroughgoing authoritarianism. Those who overthrew Sukarno did not, as they claimed, replace a rotten Old Order with something completely new, but rather realized one of the principal tendencies of the earlier regime. The New Order's triumph marked the consolidation of Indonesia's postrevolutionary elite, its achievement of self-consciousness, and its ability when threatened to reject the populism, political radicalism, and militant nationalism that had been part of its ideological baggage since the struggle for independence.

The New Order authorities have been very nearly as frank as the colonial administrators of the 1930s in their intention to separate the population from politics. They have put forward the concept of the "floating mass," which is to say a rural population kept free from contact with party politics. Golkar, often journalistically styled "the government party," is more of an anti-party, a political organization whose goal is to depoliticize. So far have thoughts of social upheaval lost any positive aspect for the ideologues of the Suharto regime that there has been serious discussion as to whether the armed struggle against the Dutch ought not to be designated officially a "war of independence" rather than a "revolution" to remove any possible association with class struggle.

It is this firm rejection of any mass mobilizational politics which, to my mind, makes the label "fascist" misleading for the New Order and similar regimes. If one is going to mean by fascism anything other than a generalized rightist authoritarianism, one must take into account the populist appeal and mass organizational emphasis so vital to the character of the classical European movements. Suharto's New Order has also differed from fascism proper in its emphasis on rules. Elections may be rigged, parties hamstrung, and parliament both helpless and stacked; but there are elections, parties, and parliament, and these forms, rather than the plebiscites, rallies, mass movement, and charismatic leader of fascism, are central legitimating elements for the regime. One of the New Order's principal slogans in the period of de-Sukarnoization was the restoration of the Rule of Law (usually given in English or as *rechtsstaat* in Dutch, there being no familiar Indonesian equivalent). This may seem a curious catchword for a leadership that was sponsoring large-scale massacres and had probably the largest number of political prisoners in the world; it is therefore the more interesting that that particular slogan was put forward.

No doubt the rule-mindedness of the military and the desire to look well internationally played a role. We might note, however, that the New Order shared this legalist emphasis with the late colonial regime, though this too tended to take the law lightly in dealing with the natives. We might suggest that constitutionalism was symbolically important for both because they were run by conservative elites whose members were sufficiently acculturated to modern Western values to accept representative democracy as ultimately the proper form of government. To conservative regimes with a gnawing sense of illegitimacy--born of the knowledge that their rule is based not ultimately but in the first instance on force--it is a considerable comfort to believe there are rules to the political game. It may be necessary to bend them at the moment, sacrificing law to order, but in the long run it can be hoped that form and content will become one. If the ruler's position is not natural, there must be some way for it to become so if he is not to resign himself to the eternal prospect of revolt.

Here the ruler's imperative combines with the historical optimism of modern Western thought, and the result is a myth developed around the symbol of modernity. This both legitimizes the differences in culture, wealth, and power between rural mass and ruling elite, and, through the concept of modernization, indicates the way by which the populace might ultimately share in the benefits and be transformed from subject to citizen. Ideologues of the 1930s colonial regime and the New Order (and indeed many other regimes of similar ilk) argued that the society's peace and prosperity rested above all on organizational, technical, and economic expertise. Administration must therefore take command over politics. It was (and is) pointed out that in the past century such population growth and structural changes had taken place that Indonesia could not allow itself the luxury of internal mismanagement or failure to respond to international economic requirements. The population had therefore to trust in the expertise and dedication of its administrators, who would not only guide the common people to material prosperity but would create the conditions under which they could be initiated into the mysteries of the modern culture which was the key to gaining full human status.

So much for the professed ideal of modernization; but what of reality? Indonesia may assert the ideals of the Beamtenstaat, but it is among the more spectacularly corrupt of the third world countries. In this feature it differed notably from its colonial counterpart of the 1930s; the Netherlands Indies bureaucracy was by no means spotless in performance, and it was hardly disinterested in the administration of its Indonesian charges, but its shortcomings were scarcely on the order of the Suharto regime. Certainly inexperience, the persistence of patrimonial traditions, need born of inflation, and the lack of effective fiscal checks contributed heavily to the corruption and inefficiency of the New Order. It seems to me, however, that there is also a structural element which makes for this distinction between the New and colonial orders. The Indies bureaucracy was, after all, effectively the employee of the Netherlands, and woe betide the official who did not deal promptly with Dutch business interests or failed to administer to Dutch satisfaction. The Indonesian bureaucracy, however, serves itself: It is (with its military component) both the dominant element in the ruling class and the agent of the ruling class; and there is no effective institution outside it.

The result is what Fred Riggs has called a "bureaucratic polity." When an agrarian society evolves--either from its own traditions or a colonial experience-- an elite which is almost wholly employed in or dependent on the bureaucracy, a business class that is weak (and most likely alien), and a passive peasantry, it is likely to assume this state. The bureaucracy modernizes enough to rout any traditional rivals and secure a firm grip on the state. It then, however, ceases to move in a modernizing direction. It has no need to do so, for there is no effective pressure on it: parties are weak or proscribed, or simply reflections of itself; economic interests are foreign or dependent on bureaucratic favor; and the main indigenous social element outside itself is a disorganized and powerless peasantry. Moreover, because it is the locus of power and of wealth (through its control of licenses and permissions, secured by a carefully nurtured statism), it becomes the arena for all meaningful political action. Real politics takes place not in parliament or whatever organs may exist outside the bureaucracy, but in the government apparatus itself. Lines of power and patronage in the administration do not follow the formal chain of command but a very different pattern: The powerful patron will have clients in several ministries or armed units; his true strength as an official will depend on his personal connections and the access his position provides to wealth. A businessman wishing to obtain favorable consideration will not necessarily seek the formally appropriate official, but the most powerful bureaucrat he thinks he can retain as his champion. Because the bureaucracy is the arena for politics, it cannot function effectively as an executive arm; it cannot be battlefield, commander, and soldier all at once. Because positions and criteria for advancement are not what they formally seem, an official's real status depends not on his formal title but on securing wealth, clients, and favor; and (quite aside from display requirements in a changing and increasingly materialistic society) this means utilizing the economic possibilities of one's position to the full. Hence the "commercialization of office" that is now a chronic Indonesian theme of complaint. Because the bureaucracy cannot administer effectively, its social role becomes largely parasitic and its members, if ever they entered with the idea of achieving anything, soon slip into the prevailing inertia. The bureaucracy thus becomes alienated functionally from the population at large, in addition to the distance created by differences in wealth, power, and cultural westernization.

Much attention has been paid to the origins of the bureaucratic polity in premodern patrimonialism and prebendary systems, viewing its emergence in postcolonial regimes as the result of a breakdown in the process of modernization and a return to more indigenous values. It has been commonly imagined as something of a culturally comfortable pit, from which the fallen society finds it almost impossible to escape, for its sole traction, the bureaucratic elite, has neither the reason nor the strength to get moving. There is certainly something to this, but one should bear in mind that in our day societies rarely remain the same, and that therefore the bureaucratic elite may be neither as all-powerful nor as incapable in the future as it is in the present. Riggs, for example, developed his theories largely from observation of Thailand in the 1950s and early 1960s. That country, having undergone neither the political nor the economic disruptions of colonialism, had had a particularly smooth transition between traditional and modern bureaucratic state. There was very little visible in terms of institutions, social forces, or ideology which offered any counterbalance, and there seemed little reason to think the system could not continue the containment and cooptation of new elements as it had before. Within less than two decades, however, social and economic changes had far outstripped the capacity of the political system to absorb them; the urban elite was deeply divided and large parts of the countryside were slipping from government control. The bureaucratic system has remained much the same, but at the cost of an increasingly visible irrelevance.

Indonesia's New Order has by no means the historical continuity and unity of the Thai bureaucratic polity; for this reason it is less stable but perhaps ultimately more flexible. The immediate pressure, it seems to me, lies not so much in demands for democracy and social justice--these are heard, but relatively faintly--as for the elimination of corruption and inefficiency--in other words, for bringing Indonesia's reality more into line with the ideal of the Beamtenstaat. It is not that Indonesians are managerially minded, but bureaucratic corruption and inefficiency are the most obvious evils and experienced by people at all levels. Moreover, criticism on these grounds offers both a stronger charge and a safer option. Not only can the government be hoisted on its own petard, but the charge of corruption has such a resonance in Javanese thought as to bring into question the legitimacy and viability of the regime.

But who, in Indonesia's bureaucratic polity, can provide meaningful pressure? One source comes from outside. We should remember that, although the New Order regime does not directly serve another master as did the colonial one. its fortunes are very much connected with the world market and foreign sources of investment and aid. Speculators may find corruption and inefficiency advantageous; serious interlocutors usually do not. Moreover, international practice is important as a model. It is after all to the international "center" that the elite of the capital looks; and it is modernization, incarnate in foreign industrial society, that the New Order has made into a principal pledge. None of this may be enough to change things--it is difficult for most people to trade in a Mercedes for a sense of virtue--but it does weaken the regime's own sense of legitimacy and confidence in success, and it provides those it rules with a criterion for judgment to which the New Order notably fails to live up.

Domestically, pressure is exerted, feebly but with increasing urgency, by the growing number of Indonesians who, having achieved an education but no place in the now restricted ranks of the bureaucratic elite, have become employees in the modern sector of the economy, entered the professions, or hang about the fringes of the student world. Within the bureaucracy itself there are allies: those who have the skills but not the connections to rise; those (and they are not so rare) who feel they should do something for the people; those who simply resent the wealth at the top. Though their demands for more honest and effective government may echo those voiced internationally they are unlikely to consider themselves on the same side. Quite the contrary: for all but the most cosmopolitan, the foreigners appear as principal corruptors, and the New Order elite's international orientation as a major reason for its neglect of its domestic duties. Hence demands for reform go hand in hand with xenophobia, a sentiment intensified by resentment of the New Order leaders' visible business connections with wealthy Indonesian Chinese. In this the protestors can look for sympathy from the elites in the more provincial towns and from the Muslim community; these were supporters of the early New Order against the threat of communism, but that was a decade ago. Now they have little in common culturally with the metropolitan elite, find its very visible wealth unreasonable against their modest estate, and resent the indifference and cupidity of the military and civilian authorities with whom they must deal.

The expression of such objections has been muffled and sporadic, but the fervor they can arouse was demonstrated in the Bandung riots of August 1973 and the "Malari" incident in Jakarta in January 1974. It is unlikely public protest will be sizeable or effective as long as the army remains united and able to take action. Suharto and his colleagues are very aware of this and have insisted that the fostering of military unity take priority over all other considerations. But curiously, the position of the army is rendered anomalous by the very bureaucratic values embodied in the Beamtenstaat model and the training of a modern professional military. By these criteria, the army should execute policy and not be a political actor itself; its business should be martial not commercial and not the infiltration of all levels and kinds of administrative and economic activity. The idea of a "dual function" of the Indonesian army, political as well as military, has been much stressed by the New Order leaders, who find it suitable in this context to resurrect the memory of the revolution; but it goes against the grain of its modernizing ideology, and it has serious practical limitations.

In the old days, prince and war leader were one; there was no separation of clientele and skills to make difficult the transition from head of the army to head of state. In modern times, control of military force makes it easy for a general to seize power in a weak state, but makes it difficult for him to keep. As a purely military leader the general has no visible right to rule; and insofar as he puts himself forth as anything more than that and devotes his time to nonmilitary affairs, he inevitably loses his grip on the military machine and thus exposes himself to the danger of being couped. He can attempt to prevent rivals from arising within the army by removing from strategic posts all who seem to pose any threat, and this Suharto has done; but this requires perpetual vigilance and a willingness to put the ruler's political survival above the leadership requirements of the army. It is also possible to give the military a leading political and economic role, ensuring both its hegemony over the society and its loyalty to the ruler--turning it, in effect, into his political machine. This, too, Suharto has done, though more by way of expanding an existing pattern than by his own invention. But this also has serious implications for the army's professional efficiency, as was vividly demonstrated in the debacle of its East Timor campaign. Moreover, insofar as the army has a hegemonic role it tends to become the arena in which political and economic interests fight their battles; the same things happen to it as to the wider administration in the bureaucratic polity.

Out of similar experiences in other countries there have arisen demands for a more spartan strongman or a return to the barracks. Professionally qualified but unconnected officers, those whose posts do not give them access to wealth, those who feel that attention should be paid to the nation and not the foreigners are a likely audience for such voices. There is now no overt sign of military disaffection; but very soon the Indonesian army will undergo a massive change as Suharto's Generation of '45 is replaced in leadership posts by younger men who have higher professional qualifications, no revolutionary experience, and a very different network of connections. It will be interesting to see whether and how they respond to the problem and how Suharto retains his powers once shorn of meaningful military connections.

Ultimately, however, the question of Indonesia's direction lies in the great silent sector of society, the peasant mass that floats--or as some would have it, sinks--under the New Order. In the parliamentary period the Communists organized them; during Guided Democracy Sukarno exhorted them; but it may be that future historians will conclude that it was Suharto who brought them decisive change. It is under the New Order and not its predecessors that social and economic transformation has proceeded apace in the countryside, with a rapid penetration of new agricultural techniques and market relationships destroying "traditional" social arrangements, and with commercial goods and improved communications providing new models for behavior and acquisition. "Onhoorbaar groeit de padi" [Paddy grows soundlessly], a colonial administrator might reflect on contemplating the too-unruffled calm of the 1930s. Whatever he may have imagined for the future, however, it is unlikely he foresaw what did take place: even after returning to the Indies in 1945 the Dutch could not believe it.

IDEOLOGY AND SOCIAL STRUCTURE IN INDONESIA

Joel S. Kahn

In this article I want to discuss a number of issues that have arisen out of my research into the structures of underdevelopment in Indonesia.[1] First, some concepts that have been used in the analysis of Indonesian social structure will be examined. I shall show that these concepts, used in many cases as analytical tools are, in fact, aspects of peasant ideology. As such they should be objects *of* analysis rather than tools *for* analysis. The three concepts discussed in the first section of this paper are: the *aliran*, or vertical alliances described by Geertz and other members of the Modjokuto research team; ethnicity; and patron-clientage.

Having argued that these are basic components of Indonesian ideology in particular periods of time, I want to attempt to account for them within the framework of a general theory of the formation of ideology. . . .

While my first aim is relatively straightforward, for reasons of space it will not be possible for me to discuss at any great length the theoretical steps necessary for an analysis of the formation and transformation of ideology. Since my argument is envisaged as an alternative to the use of conscious models for theoretical understanding, it is therefore necessary to outline briefly the general approach to ideology taken in this article. For this reason a number of general points will be made about the formation of ideology and the relation between ideology and social structure before discussion of the concepts of aliran, ethnicity and patron-clientage.

In order to understand any system of thought, whether we choose to label it ideological or not, we must recognize that every view of "reality" is the product of a cultural code. It follows from this that what is perceived, the "facts" of any thought system are, by and large, constituted by the system itself. Systems of social classification employed by Indonesian peasants, such as the aliran framework, are based on certain principles of constitution which must be uncovered by the social scientist.

Similarly, it is fruitless to distinguish views of reality according to their relative correctness simply on the basis of assumed closeness to reality. For if it is admitted that all systems of thought, both scientific and ideological, constitute their own "facts," then all systems of thought define their own separate reality with which they are, by definition, in close harmony. While, therefore, we may disagree with a Modjokuto peasant who argues that the main principles of social classification

---

1. The author would like to thank Dr. M. Gilsenan, J. R. Llobera and M. K. Stivens for reading various drafts of the paper and offering many helpful suggestions, although of course the author alone is responsible for the final form of the argument.

derive from differing degrees of religious piety, we cannot disagree that this view has what Geertz has called a certain "phenomenological reality." This is to deny that ideology, religious or otherwise, can be distinguished as a mode of thought which is non-empirical or, to use Stark's terms warped, clouded, deformed, contaminated, falsified or distorted.[2] Neither is the term "false consciousness," frequently appearing in highly materialist interpretations of Marx, an adequate description of the complexity of any accepted or shared thought system.

Indeed it often seems that "closeness to empirical reality," at times used to distinguish science from ideology, can cut both ways. In most cases it is ideology rather than science which is more directly concerned with and based on reality as it is directly perceived. The Andaman Islanders' conceptions that night is caused by the cry of the cicada[3] is based closely on directly perceivable empirical reality, i.e., that every day just before nightfall the cicadas start to sing. I shall argue similarly that the ideologies of aliran, ethnicity, and patron-clientage in Indonesia rest on certain directly perceivable aspects of personal appearance and social interaction, taking what *appears* as crucial to a definition of the structures which generate appearance.

This leads directly to a consideration of the relation between social structure and ideology. The concepts of reflection and mechanical determination of superstructure by infrastructure must be abandoned by all but the vulgar materialists (of which Marx was most definitely not one) because economic and political structures are not directly perceivable and because ideological systems are themselves semi-autonomous--the product of their own internal properties as much as of economic and political constraints.

This is not to argue that ideology must be analyzed entirely without regard to relations of production and authority within a social formation. It seems most useful to conceive of the relation between different levels of social reality in terms of what Friedman, among others, has called a hierarchy of constraints. Ideological systems thus become subject to the constraints of functional compatibility between different structures which go to make up the total formation. To quote Friedman:

> The key to the whole affair is what has been referred to as the *relative autonomy* of structures, that is, the *autonomy of their internal properties*. A contradiction between subsystems occurs as the result of a dominant structure causing intersystemic relations to strain to the limits of functional compatibility. . . . It is the relative autonomy of structures which entails the necessary existence of two kinds of relationship, those within and those between. And it is the substructures themselves which doubly determine the larger whole: first, by delimiting the kinds of functions which can serve to unite them, and second, by fixing the breakdown limits of those functions.[4]

In this analysis Friedman is largely concerned with the relationships between techno-ecological factors and economic relations. How would this hierarchy of constraints operate on the formation of ideology? I would suggest, on the basis of the preceding discussion, that it is through "empirical reality" that economic and political structures operate on thought systems. If thought systems are directly related

---

2. See Clifford Geertz, *The Interpretation of Cultures* (London: Hutchinson, 1975), p. 196.

3. Alfred R. Radcliffe-Browne, *The Andaman Islanders* (Glencoe, Ill.: Free Press, 1964), pp. 213 ff.

4. Jonathan Friedman, "Marxism, Structuralism and Vulgar Materialism," *Man*, 9 (1974), pp. 444-69.

to observable interactions, and if these interactions are generated by social structure, then it is in the generation of the raw material of ideology--social appearances--that social structure affects the perception of social reality. The relationship between social structure and ideology, when perceived in this way, becomes a negative one, in the sense that the systemic requirements are that ideology does not contradict appearance. At the same time there need be no reflective process at all, since interactions and other appearances are not themselves direct reflections of underlying social structure.

The Marxist analysis of commodity fetishism can illustrate this point. Marx argued that capitalism is associated with a particular ideological form known as the fetishism of commodities, in which material objects appear to take on a life of their own. Property conceptions, for example, are based on the principle of a relation between people and things. Similarly, producers act on the assumption that capital itself is self-expanding.[5] In these cases there is no question of a direct ideological reflection of social structure. Capital and property are social relations between classes of people. At the same time the operation of the capitalist mode of production generates a certain phenomenological reality not inconsistent with fetishism of this sort. It indeed appears as though money grows of its own accord, and that people are inextricably linked with the objects which they own. People operating with these conceptions of the structure of capitalist society are not *wrong* in any direct way. Their view of reality is directly in accord with sensual experience.

It should be clear that this conception of the relations between elements in a social formation is a dynamic one in the sense that it is predicated upon change within the various levels of functioning. Ideological change is, according to this view, a constant process depending not so much upon structural changes occurring externally as upon its own internal properties. The new phenomenal forms which are generated by economic and political changes simply serve to place limits on the direction of ideological change. At certain points these constraints may have a profound effect on the way the social universe is perceived, and it is this kind of intersystemic crisis which may have a revolutionary effect on existing modes of thought. These general points will be returned to below.

Aspects of Indonesian Peasant Ideology

Aliran. This Indonesian word meaning stream has, through the work of Clifford Geertz on Java, entered into common anthropological usage. While Geertz's definitions of the aliran are not entirely consistent, he suggests that they represent a form of social organization which arose to fulfill certain social needs in the years after Indonesian independence. The aliran were formed around the "four major all-Indonesia political parties" and consist of both local party organizations "plus a whole set of organizational appendages" such as women's clubs, youth and student groups, labor and peasant unions, religious and charitable associations and the like. To quote Geertz:

> Each party with its aggregation of specialized associations provides, therefore, a general framework within which a wide range of social activities can be organized, as well as an over-all ideological rationale to give these activities point and direction. The resultant complex . . . is usually referred to as an *aliran*.[6]

---

5. Cf. Jonathan Friedman, "The Place of Fetishism and the Problem of Materialist Interpretations," *Critique of Anthropology*, 1 (1974), pp. 26-62; John Mepham, "The Theory of Ideology in Marx's Capital," *Radical Philosophy*, 1, 2 (1972).

6. Clifford Geertz, *Peddlers and Princes* (Chicago: University of Chicago Press,

Writing of the period in which he did fieldwork, Geertz tells us that "it is the *alirans* which today form . . . the core of Modjokuto social structure, replacing the status groups of the prewar period."[7]

In spite of the relative clarity of this formulation, there is some confusion in Geertz's earlier work over the exact naming of these aliran. In *Peddlers and Princes*, as the above passage indicates, the different aliran are said to correspond to political parties--the Nationalists (Partai Nasional Indonesia), the Communists (Partai Kommunis Indonesia) and the two Muslim parties--Masjumi and the more conservative Nahdatul Ulama. Elsewhere the aliran are distinguished more on a religious than a political basis.[8] The major groups are now the Muslims (*santri*), the Hindu-Buddhist elite (*priyayi*) and the peasant syncretists (*abangan*). The santri are Muslim purists, hostile to the religious syncretism of both priyayi and abangan. Abangan religion is a mixture of Islam and aspects of Java's pre-Islamic religious heritage. Priyayi are those who adhere broadly to the traditional ideology of the Javanese court, with its emphasis on the maintenance of highly institutionalized status differentials, ascetic mysticism, and a uniquely Javanese Hinduism. These in turn are roughly associated with political allegiance: priyayi with the Nationalists, santri with the Muslim parties, and abangan with the Communists.

Finally the aliran are sometimes described in terms of the occupations of the main adherents of each stream. The santri are traders and entrepreneurs; priyayi are both the feudal landlords and the civil servants; and abangan are the peasants.

Geertz is not the only one to have used this model of Indonesian society. In one form or another it is one of the most widely used characterizations of postwar Indonesian social structure. Jay's very similar view of Indonesian history will serve as an example. In his study of Javanese religion and politics,[9] he focuses on the schism between secularism and orthodoxy or abangan and santri. In this discussion, Jay argues that the schism has both a "cultural" and a "social" basis. By "cultural" he means the ideological difference between the world views of santri and abangan. The social basis of the schism seems to refer to the fact that people subscribe to one or the other view, and define their behavior according to whether they are santri or abangan. This in turn is linked to geographically defined segments "in which the members of . . . villages, or neighborhoods band together in opposition to members of other social units."[10]

Jay seems to see the history of Javanese society, from perhaps even before the coming of Islam up to the time of his own fieldwork, primarily as a conflict between these two world views--the secular and the orthodox. The conflict is played out on the social--i.e., behavioral--level by local groups which adhere to one or the other view. While Jay protests that this conflict should not be understood to have "a dominant causal influence on the process of Javanese history," other principles of explanation are lacking. The reader of Jay's work might perhaps be forgiven for thinking that Jay's analysis of Javanese history is located within a Hegelian problematic.

1963), p. 15.

7. Ibid.

8. Clifford Geertz, *The Religion of Java* (Glencoe, Ill.: Free Press, 1960).

9. Robert R. Jay, *Religion and Politics in Rural Central Java*, Cultural Report Series no. 12 (New Haven: Yale University Southeast Asia Studies, 1963).

10. Ibid., p. 77.

That the aliran are really an aspect of Javanese peasant ideology, and not social structure as the earlier work of Geertz sometimes implies, is made clear in a more recent book by Geertz on Modjokuto. Here he tells us that he is concerned to develop a model of social structure employed by the Javanese themselves. The model, which he calls a "cultural paradigm," "is essentially a symbolic structure, that is a system of public ideas and attitudes."[11] Elsewhere in the same book he writes: "These categorizations were phenomenologically real; that is, they were objects of direct experience for the Modjokuto population taken as a unit."[12]

It is clear from this that aliran are first and foremost principles of ideological classification and not "the core of Modjokuto social structure."[13] The social aspects of the aliran might better be termed behavioral, because the models influence, or at least have influenced, the behavior of those who adhere to them. Unless it is assumed that there is an isomorphic relation between social structure and ideology we cannot use the aliran as a basis for our own models of Indonesial social structure.

While based on an acceptance of the validity of the aliran concept, this criticism of its use perhaps goes deeper than criticisms which rest on empirical refutation of the concept alone. Utrecht, for example, takes issue with Geertz by arguing that the santri-abangan distinction is unimportant to many Indonesian peasants. He cites examples of political alliances which cross-cut aliran ties in East Java and throughout Bali.[14] Wertheim in an excellent article shows how the vertical santri and abangan alliances, which Jay suggests demonstrate the unimportance of classes in the Javanese context, gave way to class struggle and the breakup of aliran along class lines during the period leading up to the terrible massacre of communists in 1965.[15]

Given, however, that aliran refers to an aspect of peasant ideology in particular periods of time in specific areas of Indonesia, it is not surprising that conflicting ideologies can and have been described for different places at different times. The criticisms leveled by Wertheim and Utrecht merely raise the question of why it should be that the ideology has been transformed, and how it is that these transformations have taken place--questions which can only be answered within the context of a general theory of the formation and transformation of thought systems.

Ethnicity. At first sight the concept of aliran appears to be uniquely Indonesian or Javanese. In fact, it is similar to concepts used in the analysis of other societies. Gunawan and van den Muijzenberg,[16] for example, compare it to the concept of "pillarization" developed by sociologists in the analysis of Dutch society. Ethnicity, however, is more explicitly used in a wide variety of settings to analyze group solidarities, and to attempt to explain them.

---

11. Clifford Geertz, *The Social History of an Indonesian Town* (Cambridge, Mass.: MIT Press, 1965), p. 8.

12. Ibid., p. 124.

13. Geertz, *Peddlers and Princes*, pp. 14-15.

14. Ernst Utrecht, "Some Remarks on Class Struggle and Political Parties in Indonesia," in *Indonesia's New Order* (Association for Radical East Asian Studies and the British Indonesian Committee, 1972), pp. 24 ff.

15. W. F. Wertheim, "From Aliran towards Class Struggle in the Javanese Countryside," *Pacific Viewpoint*, 10, 2 (1969), pp. 1-17.

16. Basuki Gunawan and O. D. van den Muijzeberg, "Verzuilingstridents en sociale stratificatie in Indonesia," *Sociologische Gids*, 14, 3 (1967).

Ethnicity has become very much a part of Indonesian thinking, used by some to explain the obstacles to true nationalism, economic development and the like, and by others to describe the particular strengths, or weaknesses, of some groups as opposed to others. Swift, for example, uses what seems to be the spirit of the Minangkabau ethnic group to explain economic structures in West Sumatra, manifested in the great success of small-scale entrepreneurial activity:

> I suggest that the intense competitiveness of the Minangkabau is such that success as a part of a group is not satisfying for the personality and culture drives involved. I see the genius of the Minangkabau as most suited to a quick perception and grasping of short term opportunity, best exemplified in the world of petty trading.[17]

Ethnicity has also been used to analyze political behavior. Liddle, for example, has "explained" voting patterns in the 1955 elections in part on the basis of ethnic identification. He concludes his study of political organization in East Sumatra by saying that ethnicity "has provided a focal point . . . for the individual's . . . conception of his relationship to the Indonesian polity."[18] As a result particular ethnic groups--the North and South Tapanuli Bataks and the Javanese--have allied themselves with particular political parties.

Similarly Bruner's analyses give primary importance to ethnic identification. He compares the "structures" of two Indonesian cities, Medan and Bandung, concluding that "The major line of social differentiation and cleavage in Medan society is undoubtedly ethnic. . . ."[19] For Bruner, ethnic groups in Indonesia are determined according to linguistic and geographical criteria, as well as by stereotypes formed by other Indonesians. Some, he argues, are known as good businessmen, others as puritans, and others because they fight with knives.

Urban Minangkabau and non-Minangkabau in Jakarta with whom I talked gave me similar criteria of ethnic identification. The Minangkabau, they said, were good businessmen (on a small scale), puritanical Muslims, firm adherents to matrilineal *adat* (custom), bad employees because they were generally unwilling to relinquish their independence and, if they turned to crime, pickpockets.

Ethnic identity, of course, takes different forms in different periods of time. In the period of my own fieldwork in West Sumatra (1970-72) there was a strong feeling of Minangkabau ethnic solidarity. This was continually expressed in the stress placed on adat, the independence and strength of Minangkabau culture, and so on. It is also interesting to note that non-Minangkabau, or Minangkabau who identified with the national elite, often cited the strength of adat as the main obstacle to economic development.

Similarly in the period of the regional rebellions in the late 1950s the solidarity of the Minangkabau was a constant theme of discourse. Again solidarity was directed against the cultural domination of the Javanese, as well as Javanese economic and political hegemony. In contrast to this it was the splits within Minangkabau,

---

17. Michael G. Swift, "Minangkabau and Modernization," in *Anthropology in Oceania*, ed. Lester R. Hiatt and Chandra Jayawardena (Sydney: Angus & Robertson, 1971), p. 265.

18. R. William Liddle, "Ethnicity and Political Organization: Three East Sumatran Cases," in *Culture and Politics in Indonesia*, ed. Claire Holt et al. (Ithaca: Cornell University Press, 1972), p. 174.

19. Edward M. Bruner, "The Expression of Ethnicity in Indonesia," in *Urban Ethnicity*, ed. A. Cohen (London: Tavistock, 1974), p. 261.

rather than ethnic solidarity, which received greater emphasis in the period leading up to the abortive communist uprisings of the mid-1920s.

Ethnicity, then, is clearly a part of the Indonesian ideological formation. As a shared system of thought it also motivates behavior based on ethnic solidarities and divisions. Ethnicity alone, however, is of limited explanatory value. To ask ethnicity to "explain" voting patterns, or social interaction as do Liddle and Bruner, is to become trapped in the tautological circles of ideology and behavior. Why certain ethnic characteristics should be significant in some periods, and insignificant in others no amount of allusion to the relativity of ethnic identification can explain.

Patron-clientage. Along with ethnicity, the patron-client model has been used widely by sociologists and anthropologists, particularly with reference to precapitalist or transitional societies. Perhaps most frequently patron-clientage has been used to describe a dyadic tie between individuals with differential access to wealth and/or power. In Landé's study of Philippine politics it is a "behavioral pattern according to which the little people anticipate the crises of life through the cultivation of dyadic ties with specific big people."[20] As such patron-clientage is one "of the patterns of behavior which takes place within the framework of" the kinship and class systems.[21]

As a model of social structure patron-clientage is something quite different. For Barth, for example, the nature of patron-client contracts appears to determine political structure.[22] This has been criticized recently as a political formalism.[23] Perhaps more important, however, recent studies of patronage[24] show that in particular cases patron-clientage is an aspect of the folk model, built up on the perception of structural relations of economic exploitation and political domination.

Patron-clientage then becomes a conscious model for behavior in particular kinds of social formation. It is also a model of social structure built up on the observance of all interactions between inferiors and superiors whose differential access to wealth and power are defined by their place in the class structure. The existence of this model in Java, as Wertheim clearly shows, corresponds with the aliran system which serves as an overall framework for linking patrons and clients within the same social group.

Aliran, ethnicity and patron-clientage all have this in common--they are all aspects of peasant ideology in Indonesia, or, more accurately, they have all been a part of Indonesian ideology in particular periods of time. As, to use Geertz's terms, models of the appearances *of* social reality (interaction), they are clearly at the same time conscious models *for* behavior. To equate ideology with idealization is to take an extremely narrow view of ideology.

---

20. Carl H. Lande, *Leaders, Factions and Parties: The Structure of Philippine Politics*, Monograph Series no. 6 (New Haven: Yale University Southeast Asia Studies, 1965), p. 1.

21. Ibid., p. 9.

22. Fredrik Barth, *Political Leadership among Swat Pathans* (London: Athlone, 1959).

23. Talal Asad, "Market Model, Class Structure and Consent," *Man*, 7 (1972), pp. 74-94.

24. L. Li Causi, "Anthropology and Ideology: The Case of 'Patronage' in Mediterranean Societies," *Critique of Anthropology*, 4 and 5 (1975), pp. 90-109; Michael Gilsenan, "Against Patron-Client Relations," in *Patrons and Clients*, ed. Ernest Gellner and John Waterbury (London: Duckworth, 1977), pp. 167-83.

Ideology and Reality

I have argued that in many cases the formation of ideology rather than taking place in a vacuum is directly based on empirical reality. The relation between aliran, ethnicity and patron-clientage as thought systems and reality as it is perceived by Indonesian peasants--and anthropological fieldworkers--is a very close one.

Folk models based on ethnicity, patron-clientage and aliran all rest, in one way or another, on an equation of social grouping on the one hand and physical space or distance on the other. In Geertz's discussion of aliran, for example, it will be noted that the different layers are distinguished according to spatial distance from the urban centers.[25] The distance from the rural mass at the bottom end to the intelligentsia at the top is a spatial distance, the product of the application of a geogrphically defined rural-urban continuum to groups of people. In other words one of the principles of social classification employed by people of the Modjokuto area in the period of Geertz's research was not social at all, but geographical.

While perhaps not so crucial for ethnic identity, geography also serves partly to define ethnicity. People are grouped together not according to social criteria but according to place of origin or in terms of residential proximity. At the conceptual level, then, spatial affinity is equated with social similarity in the ideology of ethnicity.

Spatial concepts also enter into the patron-client concept, although in a slightly more complex way. Patron-client is based on the perception of a social gap, which is bridged by the patron or the "broker." In fact, it will be noted that this gap is a physical one, in many cases corresponding to the rural-urban gap itself. The gap separates town and country and, more precisely, village from the outside world. This gap is experienced by villagers if only because to bridge it themselves they have to leave the village periodically--to go to market, to visit government offices and the like. While this is not a gap in social structure--villager and town dweller already form part of a social unity, their roles not defined by place of residence so much as by social factors--for the villager it is real because it is experienced. When an outsider bridges this "gap" the act is taken to be a basic social relationship linking town and country. The ideological model of social structure, based on this vertical linkage, again fuses physical with social space.[26]

Finally for the aliran, as described by Jay, the whole basis of the santri-abangan split is geographical, as we have seen. Jay describes the associations of "social" units--residential groups, neighborhoods, villages--with the one or the other of the secular-orthodox positions. In fact, what is taken for social affinity is geographical proximity. The fact that people live together does not mean, of necessity, that they occupy similar places in the social structure. But in the folk model the two ideas are fused. The ideology aliran implies on the one hand a concept of the social solidarity of geographical units, and on the other their association with or opposition to other spatially defined units. This assumed homology between social and geographical space is, then, an important feature of the three ideological systems.[27]

---

25. See Geertz, *Social History of an Indonesian Town*.

26. Cf. Gilsenan, "Against Patron-Client Relations."

27. A similar disjuncture between spatial models of social structure and social structure itself has been noted by Levi-Strauss in very different circumstances. Levi-Strauss writes that he has attempted to demonstrate that, among the Bororo, spatial configuration reflects not the true, unconscious social organization but a

A second important feature of these systems is the emphasis given to observable behavior and social interaction. These are taken, in the ideology, to be reflections of social structure, and hence in themselves used to define the structural relations of society. For example local, geographically defined units acquire a semblance of structural solidarity because people in these units interact with each other. Patron-clientage seems to be a basic structure of social organization because this is one of the few interactional ties between these different categories of people. Where patron-clientage has become part of local ideology then it is based on an assumed coincidence between interaction and all the important social (economic and political) relations.

This confusion of the structural with the observable is a characteristic of some anthropological models as well. Radcliffe-Brown's proposition of the convergence of social structure with observable relations[28] has been frequently criticized.[29] Yet social scientists in the study of Indonesia continue to accept the empiricist view of structure. Bruner, for example, argues that the "major line of social differentiation and cleavage in Medan is undoubtedly ethnic."[30] This conclusion is derived by Bruner from an evaluation of people's interaction networks outside work. This equation of interaction with social structure is basic both to Indonesian ideology, as well as to some social theory in Indonesia as well.

A third characteristic of these systems, and of aliran and ethnicity in particular, is their similarity to the taxonomies produced by Levi-Strauss's *bricoleur*, who builds with a repertoire given to him. He "has to use this repertoire . . . whatever the task in hand because [he] has nothing else at [his] disposal."[31] The repertoire here is that array of observed odds and ends thrown up by ethnic differentiation: language, dress, eating habits, styles of interpersonal behavior and the like. The "ethnic bricoleur" draws on this source of readily identifiable characteristics to build his models of society, and then to act on them. What his informants tell him is often taken at face value. When I was in Jakarta talking to Minangkabau and non-Minangkabau alike I was constantly reminded of the reputation of the Minangkabau as fanatical Muslim purists. This contradicted my own experience in Minangkabau villages of a rather tolerant people whose observance even of required ritual tended to be rather lax. What counted, of course, was not ritual observance or textual expertise, but the universal proclamation by the Minangkabau themselves of their attachment to Islam. In many cases one would suspect that the difference between santri-abangan has little to do with secularism or orthodoxy, but rather with external proclamations of faith, and the cultural trappings of Islam --dress, the use of a few Arabic utterances at appropriate times, obtrusive disappearances at prayer times, and breaking of the fast only behind closed doors. Ethnicity and aliran are in this way most directly concerned with things as they appear,

---

model existing consciously in the native thought, though its nature is entirely illusory and even contradictory to reality." Claude Levi-Strauss, *Structural Anthropology* (New York: Basic Books, 1963), p. 292.

28. Cf. Alfred R. Radcliffe-Brown, "On Social Structure," in *Structure and Function in Primitive Society* (1940; London: Cohen & West, 1963).

29. Edmund Leach, *Rethinking Anthropology* (London: Athlone, 1961); Levi-Strauss, *Structural Anthropology*, pp. 204 ff.

30. Bruner, "Expression of Ethnicity," p. 261.

31. Claude Levi-Strauss, *The Savage Mind* (London: Weidenfeld & Nicolson, 1966), p. 17.

and remind one of nothing more than the taxonomies produced by Leach's butterfly collectors.

In a very real sense, then, ideology in Indonesia is directly related to, if not obsessed with, reality, if reality is defined at the empirical level. In spite of the apparent superficiality of its underpinnings, Indonesian ideology is a strong force for motivating behavior, and its strength must not be underestimated. Nonetheless while it seems to be compatible with existing social structure it must not be confused with social structure. In spite of the phenomenological reality of these principles of ideology, other approaches to the analysis of Indonesian social structure yield different models altogether. A structural analysis of political and economic organization would reveal a disjuncture between the categories of ideology and the principles of social structure. It is precisely because these underlying structures do not receive physically perceivable verification--and it is the perceptual level which provides the raw material for the ideological *bricoleur*--that a disjuncture develops between ideology and social structure.

Social Structure and Ideology in Indonesia

Indonesian peasant ideology, in particular historical periods, is then based on taxonomic principles which derive from the phenomenal forms thrown up by underlying social structure. People are categorized according to spatial, geographical and ethnic principles. As a result, ideology is in no way a reflection of economic and political structures--rather there is a clear disjuncture between the levels of social structure.

Elsewhere[32] I have provided a preliminary analysis of the economic relations which link Indonesian peasant producers to other classes in the social formation. A brief summary of the argument is called for here, in order to demonstrate the existence of a disjuncture between class relationships and the way these relationships are perceived. What I have argued is that the Indonesian social formation is best seen as the articulation of three modes of production: capitalism, petty commodity production, and a subsistence mode of production. The social formation is dominated by capitalism in the sense that the other modes of production are articulated into the reproduction of capitalism. I pointed out that the formation of prices in the petty commodity sector differed from that found under capitalism because of the existence of subsistence production. Individual producers, in competition with each other, do not calculate prices of production in terms of the cost of reproducing their own labor power. Rather they are forced through competition to peg their prices below the level at which they can reproduce their own labor power. This is the result of the alternative possibility of subsistence cultivation.

The exchange values of peasant commodities are therefore lower than their values. Together with the fact that exchange values in capitalist production may be higher than value, the result is a flow of value, i.e., labor time, towards capitalism through unequal exchange between classes defined by capitalism and petty commodity producers.

Indonesian class structure differs from that described by Marx for the capitalist mode of production. Nonetheless, the pervasiveness of commodity production in many parts of Indonesia, the long history of Indonesian involvement in long-distance

---

32. Joel S. Kahn, "Imperialism and the Reproduction of Capitalism," *Critique of Anthropology*, 2 (1974), pp. 1-35; idem, "Economic Scale and the Cycle of Petty Commodity Production," in *Marxist Analyses and Social Anthropology*, ed. Maurice Bloch (London: Malaby Press, 1975).

trade, and the dependent (i.e., non-"traditional") nature of the subsistence sector[33] demonstrate the close integration of all sectors of the Indonesian economy. The importance of petty commodity production and underdevelopment are a result of capitalist domination, and not of the survival of precolonial economic forms. This means that we cannot speak of autonomous or even semiautonomous sectors of the Indonesian economy.[34]

There are no autonomous groups within the commodity-producing regions of Indonesia. The urban bourgeoisie and small entrepreneurs, the employees of and representatives of foreign capital, and the small commodity producers are classes, and as such are defined not in isolation but in terms of their relationships to other classes. Value flows from one class to another, prices are determined in competition regardless of the nature, location or ethnic group involved in production; economic stagnation in one sector is the result of economic growth in another; and there is a national--indeed an international--division of labor such that no village or class is self-sufficient. In short in most of Indonesia, where commodity production is dominant, it is impossible to speak of economic gaps or autonomous sectors. There are nonvisible economic relations without which it would be impossible to understand economic conditions. While it is not being argued that economic forms are identical throughout the world economy, it is being argued that all its sectors, in those areas dominated by the world capitalist system, are inextricably linked.

An analysis of the political structure of Indonesia would show a similar pattern. The Indonesian state and its administrative branches reach into all corners of the nation. Indeed, rather than there being any internal political autonomy, it should be argued that under present conditions Indonesia itself does not form an autonomous political unit. As is the case with the economy, the Indonesian political system is all-pervasive.

An analysis of economic and political structures of the Indonesian social formation does not coincide with the folk models nor with appearances. Economic and political structures, for example, are in no way determined by physical space. Villages which are associated with one aliran or another are distinct neither in economic nor in political terms, although they may be separated in their ideology. Two villages may both produce cash crops for national and international markets. The subsistence sector in both villages helps equally to reproduce commodity production within the villages and outside them. Neither are the two villages politically autonomous--they occupy the same niche in the state administrative structure. In economic and political terms there is no way of distinguishing the two. Nonetheless they may be opposed in the local folk model, one being a santri, and the other an abangan village.

Similarly the Indonesian village economy is an integral part of a total economy which is rural, urban and international. Village producers stand in a class relationship to others, not on the basis of whether they live in rural or urban areas, but according to their productive or distributive role. Petty commodity producers are not restricted to any particular residential niche. And yet in ideological terms

---

33. Joel S. Kahn, "'Tradition,' Matriliny and Change among the Minangkabau of Indonesia," *Bijdragen tot de Taal-, Land- en Volkenkunde*, 132 (1976), pp. 64-95.

34. For other critiques of dualism, cf. Andre Gunder Frank, *Latin America: Under-Development or Revolution* (New York: Monthly Review Press, 1969). Clifford Geertz also criticizes the dualist thesis for Indonesia in his *Agricultural Involution* (Berkeley: University of California Press, 1963).

the rural is distinct from the urban. There is an ideological--not a social--gap between town and country. Indeed the relationship between town and country appears to be restricted to dyadic relations across this "gap." Political patrons recruit followings in villages. The patron appears to come from nowhere, although in fact he is only a representative of a preexisting political hierarchy.

Similarly both town and country reproduce themselves only through a division of labor, and yet they seem to remain autonomous when individuals are linked as buyers and sellers in the market. The structural links become fetishized such that structural relations are perceived as relations either between material goods which flow in and out of the villages, or dyadic links between producer and shopkeeper. The market, and the dyadic market relations, however, only serve to link producers and nonproducers who already stand in an economic relation to each other. For this reason it is not difficult to understand why it is that personal interaction should be incorporated into the ideology as the basis of the whole system. For while the existing political and economic structures are not given any physical confirmation, they give rise to interactions which are, as it were, within the field of vision. This analysis could be extended to include the structural relations of underdevelopment as well. Here the apparent gap is even greater, bridged even less often, in many cases by the anthropologist himself.

Ethnic solidarity is based in the same way on appearances. As Bruner himself points out there are important differentials within ethnic categories. In economic and political terms the Minangkabau blacksmith and a Javanese smallholder occupy similar slots in the social structure. And yet again this is not confirmed by direct observation and experience. In the ideology of ethnicity the more directly perceivable aspects of ethnic identity, as well as observable interactions, are taken to illustrate the basic principles of social structure.

What I have tried to show is that a model of Indonesian social structure which distinguishes different systemic levels illustrates a disjunction between economic, political and ideological systems. There is no neat isomorphism between levels. An analysis which goes beyond the conscious models of peasant villagers allows us to understand the discontinuities in the system.

To argue that the levels are not isomorphic reflections one of another, is not necessarily to suggest that there is a functional incompatibility among them. Appearances do not coincide with the structures themselves, and it is empirical reality as it is perceived, not unseen structures, which becomes the raw material for ideology. The Indonesian social formation generates interactions which, in a sense, conceal the underlying structural realities. It has also generated a diversity of forms, in space and time; and models of aliran, ethnicity and patron-clientage are built up on this diversity. . . .

INDONESIA'S NEW ORDER AS A BUREAUCRATIC POLITY, A NEOPATRIMONIAL
REGIME OR A BUREAUCRATIC-AUTHORITARIAN REGIME:
WHAT DIFFERENCES DOES IT MAKE?

Dwight Y. King

It has become increasingly apparent that disagreements exist among observers of Indonesia's New Order about the nature of the regime, about where it is going, and about how it got where it is. I assume that better understanding of Indonesia and possibly more scholarly agreement require clarification of concepts and more self-consciously comparative analysis which utilizes general social scientific models and theories.[1] My purpose, then, is to examine critically on logical and empirical criteria some recent concepts and models and to begin to set forward more adequate ones. In conclusion I hope to suggest a more defensible approach to comparative, empirical analysis than those which have been (rightly) accused of being universalistic-cum-imperialistic/ethnocentric.[2]

Bureaucratic Polity: A Criticism

The model of a bureaucratic polity, earlier utilized in the study of Thailand by Fred Riggs, has recently been applied to Indonesia by Karl Jackson.[3] "My major thesis," Jackson writes, "is that at least since 1957 . . . the basic form of government has not changed fundamentally" (p. 3). A subsequent note that "there is nothing peculiarly Third World about bureaucratic polity" and that Dutch colonial government was "similar" reinforces Jackson's stress on *continuity* in the pattern of political domination, except for the so-called Liberal Period, 1950-57. Concomitant with this emphasis on continuity, however, Jackson sees "important modifications of the Suharto era" (p. 4), especially "a steadily increasing concentration of power" resulting in basically a monistic rather than a dualistic power center (p. 8). This concentration of power does *not* include (is not accompanied by) an increase

---

1. I do not find in historicism, evolutionism, or diffusionism insuperable obstacles against the possibility of constructing an empirical social science based on cross-systemic uniformities. For a brief but persuasive discussion, consult Moshe Czudnowski, *Comparing Political Behavior* (Beverly Hills: Sage, 1976).

2. Benedict R. O'G. Anderson, "Perspective and Method in American Research on Indonesia" (unpublished manuscript, 1972), see above, pp. 69-83.

3. Karl D. Jackson, "Bureaucratic Polity: A Theoretical Framework for the Analysis of Power and Communications in Indonesia," in *Political Power and Communications in Indonesia*, ed. Karl D. Jackson and Lucian W. Pye (Berkeley: University of California Press, 1978), pp. 3-22.

in power, which only derives, in Jackson's view, from greater ability or willingness to organize and mobilize the masses into politics (including central government programs) on a regular basis (p. 8). One might question already whether a change from a dualistic to a monistic power center does not represent more a transformation than a transition, whether political participation is the basic source of political power, and whether concentration and centralization of power may be only one of alternative policy strategies for an increasingly sophisticated regime. But let us first note how Jackson distinguishes a bureaucratic polity from other types.

A bureaucratic polity is distinguishable by "the degree to which national decision-making is insulated from social and political forces outside the highest elite echelons of the capital city" (p. 4). It differs from a one-man, sultanistic or personalistic regime in that an incumbent president's power is based on legal authority rather than traditional legitimacy, "must be backed by at least a minimal consensus among the military and bureaucratic elite" (p. 6), and thus "is in the long run accountable to the bureaucratic and military elite" (p. 17). It differs from military rule or military dictatorship in that "the basic style and goals [policy priorities] of the government are bureaucratic and technocratic rather than military" although "bureaucratic polities rarely maximize economic rationality, organizational efficiency, and economic development" (p. 13). These distinguishing characteristics are also problematic.

Jackson's use of quantitative phraseology ("degree") is misleading because he is speaking of attributes that are *not* variables in any proper sense (i.e., do not permit gradations and measurement). In fact, the bureaucratic polity is nothing else than a qualitative classification. This does not make it more or less useful; it should remind us, however, that concept formation stands prior to quantification, categoric concepts cannot give way to gradation concepts, and the logic of classification building requires mutually exclusive classes and precise definitional limits--otherwise "conceptual stretching" occurs and we lose connotative precision.[4] Jackson's analysis neither advances us toward quantification nor does it supply the definitional limits needed for a useful concept. Rather, we find almost every attribute subject to qualification. For example, political power and participation are said to be limited almost entirely to high employees of the state; yet "large numbers of citizens" regularly obtain relief from government regulations at the local levels (p. 5), Muslim elites have used Islamic doctrine "with telling effectiveness to rouse the traditional peasant masses to political violence" (p. 7), and "the cleavage between orthodox and nominal Muslims, which cuts across Indonesian society, further limits the actions that may be taken by the official class" (p. 9). Power is said to be markedly more centralized now than during Guided Democracy, yet even Suharto is "accountable to the Army and the bureaucracy."

In what ways do bureaucratic and technocratic style and goals differ from military style and goals? Certainly most observers of modern military rule have noted the attraction of generals to modern technology, in terms of weaponry, infrastructure, and fast, politically "neutral" solutions to social problems. In my own research I have documented the increasing bureaucratization of labor-management conflict under the New Order. With reference to Indonesia, Jackson seems oblivious to the way popular and technocratic policy goals have been subordinated to military imperatives during implementation,[5] evidence of the clear power differential between

---

4. Giovanni Sartori, "Concept Misinformation in Comparative Politics," *American Political Science Review*, 64 (1970), pp. 1033-53.

5. Martin Rudner, "The Indonesian Military and Economic Policy," *Modern Asian Studies*, 10 (1976), pp. 249-84.

ABRI and the civilian bureaucracy, and his assertion of a drastic reduction in Indonesian military establishment is contravened by the system of unconventional financing,[6] bureaucratic capitalism,[7] a substantial increase in *para*military forces,[8] and a sharp increase in the share of the development cake going for defense in 1979/80.[9] . . .

[In Jackson's bureaucratic polity, the political sphere is self-determining and autonomous vis-à-vis the domestic environment. "Like islands cut off from the social sea surrounding them, bureaucratic polities are largely impervious to currents in their own societies and may be more responsive to external pressures emanating from the international arena" (p. 4). The ruling elite "is accountable to fewer than 1,000 out of 130 million citizens" (p. 13). Politics occurs as competing circles of high-ranking bureaucrats and military officers seek a mixture of organization objectives and "nonservice goals" such as prestige and wealth. In Jackson's view, elite choices, especially those of the president, "are critical in determining whether continued socioeconomic change leads to (*a*) development of a competitive democratic system based on mass political parties and a participant citizenry, (*b*) movement toward a single-party, ideologically based mobilization regime, or (*c*) continuation of a bureaucratic polity" (p. 21).

Jackson recognizes, however, that certain structural and cultural variables affect the maintenance and durability of the bureaucratic polity. But the geographically dispersed quality of the archipelago, weaknesses in communication and transportation, ethnic, linguistic, and religious differences, overwhelmingly rural character of the population, social structure emphasizing predominantly vertical rather than horizontal affiliations and the political culture emphasizing deference, self-control, and indirectness have all conspired to maintain the bureaucratic polity in Indonesia, giving the elite virtual decisional autonomy. Socioeconomic changes such as expansion of education, urbanization, and industrialization may create "instability" (p. 19), but any fundamental political change "over the next several decades" is unlikely (p. 21). Structural and cultural variables affect regime type but have not changed it in any major way and have little influence on policy outputs of the New Order both now and for the foreseeable future.][10]

Conceiving of the polity in such isolated fashion ignores the political consequence of delayed, dependent capitalist development, and obscures the importance of economic stabilization for the legitimacy of the New Order and economic growth for its cohesion. The domination of the modern economic sector by foreigners and Chinese ethnic minority after independence was a main source of social conflict and ineffectiveness of the parliamentary regime and inhibited the growth of an indigenous, middle stratum. The growth of bureaucratic capitalism once the bureaucratic polity was "restored" must be a major factor in any explanation of the social conservatism of Guided Democracy and the New Order. Foreign aid averaging over 20 percent of total government revenues annually since 1968, together with the windfall from dramatic increase in world oil price, made possible a boom in (non-oil)

---

6. Harold Crouch, "Generals and Business in Indonesia," *Pacific Affairs*, 48 (1975-76), pp. 519-40.

7. Richard Robison, "Toward a Class Analysis of the Indonesian Military Bureaucratic State," *Indonesia*, 25 (April 1978), pp. 17-39.

8. ISS, *Military Balance* (various issues).

9. *Far Eastern Economic Review*, January 19, 1979.

10. The author added these two paragraphs in 1982 as a revision of arguments made in the original paper.

public sector investment and a decrease in the proportion of government revenue extracted from Indonesian taxpayers. Public sector expenditure and the inflow of private foreign investment has substantially benefited a small, but strategically placed elite. This policy of dependence on foreign capital, technology, and managerial expertise has created pressure to control the wages of the popular sector and to control the political parties and unions that represent that sector's interests, in order to create an attractive investment climate. A development strategy heavily biased toward import-substitution and capital-intensive industrial growth has resulted in growing numbers and political importance of technocrats who favor technical solutions to economic and social problems. Like the Indonesian military, they feel that political demands of the popular sector should not play a role in shaping public policies. In these ways, then, we can see interactions between recent economic and political changes and interaction that follows *patterns* similar to those in other delayed, dependent, capitalist developing countries. . . .

A Neopatrimonial Regime?

Indonesian politics under the New Order most resembles the neopatrimonial model in the view of several other scholars.[11] In this model of "detraditionalized, personalized patrimonialism," a reinterpretation of Weber's notion of patrimonial rule by Eisenstadt and Guenther Roth, beliefs about legitimacy, actual operating modes and administrative arrangements are "inextricably linked to material incentives and rewards."[12] While this model may provide us greater analytical precision due to clearer boundaries, it does not fit the Indonesian case well either and use of it may be misleading.

Despite the prefix and Roth's assertion that he is conceptualizing a *detraditionalized* type of rule, I suspect part of the appeal of the neopatrimonial model derives from its connotation that more or less fixed cultural or historical traits characterize the regime. Like the bureaucratic polity the accent is on continuity, but it is continuity of norms, sociopolitical ideas and process instead of continuity of structural division between court-bureaucracy and a great apolitical mass. Although the neopatrimonial model can be applied to contemporary political structure and process (which I prefer in evaluating the model) without necessarily connoting permanent traits,[13] the difficulties in stressing continuity in Indonesian politics should be noted in passing.

---

11. Herbert Feith, "Political Control, Class Formation and Legitimacy in Suharto's Indonesia," Paper presented at Melbourne Conference of the Asian Studies Association of Australia; Robison, "Toward a Class Analysis"; Donald K. Emmerson, "Comments: Modernizing the Nation," in *What is Modern Indonesian Culture?* ed. Gloria Davis (Athens: Ohio University Center for International Studies Southeast Asia Program, 1979), pp. 225-29. Robison vacillates between labeling the state under the New Order neopatrimonialist and military-bureaucratic and thus confuses two distinct models.

12. Guenther Roth, "Personal Rulership, Patrimonialism, and Empire-Building in the New States," *World Politics*, 20 (1968), pp. 194-206.

13. This connotation is reinforced if not created by Willner and Anderson, see Ann Ruth Willner, "The Neotraditional Accommodation to Political Independence: The Case of Indonesia," in *Cases in Comparative Politics: Asia*, ed. Lucian W. Pye (Boston: Little Brown, 1970), pp. 242-306; and Benedict R. O'G. Anderson, "The Idea of Power in Javanese Culture," in *Culture and Politics in Indonesia*, ed. Claire Holt et al. (Ithaca: Cornell University Press, 1972), pp. 1-69.

The analysis of ideas is an important task in the social sciences, but one cannot assume the continuity much less the current impact on behavior of old, pre-Western Javanese conceptions of politics. Ideas and norms deemed once again flourishing as an operative if not always conscious ideology despite colonialism, revolution, egalitarianism (from Islam), individualism and pluralism, changes in ecological setting and in social stratification, amorphous political socialization in the family and schools, and vague, inconsistent and superficial political indoctrination, would be remarkably persistent ideas and norms indeed. As a preliminary step, it would be necessary to undertake an analysis of the current system of ideas to determine both the nature and prominence of the pre-Western conceptions still to be found in Javanese politics. MacDougall's and Liddle's work on the thinking of *civilian* elites suggests sharp discontinuity in ideas about the sociopolitical order.

The New Order has come to exhibit political characteristics that, when taken together, indicate a pattern of political domination that is different in kind from earlier regimes. It is important to note that the increased centralization/consolidation which has occurred under the New Order has ended the basic dualism of the Guided Democracy regime that arose from the conflict between Sukarno and the Army and which resulted in that regime retaining a good deal of the earlier pluralistic character of the liberal parliamentary regime. Second, Guided Democracy until 1963 was largely a holding operation perhaps because the government was continually distracted with maintaining territorial integrity, whereas the Suharto regime has given far more attention to bringing about the integration of contending forces after destroying the strongest one (PKI). Third, the ideological dynamism of Guided Democracy when it was coupled with mobilization of the lower strata in order to effect radical social politics after 1963, contrasts sharply with the pragmatism and the social conservatism of the present regime. Fourth, the systematic and widespread use of violence against nonsuccessionist political adversaries by the present regime represented a departure from the old rules of the political game. Finally, the New Order's reliance on foreign aid and investment allows greater external control over scarce economic resources (continuity with 1950-58 liberal period?) and greater monopolization of Indonesian access to them by compradores than under any previous regime.

The problematic connotation of continuity aside, the neopatrimonial model faces other difficulties. Personal rulership is, by definition, unchecked leadership; the ruler's discretionary power is the predominant form. Yet, most observers would agree that Suharto's leadership style has been deliberate, predictable and, above all, *consultative.* Key policy decisions seem far more the product of a military-technocrat oligarchy than the discretion of a military dictator. A second problem pertains to the character and political role/function of the bureaucracy. In Roth's formulation, personal rulership may be extended through the instrument of the bureaucracy. Patrimonialism, in other words, may work through bureaucratic domination; there is no need to juxtapose them as fundamentally different types of rule. In neopatrimonial regimes having a large and politically important public apparatus, authority is based, presumably, on "substantive" rationality rather than "formal-legal rationality" which characterizes bureaucratic domination in Western, industrialized states. Does *substantive* rationality predominate; is it the general tendency in the bureaucratic process at the national level? Emmerson has documented administrative reform and rationalization,[14] Glassburner and others have lauded the economic policy performance, and the handling of the Pertamina crisis reflected and increased the political influence of the technocrats in the cabinet--

---

14. Donald K. Emmerson, "The Bureaucracy in Political Context: Weakness in Strength," in *Political Power and Communications*, ed. Jackson and Pye, pp. 82-136.

factors that are not easily reconciled with the model of neopatrimonial bureaucracy operating primarily on substantive rationality.

Neither the neopatrimonial model nor the bureaucratic polity model handles the problem of legitimacy well. In Jackson's bureaucratic polity, legitimacy is an issue only between the ruling circle and the approximately 1,000 member official class. Presumably it is a nonissue for the remainder of the population (140 million!) who lack modern political attitudes. The Suharto ruling circle's legitimacy is based on a combination of legal authority and sharing of the perquisites of power and office with the official class and thus is based on distinctly modern principles. In Roth's version of the neopatrimonial model, as Feith points out, the regime has a constant legitimacy problem and is particularly vulnerable to legitimacy challenges from modern urban groups which demand more charismatic forms of leadership. Can one find sufficient empirical evidence of a *constant* legitimacy problem? Without wishing to become involved in a debate over how much of what kind of evidence might be sufficient or to obscure the heavy-handedness and repressiveness of the regime, a neopatrimonial model may imply less legitimacy and more instability than has characterized New Order rule. This is reinforced by the basic instabilities which are built into the patrimonial state, at least in the Weberian version, resulting from the impetus to centralization of the monarch and the localizing, fissiparous tendencies represented by provincial notables and royal princelings.

The implications about the lower strata when the neopatrimonial model is applied to New Order Indonesia and the situation of relative political stability may be erroneous. Would not the model lead us to explain relative quietude and obedience of the lower urban and rural strata as resultant from their having received material benefit? A growing corpus of factual evidence points to the contrary and that patronage relationships that existed during Sukarno's rule are rapidly crumbling. But an alternative basis for allegiance and obedience, traditional legitimacy, is excluded from the model. So is obedience from fear of incipient class-based violence or the regime's threat or selective use of force? In sum, the neopatrimonial model explains lower strata/mass allegiance and obedience by reference to material gratification; the bureaucratic polity model explains allegiance and obedience by reference to traditional, backward attitudes. Logically, neither allow for obedience from fear, manipulation by more subtle mechanisms of social control or rational calculation of least risk.

Toward a More Adequate Model: A Bureaucratic-Authoritarian Regime

In my own analysis of national level politics under the New Order, I have found the concept and model of a bureaucratic-authoritarian regime more useful than the models discussed above. Originally formulated by Juan Linz[15] on the basis of his empirical study of Spain under Franco, and subsequently elaborated by a number of scholars while studying Latin American cases,[16] use of the model carries both

---

15. Juan Linz, "An Authoritarian Regime: Spain," in *Cleavages, Ideologies, and Party Systems*, ed. Erik Allardt and Yrjo Littunen (Helsinki: Academic Bookstore, 1964); and "Totalitarian and Authoritarian Regimes," in *Handbook of Political Science*, vol. 3, ed. Fred Greenstein and Nelson Polsby (Reading, Mass.: Addison-Wesley, 1975), pp. 175-411.

16. Guillermo O'Donnell, *Modernization and Bureaucratic-Authoritarianism: Studies in South American Politics* (Berkeley, Calif.: University of California, Institute of International Studies, Politics of Modernization Series No. 9, 1973); Fernando Henriques Cardoso, "Associated Dependent Development Theoretical and Practical

the hazards and promise of placing Indonesia in a more comparative perspective. I find the hazards fewer and the promises greater than with the above models because of the larger and more elaborated theoretical literature on bureaucratic-authoritarianism and, paradoxically perhaps, because of the greater historical-contextual sensitivity of the model.

The bureaucratic-authoritarian model postulates a distinct, modern, relatively stable pattern of political domination that emerges under certain historical, environmental, and political conditions and which has, by virtue of its structure and process, remarkable capacity to maintain itself and control various potentially destabilizing pressures produced during modernization. Unlike the bureaucratic polity in which legitimacy of ruling circle vis-à-vis the official class is based on legal- and substantively-rational principles and on habit vis-à-vis the populace, and unlike neopatrimonial regimes which base their legitimacy heavily on material incentives and consequently suffer chronic legitimacy problems, bureaucratic-authoritarian regimes deliberately cultivate a multiple legitimacy base--a calculated mixture of traditional, charismatic, legal- and substantive-rational, and technical efficiency principles. I submit that the latter more accurately describes the legitimacy base on the New Order and helps explain why differentials and changes in the distribution of material benefits has not been more politically destabilizing, e.g., recent reduction in Pertamina-financed extra-budgetary allotment for the Armed Forces; increased maldistribution of income (household, regional, and urban-rural). This complex, subtle, often contradictory basis of legitimacy provides one criterion for distinguishing a bureaucratic-authoritarian regime from narrowly tyrannical or expediently dictatorial regimes and helps to explain its unwillingness to enforce rigid ideological conformity and its lack of compulsion to expand power exclusively through mass participation/mobilization. With reference to a research agenda, this perspective on legitimacy suggests potential insights are to be gained about regime sensitivity to the social environment and the relative efficacy of various types of legitimacy principles, by attention to changes in the mixture over time and variations in the mixture being cultivated among different groups and population sectors.

In the bureaucratic-authoritarian model, ultimate authority resides in an oligarchy or the military as an institution, rather than exclusively in an individual ruler. Where a group of military men or the military as an institution hold power, they adopt a technocratic, bureaucratic approach to policy making. The accent is on a consultative and consensual (and relatively predictable) decision-making process among a ruling group and the central role of a larger bureaucratic structure, not the *military* per se. The bureaucratic-authoritarian model thus avoids juxtaposing military and technocratic goals and style (bureaucratic polity) or overestimating the discretionary power of a single individual (neopatrimonial model).

The prevalence of a technocratic mentality, as opposed to any more elaborated form of ideology is a second criterion for distinguishing a bureaucratic-authoritarian regime, particularly from a totalitarian regime. New Order efforts to effect a political cultural transformation have consisted mainly of negative acts, such as persecution of radicals and critics and imposition of diffuse censorship on all media and

---

Implications," in *Authoritarian Brazil: Origins, Policies, and Future*, ed. Alfred Stepan (New Haven: Yale University Press, 1973), pp. 142-76; Philippe C. Schmitter, "Paths to Political Development in Latin America," in *Changing Latin America*, ed. Douglas Chalmers (New York: Columbia University Press, 1972), pp. 83-105, and "Liberation by *Golpe*," in *Political Participation under Military Regimes*, ed. Henry Bienen and David Morell (Beverly Hills: Sage Contemporary Social Science Issues, No. 26, 1976), pp. 86-114.

attempts to create a conformist mentality by invoking vague and generic values or inclusivistic doctrines (e.g., Panca Sila)[17] and manipulating patriotic and chauvinistic symbols. What binds together the current ruling elite, military and civilian, is less an ideology of modernization than a programmatic consensus. Their ideas about modernization are contradictory and unelaborated, not to mention fluctuating.

Another characteristic of a bureaucratic-authoritarian regime is the willingness to work within the framework of an apathetic acceptance of the regime by the mass of the population and a corresponding lack of interest on the part of the ruling elite in mobilizing mass support on a continual basis. The applicability of this criterion to the New Order seems obvious enough, given its concern for depoliticalization, "de-party-ization," "floating mass," and view of non-Golkar political activity as unprofessional and archaic. Only twice, in the form of general elections, has the New Order made an active effort to mobilize popular support as a source of legitimacy. This characteristic and the one above differentiate bureaucratic-authoritarianism from German and Italian fascism, which were characterized by a highly elaborated nationalistic ideology and by high levels of popular mobilization.

A final distinguishing feature of a bureaucratic-authoritarian regime is its attempts to achieve a limited pluralism, using repression, cooptation and, typically, a network of corporatist organizations, and thereby control opposition to the regime. According to several theorists, limited pluralism is the most distinctive feature of bureaucratic-authoritarian regimes and research and analysis of this aspect is likely to be most revealing about how the bureaucratic authoritarian pattern of domination is maintained and about emergent sources of political change. It is important to note that corporatism is *one* among alternative patterns and strategies of regime-civil society relationship, and thus should *not* be viewed either as a synonym for this regime type or as an alternative/competing model.[18] Second, while corporatism may be compared with pluralism as alternative ideal-typical patterns and strategies for linking the associationally organized interests of civil society with the decisional structures of the regime, corporatism needs to be further specified in order to make it useful in analysis of empirical cases. I have found "state" corporatism, in which constituent units are created and kept as auxiliary and depen-

---

17. The Panca Sila should not be labeled an ideology (even a rudimentary one) because of its original instrumental character (a compromise establishing limits on parties), lack of logical consistency (one, supreme God vs. democracy), and lack of any future orientation. S. B. Joedono labels it, appropriately, an "anti-ideological device" (see his "Notes Toward the Understanding of the Indonesian Revolution" [Ph.D. dissertation, State University of New York at Albany, 1971], ch. 4). Among the wide and vague assortment of ideas relating to modernization and development, sharp contrasts are noticeable between civilian and military circles on the scope and permanence of the military's dual role and on the most appropriate structure for a modern Indonesian society (pluralist model of Western social science vs. organic and corporative arrangements).

18. Corporatism does not belong to the same class of models/constructs with neopatrimonial regime and bureaucratic-authoritarian regime; hence, Donald Emmerson's (1979) juxtaposition of corporatism and neopatrimonialism is inaccurate. The reason for not equating bureaucratic-authoritarianism and corporatism is to allow for the possibility that a bureaucratic-authoritarian regime may achieve limitation of pluralism without a corporatist strategy. On this possibility, see Clement Henry Moore, "Authoritarian Politics in Unincorporated Society: The Case of Nasser's Egypt," *Comparative Politics* (January 1974), pp. 193-218.

dent organs of the state, more applicable to New Order politics than "societal" corporatism in which the legitimacy and functioning of the state depends on the support and recognition of constituent autonomous associational units.[19] Through state corporatism, a regime attempts not only to structure relations *between* civil society and the public authority in a polity but also to structure many crucial relationships within civil society as well.

The bureaucratic-authoritarian model alerts us to major gaps and shortcomings in the existing literature on New Order politics by giving more independent weight to the role of the state in politics and by emphasizing state-societal linkages or the strategies and mechanisms for limiting pluralism. Preoccupation with "basic" sociocultural phenomena and variables (e.g., *aliran*), and the dominant theoretical approaches to politics--liberal-pluralist and Marxist alike--have downplayed and/or denied a purely and calculatedly political role to the Indonesian state, arising from the *relative* but significant autonomy of the state's executive decisional element from immediately enforceable accountability to any single social group, faction, class, aliran, or institution.[20] The model redirects us to investigate the devices and/or practices through which executive power becomes progressively more autonomous and suggests that the regime's dynamic conservative properties may provide it more policy flexibility, general structural stability, and thus capacity to survive international pressures and the endogenous clashes of national "classes" than we think possible. It also implies that the contradictions of bureaucratic-authoritarian rule, the nature of its vulnerability, are peculiarly political and administrative-- "more closely linked to the *forms* in which state power is organized, the distributional effect of policy on agents of the state, and the means whereby state authority is transferred from one set of supporters to another."[21] In other words, the course of internal political change will likely be determined less by social mobilization, class, sectoral, and regional group conflict, electoral activity, legislative debates, ideological pronouncements and even revolutionary struggle--main concerns in much journalistic and academic literature--and more by

> shifting coalitions currying for special favor with their national leader; infighting between bureaucratic agencies for control over policy areas and within agencies for personal power and status; complex maneuvers in the hierarchy of military command; discrete devolutions of decisional authority from peripheral to central political institutions; defensive efforts by corporatized interest groups to protect existing privilege against further incursions of the state; preemptive co-optation of emergent class and sectoral leaders; unreported and unobserved acts of intimidation against individual opponents; prudent self-censorship by intellectuals and mass media; and the mobilization of legal violence through repressive police and judicial actions.[22]

The gathering of this type of information requires attention to behaviors that are difficult to measure, extraordinary attention to context, and a special sensitivity to

---

19. The frequent failure among scholars to delineate these very different subtypes of corporatism, perhaps as a result of thinking about corporatism only in terms of the estate structure of feudal domination (Weber), may explain why some have facilely pronounced it to be inapplicable to the New Order.

20. See, for example, the students' accusation that state institutions have been fixed so as not to interfere with the buildup of executive power, "White Book of the 1978 Students' Struggle," *Indonesia*, 25 (April 1978), pp. 151-82.

21. Schmitter, "Liberation by *Golpe*," p. 102.

22. Schmitter, "Paths to Political Development," pp. 104-5.

what does not occur as well as what does. The models utilized or implied in much of the existing literature on New Order politics have led scholars to focus almost exclusively on state-societal linkage through informal, personalistic, dyadic ties (political clientelism) and political parties. Because of the New Order's simplification and manipulation of electoral politics, fascination with the latter may be waning; what continues to be stressed are clientelistic networks and factions that channel patronage, although the extent of downward reach varies depending on the model, and the maintenance of regime hegemony through force or the threat of it.

Patron-client exchange is central to both the bureaucratic polity and neopatrimonial models and is to a considerable extent complementary with an underdeveloped-dependency perspective as well; it constitutes the most important basis of interest articulation and sociopolitical control. However, insufficient attention has been given to several problems that occur with so heavy reliance on clientelism to describe power relations and political process. One problem is the confusion that results from attempting to treat several analytically separate levels (individual, small group, large scale organization, national, and international) simultaneously. Whereas most writers who mention political clientelism start out with elaboration of individual orientations or dyadic relationships (micro-level), their focus expands rather quickly to some larger unit of analysis--to parties, bureaucracies, or even entire national political systems. Simply spelling out the way in which clientage bonds aggregate into large-scale systems of collective behavior is not sufficient.[23] It leaves unanswered the question, to what level can the patron-client concept be extended without at the same time risking the reductionism that inheres in any attempt to derive and describe macro-units in terms of micro concepts? Robert Kaufman points out,

> The conceptual distinction between a purely clientelist macrosystem and its non-clientelist environment, however, becomes less viable as the analytical focus shifts to levels larger than the "little community"--i.e. to large-scale organizations and national systems. *The larger the macro-unit, in other words, the more necessary it becomes to introduce into the analysis properties and assumptions which are not implied by and cannot be derived from the patron-client concept. And what is still more important, it would seem advisable to treat many of these not merely as environmental "givens" but as integral parts of the macro-system itself.*[24]

The larger the level of analysis the more important it is to consider "nonvertical" peer group relationships (e.g., class or interest coalescence or rivalry, more or less formally organized relationships within elite sectors such as CSIS cf. HANKAM), interplay among subunits that are themselves more complex than the interchange between individual patrons and clients (e.g., the military, the Chinese, the expatriate business community, the santri Muslims),[25] legal structures and codes

---

23. The two most common ways of applying the patron-client concept at the macro-level of analysis is to treat clientelism as a variable attribute of macrosystems and to conceptualize large-scale, "clientelist" social formations which are derived logically from the basic patron-client dyad, e.g., clusters, pyramids.

24. Robert R. Kaufman, "The Patron-Client Concept and Macro-Politics: Prospects and Problems," *Comparative Studies in Society and History*, 16 (1974), p. 293.

25. "Sub-structures organized internally along clientelist lines may relate to one another through confrontation, bargaining, and alliance, as well as through hierarchical, reciprocal relations. . . . Even if this were not the case, however, the postulation of a patron-client relation among *groups* rather than individuals risks

which, even where public law is weak, provide an important framework of roles, privilege, and resources which advantage some sectors and disadvantage others (e.g., police permits required to hold an associational meeting, regulations granting public facilities to KNPI and FBSI affiliates, compulsory arbitration of labor disputes in tripartite councils), nonclientelistic opposition movements (e.g., student movement of 1977-78), and nonclientelist factors in linkage between the national and international systems (e.g., TNC's, preferential trade agreements, IGGI, OPEC).

Another problem is defining large scale clientelist systems and distinguishing them from other types of large-scale collectivities. Clientelist organizations, allegedly, are characterized by the exercise of personal power, by the permeation of formal structures with informal cliques, and by the particularistic, private goods distributed to followers.[26] The difficulty with the last two defining characteristics is that they describe characteristics of virtually all large-scale organizations. All bureaucratic organizations and formal associations are permeated in some degree by informal cliques[27] and substantial individual contributions of time and effort will depend on the capacity of the organization to deliver some sort of narrow, selective benefit or sanctions.[28] Furthermore,

> the tendency to dismiss formal rules and norms as "facades" which disguise the reality of personal rule is much overemphasized in analyses of clientelist organizations. The persistence of any large-scale organization, clientelist or not, implies at least some regulative matrix of rules and norms. And even where public definition of authority roles are subordinated to the direct personal "enforcement" of the patron-client contract, these formal structures do provide organization leaders with the means to hire and fire, to grant favors, and to appropriate funds for private use. At the very least, formal structures are relevant to patron-client systems, if only because they provide the critical resources necessary to build and sustain such a system.[29]

The bureaucratic-authoritarian model, by drawing attention to regime attempts to achieve a limitation of pluralism, often through corporatism, can assist us in finding solutions to these conceptual and empirical deficiencies. I have described the New Order's attempt to establish a corporatist network of interest intermediation and argued that it is an increasingly important channel of interest articulation and sociopolitical control.[30] I am suggesting that corporatism, similar to clientelism in being hierarchical but contrasting in being a *macro* concept or operating principle, is a useful addition to our conceptual arsenal because it enables us to describe and understand a larger portion of New Order political structures and processes than clientelism alone.

---

reification of the groups (how can groups be related on a face-to-face basis?) and suggests that other concepts, besides those of clientelism, are required." Ibid., p. 294.

26. Roth, "Personal Rulership," pp. 194-206.

27. Peter M. Blau, *Exchange and Power in Social Life* (New York: Wiley, 1961).

28. Mancur Olsen, *The Logic of Collective Action* (New York: Schocken Books, 1971).

29. Kaufman, "Patron-Client Concept," p. 301.

30. Dwight Y. King, "Social Mobilization, Associational Life, Interest Intermediation and Political Cleavage in Indonesia" (Ph.D. dissertation, University of Chicago, 1978).

First, it enables us better to comprehend and delineate nonclientelistic forms of organization (e.g., based on group identification/goals, or coercion/manipulation rather than personal authority) that can be expected to become more salient as modernization proceeds. In my research I found that, despite the decimation of the PKI and affiliates, manipulation of the surviving political parties, and close surveillance of spontaneous collective activity, 47 percent of rural household heads (N = 700) in West Java (Keb. Bandung and Cianjur) claimed membership in at least one type of more or less formal secondary group or voluntary association and another 34 percent were members of two or more. As pointed out above, the student movements of 1973-74 and 1977-78 do not appear to have had clientelist bases. In Jakarta, I found about fifty business and professional representative associations, some of which appear to have evolved continuously since the pre-Independence period (e.g., INSA, PERPADI, SPS), the Republican period (e.g., PERBANAS, GKBI, IKAPI), or Guided Democracy (former OPS) and others of which emerged spontaneously (e.g., PIBA, IKINDO, HIPMI) or were established by the authorities during the New Order (GAAKINDO, KADIN).

Second, corporatism draws attention to a large realm of public policy activity, neither particularistic nor generally instrumental in nature, intended to promote modernization defensively. The corporatist concept can be understood as the monopolization of interest representation by noncompeting, officially sanctioned functional organizations which are supervised by agents of the state bureaucracy. In ideal typical terms, state corporatist systems are vertically segmented societies, encapsulating individuals and groups within a network of legally defined structures which derive their legitimacy from and integrated by a single bureaucratic center. It thus alerts us to the possibility that, unlike the experience of Europe and the US, Indonesia's rulers seek to avoid the great historical discontinuities and profound social cleavages associated with modernization and the capitalist development process by obfuscating authority and expanding privilege in ways that preempt and co-opt new social forces and defuse their revolutionary potential, e.g., establishment of semicompulsory associations for labor (FBSI), middle peasants (HKTI), youth and students (KNPI), national entrepreneurs (KADIN), Islamic religious leaders (MU).

Third, it can help us make sense of or accommodate the seemingly contradictory findings of fluid, clientelistic patterns on the one hand, and the trend toward formal centralism on the other. The relationship between corporatism and clientelism can be seen as highly functional or symbiotically interconnected. "On the one hand, corporatist arrangements discourage autonomous group competition and perpetuate more particularistic forms of individual problem-solving behavior. Clientelistic forms of problem-solving behavior, in turn, vastly increase the flexibility of what would otherwise be quite rigid corporatist legal structures."[31]

Is it really worthwhile to expend time and energy studying interest intermediation and corporatism which, admittedly, is a dependent (affected) aspect of the Indonesian political system at the present time? A negative reply, I suspect, might refer to the evidence that corporatism is being implemented gradually, pragmatically, and often nominally and contradictorily. More likely, the skeptic would mention that we lack evidence of much transmittal of interests upward or of the delegation of authority to semiautonomous bodies who govern their respective fields on behalf of the state. Although I found some evidence of such positive functions,[32]

---

31. Robert R. Kaufman, "Corporatism, Clientelism and Partisan Conflict: A Study of Seven Latin American Countries," in *Authoritarianism and Corporatism in Latin America*, ed. James M. Malloy (Pittsburgh: University of Pittsburgh, 1977), p. 113.

32. Although I concluded that business and professional interest associations are

the best rebuttal is that state corporatism should be assessed not primarily in terms of what it openly and positively accomplishes, but in terms of what it surreptitiously and negatively prevents from happening. Corporatism has functioned admirably elsewhere to prevent the emergence of obvious class hegemony or polarized group confrontation that would have likely jeopardized the autonomy of state executive power.

Another cause of skepticism may be rooted in the confusion of two types of mobilization, one delineated by Karl Deutsch and the other by David Apter. Different strata of the population may be mobilized and different political processes may be associated with each type. If mobilization is used in the Deutschian sense, a strategy of corporatist organization will be viewed as *exclusionary*, as squelching participation. For persons who value participation, who view it as evidence of political development or who view it to be the fount of political power, state corporatism will be a negative thing and, perhaps, not worthy of serious study. But if mobilization is used in the Apterian sense, a strategy or corporatism can be viewed as *inclusionary* or as directed toward mobilization without participation. It is in this latter sense that one can detect a shift in New Order strategy following the 1971 elections toward increased, controlled mobilization of the urban population through corporatist structures.

Finally, I wish to return to my earlier assertion about the historical-contextual sensitivity of the bureaucratic-authoritarian model. It has been formulated out of rethinking about the interaction between political, economic, and social spheres that occurs in the course of industrial modernization. The formulators have sought to avoid the mistakes of earlier modernization theory, resulting from the presumed universality of assumptions about political change, by taking greater care to specify the particular context under analysis in terms of theoretically relevant variables. It is postulated, for example, that the interaction among patterns of economic, social and political change that have occurred in the context of late, dependent, capitalist industrialization help to explain the emergence of the bureaucratic-authoritarian type of political domination. I doubt, however, that these economic arguments are sufficient in the case of Indonesia or that this greater contextually sensitive modeling is entirely free from the interaction between American academic culture and American interests abroad.[33] In addition to the economic arguments, I have pointed to the influence of Old-Java political traditions, cultural predispositions, cultural pluralism and social polarization, clientelistic forms of electoral mobilization and weakness of prosystem conservative and moderate parties, fragmentation of national leadership, centrality of the civil bureaucracy, political orientation of the army, and international pressures fomenting the protracted coup and helping to consolidate power in the New Order.[34]

---

not very salient political forces and have only limited capacity to influence policy making, still nearly two-thirds reported initiatory activity or having pressed upon an authority group a specific project and most claim a measure of success. Associations tend to concentrate on certain stages of the decisional process: signaling or bringing problems to attention, consultation and negotiation, and above all, revision and renegotiation.

33. Anderson, "Perspective and Method." The central thrust of political research on the Third World shifted in the 1970s from a concern with democratization and "Westernization" to a concern with the difficult issues of national political economy.

34. Dwight Y. King, "Authoritarian Rule and State Corporatism in Indonesia," Paper presented at annual meeting of American Political Science Association Meetings, Washington, D.C., 1977.

INDONESIA SINCE 1945--
PROBLEMS OF INTERPRETATION

Jamie Mackie

This paper had its origins in two sets of arguments about contemporary Indonesian politics. One of these, to which I will be returning in due course, is a debate that Herb Feith and I have been conducting for several years (or perhaps something less grandiose and structured than that, a low-level skirmishing engagement) over the relative merits or otherwise of various radical critiques of the Suharto regime as against the views commonly advanced in defense of it. The other was a discussion I had recently with two colleagues who are also involved in teaching undergraduates what present-day Indonesia is all about, in the course of which we talked about the difficulties that arise when we try to incorporate the whole story of Indonesian politics since 1945 within a single analytical framework. For we then have to embrace under one overarching explanatory theory such sharply contrasting political systems as President Suharto's "New Order" and President Sukarno's "Old Order," not to mention the very different political dynamics of the "liberal democracy" period (1950-59) and of the 1945-49 "revolution" or struggle for independence. As soon as one begins to think about this problem, one has to assess the relative significance of the radical discontinuities in Indonesian political and social life to which these labels draw attention, as well as the underlying continuities in Indonesian society, culture and history which equally deserve attention.

I am not proposing that we should attempt to formulate some kind of new generalized theory along these lines, but I would emphasize that it is important to see the changes that have taken place in Indonesia since 1965-66 within a broader historical perspective, which also takes into account other long-term processes that have been working themselves out there ever since 1945--and, indeed, much longer. In that context, the policies pursued by the Suharto government since 1966 are, I believe, more explicable and more defensible than they appear if presented, as they often are, solely in the light of recently fashionable theories of "dependencia" or neo-colonialism, or the view that an all-powerful Army-backed government should be capable of remedying many of the ills that still afflict the country, if it really wanted to do so. I would argue that in most respects it probably does *want* to do so, but simply has not always been able to: first, because it is often not sure how to go about it,[1] and second, because while the government and the Army are,

---

1. The Indonesian authorities have absorbed into their own rhetoric many of the ideas and policies advanced by opponents of the regime, about more egalitarian distribution patterns, popular participation and basic human needs, thereby depriving them of some of their force and meaning. In many respects, some of them seem quite genuinely to want to achieve the objectives stated, though not by the same

indeed, vastly more powerful than either was before 1965, they can only accomplish their will with the means available to them--and the means are still very limited in the Indonesian situation, for various reasons which are rooted deeply in the nation's culture and history. In this respect, continuity is still a powerful and pervasive fact of life there. So many features of the political system have not changed very greatly, even though others have.

I do not mean here simply to offer excuses for the many shortcomings of which the Suharto government can be accused; on the contrary, I believe it would and should have pursued very different policies in numerous respects, from the treatment of ex-communists and political prisoners to corruption, extravagance and social inequalities.[2] But in making judgments on these matters, we must avoid excessively mechanistic or deterministic theories--as well as extraneously moralistic or utopian ones--about why governments or officials behave as they do and try to take into account the particular historical reasons why they have responded to the situations confronting them as they did, why they have given priority to some sets of considerations and objectives over others for reasons which we may not readily comprehend. Essentially I am arguing for a more pluralistic and historically grounded approach to the task of explaining recent events in Indonesia and interpreting their significance, not the superimposing of externally derived explanatory models or irrelevant ethical standards.

One of the major shortcomings of some of the currently popular theories which seem *prima facie* to account for Indonesia's "underdevelopment" is that while they may seem to fit the most salient facts of the New Order period, they do not serve nearly as well if we try to apply them to the earlier years of Indonesia's independence. Interpretations in terms of neocolonialist dominance of the Indonesian economy by foreign investors since 1967 do not fit comfortably against the facts that Dutch business interests there (and British and American) found themselves forced increasingly on to the defensive during the 1950s and early '60s, or that there was only a negligible flow of foreign capital into Southeast Asia from any of the advanced capitalist countries at that time--for reasons which had little to do with the Asian countries themselves. Hobsonian or Leninist theories of imperialism just did not match the facts of that period at all well.[3] So if one is going to try to apply them

---

routes as their critics have in mind. In a 1973 seminar at Monash, Centre of Southeast Asian Studies, Lt. Gen. Ali Moertopo spoke about the need for "alternative development strategies" with an almost glowing enthusiasm.

2. Some of the most trenchant criticisms of the Suharto government's economic policies I have encountered have been made by staunch supporters of the regime and of the "technocrats" advising it on economic policies; see, for example, Bruce Glassburner's comments on monetary policy and inappropriately capital-intensive investments in "Political Economy and the Soeharto Regime," *Bulletin of Indonesian Economic Studies* (hereafter *BIES*), 14, 3 (Nov. 1978), pp. 37, 43-45; also H. W. Arndt, "Survey of Recent Developments," *BIES*, 14, 1 (March 1978), pp. 27-28.

3. I know of no neocolonialist interpretation of Indonesian politics (or of any other Southeast Asian country) which has actually dug out the statistics of capital inflows at different times or from different countries. Nor does any point out that despite the high levels of foreign investment *approvals* in Indonesia since about 1970, the rates of actually *realized* investment have been very low, averaging about $200 million p.a., a rate well below Singapore's rate of capital inflow. I am indebted for this information to Peter McCauley, *The Indonesian Economy Under Suharto* (forthcoming).

to the New Order period, one must be able to show (within the terms of such theories themselves) why they did not work for the earlier years.

I do not want to say much here about the debate over the strengths and weaknesses of the various radical critiques, which would need more extensive treatment than I can spare them here. But although I reject many of the more mechanistic theories on which these critiques are based and am trying to offer here an alternative approach to the problem of characterizing and explaining Suharto's "New Order" in Indonesia, two things should be said about them at the outset. First, these theories, although often crudely formulated and overstated, in my opinion, do pose a challenge even to those of us who are reluctant to espouse them, just because they come uncomfortably close to the truth in many respects and because they direct attention to shortcomings of the Indonesian government and its policies which cannot be disregarded, however little we may like to face them in plain terms. There is simply too much corroborating evidence that they are at least partially right, though we may argue at length about how far. Second, one must admit that there are some elements of these theories which, if formulated with due care and precision, do seem to provide a plausible explanation of key characteristics of the present regime--e.g., its repressiveness, the elite-orientation of many of its policies and its lack of effective action on behalf of the poorest segments of the rural and urban population.[4] (There is nothing unique about Indonesia in that last respect, of course!) I do not advocate, therefore, that these theories should be altogether thrown out and disregarded; but neither do I find them wholly satisfactory or acceptable.

My objections to these interpretations of the present regime in Indonesia center mainly around their underlying logic rather than the empirical evidence on which they rest.[5] First, they are frequently oversimplified, excessively deterministic or mechanistic in establishing causal connections and sometimes intrinsically unverifiable (i.e., of a kind that cannot be shown to be false by the production of contrary evidence). One of the strongest reasons why these theories have had such a widespread appeal has been the fact that they seem *prima facie* to offer such a rounded watertight explanation of so many striking features of the current regime and to have an exact "fit" with the salient political events and data about socio-economic

---

4. It is difficult to deny the force of the systemic connection between these elements in Benedict Anderson's charge that "the treatment of political prisoners is not an isolated blemish on an otherwise humane record. . . . Although there are many sincere and idealistic people both inside and outside the Indonesian government who are seriously concerned about the situation and would very much like to improve it . . . the channels for expressing concern are being steadily closed and the risks involved increasing. . . . The problem lies not in individuals abusing their authority but with a government that has shown itself over a whole decade to be increasingly authoritarian, suspicious of its own citizens and indifferent to the rights of the weak and vulnerable." Prepared Testimony of the Question of Human Rights in Indonesia; Subcommittee on International Organizations of the Committee on International Relations, House of Representatives, US Congress, May 3, 1976.

5. In their more popularized forms, theories that purport to explain Indonesia's ills in terms of "neocolonialism" or "dependency" are often expressed in tautologous fashion, impervious to contrary arguments and evidence. Even in *Showcase State*, ed. Rex Mortimer (Angus & Robertson, 1973), which gives a fully worked out formulation of these arguments, one finds in the best chapter, Rex Mortimer's "Indonesia: Growth or Development," a tendency to couch his definitions in such a way that the conclusions he wishes to draw are logically inescapable under that definition, hence empirically untestable (e.g., pp. 54 and 57).

trends they purport to deal with, describe and explain, although the situation is almost always more tangled than they allow for and the causal factors more complex. But complex explanations are rarely as appealing as simple ones. Moreover, the latter kind frequently imply a ringing condemnation of the regime, on impeccably high-minded grounds, pointing towards the conclusion that only through a root-and-branch "revolutionary" transformation of the socio-political order can the country's present ills be remedied. No good can come of piecemeal technocratic reforms or administrative tinkering at the fringes of the problems, according to this line of argument. They need to be tackled at a more fundamental level--whatever that means in Indonesia's circumstances.

My second objection is that these views generally fail to take account of the multilayered, or overlapping, character of so many of Indonesia's most crucial socio-economic problems, which are simply not susceptible to easy solutions at one level of any kind, radical or conservative. While radical theories may highlight much that is true about the seamier side of Indonesian political and economic life, they do not present the whole truth. Above all, they tend to neglect the historical dimensions that must be taken into account in explaining the main socio-economic changes taking place there in recent decades, especially overpopulation, poverty and social stagnation. The root of these problems must be sought several generations back in the past in most cases, not just in what has been happening since 1965-66, critically important though the latter changes have certainly been. It is not only that problems like the inexorable, long-term pressure of overpopulation and deteriorating man-land ratios also have to be taken into account in any analysis of poverty, for example, but also the development over the last 80 years or more of societal values, both of rulers and the ruled, as well as traditional attitudes towards government, authority, fate (*nasib*) and free will, and the ideas of "progress" (*kemajuan*) and modernization or "development" (e.g., what Indonesians envisage by *pembangunan*), all of which must be taken into account as objective givens in the situation confronting any government attempting to change the social order.

A third objection is related to that. Many of these critical theories attribute too much of the blame for the country's ills solely to the current policies of the government, whereas most of the problems have been defying attempts to solve them since 1900. These theories assume that governments have a far greater degree of capacity to control or direct social processes in Indonesia than has been, in my experience, the case since 1945. Yet by 1965-66, the country's tax revenues amounted to a mere 4 percent of GDP and the atrophy of the various instruments of control available to the government had utterly wrecked its capacity for effective planning and administration.[6] Since then, the government has restored these mechanisms quite remarkably (e.g., that 4 percent is now 21 percent) and greatly enhanced its administrative potentialities, but anyone who knows Indonesia (or any other developing country) will be familiar with the tremendous limitations upon what her bureaucratic machinery can accomplish by way of social engineering. It can exert some influence where the granting of resources can be made conditional on the adoption of desired policies or where repression can have a preventive effect. It has become administratively more effective mainly because foreign aid, initially, and oil revenues, later, have provided it with far more resources to dispose in this way. But it has had a feeble record in matters like the levying of personal income or land taxes, or preventing illegal occupation of forest lands, or reducing the size of an overbloated bureaucracy, to mention only the most obvious. And it has not only

---

6. I have dealt more fully with this point in "The Atrophy of Control Mechanisms" in my *Problems of the Indonesian Inflation* (Ithaca: Cornell Modern Indonesia Project, Monograph Series, 1967), pp. 53-60.

been unable to prevent widespread corruption, but unable even to prevent it becoming worse over the last decade, for reasons which have to do with both the socio-political structure of the regime and deeply ingrained cultural attitudes. Yet anyone who has looked at all closely at the profession of accountancy in Indonesia, its virtual collapse during the years of inflation, the feeble traditions of financial accountability or the sanctions behind the concept, and even the paucity of trained accountants, would hardly find that surprising. In circumstances like that any government would be critically handicapped, no matter whether communist or capitalist, colonial or independent, made up of saints and sinners, or of Jacobinical root-and-branch revolutionaries rather than hard-nosed technocratic incrementalists. Even with the record of China's transformation after 1949 in mind, I am skeptical that Indonesia's problems are susceptible to drastic political surgery or sweeping solutions of the Chinese variety.[7] Her problems are not just the outcome of the policies pursued since 1966 (e.g., high foreign investment levels, IMF-World Bank monetary policies, adoption of advanced technology, etc.), although it could not be denied that in some respects these policies have created or reinforced structural tendencies in the political system which make solutions harder to achieve. The roots of her problems go much further back into the past, as Geertz showed well in *Agricultural Involution*, and their solutions will require measures which are bound to be slow and piecemeal. Likewise, their analysis will have to be both piecemeal, intricate, and above all precise.

When one takes these kinds of considerations into account, one is less inclined to jump to sweeping judgments about the shortcomings of the country's present leaders or the policies they have been trying to follow than if one measures them against some abstract standard that is simply inappropriate to the country's situation. Conversely, criticisms of the regime by Indonesians such as the poet Rendra or the legal aid activist, Bujung Nasution, or Islamic leaders, all of whom invoke an idiom and standards of behavior which are meaningful to other Indonesians, carry far more conviction than cliches which depict the ruling generals as mere puppets of neocolonialist masters. This point is so obvious that it should hardly need to be mentioned were it not for the fact that many of the more superficial critics seem to find the generals so distasteful that they are not interested in learning what makes them tick in the way they do.

But I do not want to pursue these points further here. My primary purpose is to argue the case for using a broader frame of reference, which will enable us to formulate a more coherent analysis of Indonesian social and political developments over the last 30-40 years, so that our picture is not unduly dominated by the pattern of events that has been emerging since 1966. I want more stress on the continuities over that broader period, since these will undoubtedly stretch forward into the future also, as well as on the striking discontinuities of 1965-66 and 1959.

At the same time, we must remember that our interpretations of earlier events are inevitably colored by our awareness of what has happened subsequently and the significance we attribute to them is bound to be affected by that. Earlier writers on Indonesia saw events in a very different light, partly because what they

---

7. Robert Reid Smith has made a persuasive case for the relevance to Javanese rural conditions of the Chinese model of collectivization in "Impasse in Java's Agriculture: The Case for Chinese Style Collectivization" (M.A. thesis, Monash University, Politics Department, 1974). But the political feasibility of carrying through such policies seems so remote as to be out of the question. Even when the PKI was at the peak of its strength in 1964-65, if it had made any bid to seize power in Java and carry through a collectivization of land, it would almost certainly have precipitated the secession of the islands controlling the country's main export resources.

then took to be the end-point of the story they were telling, the culmination of the course of events they were describing, seemed to them to give their story quite a different character and significance from that which they would attribute to it today. A classic example of this effect can be seen in George Kahin's admirable pioneering study of *Nationalism and Revolution in Indonesia*, published in 1952; this told the story of post-independence politics largely in terms of a power struggle between political parties within a quasi-parliamentary system of government, for these seemed then to be the key features of the political structure in the 1945-50 period. Yet later we discovered that political parties and the parliamentary system had put down only shallow roots in Indonesian soil. When they came under challenge in 1957-58, very few prominent political leaders were prepared to defend them. (One exception was Mohammed Hatta, but in a very qualified vein.) So liberal democracy collapsed, largely through sheer lack of supporters, as Herb Feith showed so well.[8]

Feith himself wrote another account of Indonesian society and politics in 1958-59, which seemed at the time to give an entirely satisfactory, illuminating characterization of a puzzling, unfamiliar process. Yet twenty years later, nearly all the key features of that society and the changes taking place in it seem utterly irrelevant to the Indonesia we see today:

> No single adjective better characterises present-day Indonesia than 'post-revolutionary'. Indonesian society today is vastly different from Indonesian society twenty years ago, because of independence and the way in which it was achieved and because of the tumultuous political and society changes of the Japanese occupation and particularly of the revolution.[9]

He went on to elaborate this picture of tumultuous changes in terms of the collapse of the old colonial caste structure and the emergence during the revolutionary struggle for independence of new groups of leaders with new types of qualifications; new mass organizations had arisen, "undermining local loyalties and replacing them with loyalties to the nation and to political ideologies," while thousands of Indonesians experienced the profound disruption of being uprooted from their villages during the war and revolution, when they were mobilized for forced labor or military service. It was a picture of a society in ferment, undergoing intense political and ideological mobilization. No one could seriously question the accuracy of his account. But one must wonder how it can possibly be that Indonesian society twenty years later seems so utterly different, depoliticized to a quite depressing degree. One of the best characterizations of that society in the 1970s was given by Lance Castles in a paper which put the emphasis at quite the other end of the spectrum, on the stifling dominance of the bureaucracy and the almost complete lack of alternative channels for political activity. One might almost ask if they were talking about the same country.

* * *

As is so often the case, we find in the writings of Clifford Geertz a revealing clue to the problem of sorting out these contradictions and imposing some kind of order upon our interpretations of recent events in Indonesia. How can we decide what meaning or significance to attribute to particular events or phenomena in such

---

8. Herbert Feith, *The Decline of Constitutional Democracy in Indonesia* (Ithaca: Cornell University Press, 1963), pp. 597-608 and passim.

9. Herbert Feith, "Indonesia," in *Governments and Politics of Southeast Asia*, ed. George McT. Kahin (Ithaca: Cornell University Press, 1959), p. 181.

a richly variegated socio-cultural landscape as Indonesia's, in which Indonesians themselves attach such diverse metaphysical meanings to all that goes on around them? We are confronted, says Geertz, with a veritable "garden of metaphors" which they use to describe the complexities of the world around them in an attempt to bring it into some sort of comprehensible order and coherence.[10] All of these need to be taken seriously just because they carry meaning for those who use them, but the consequence is that we face a formidable task of deciding which to accept or reject as we construct our own conceptual models. Because of the Byzantine complexities, ambiguities and subtleties of Indonesian (especially Javanese) social and political phenomena, it is, says Geertz, "really impossible to frame an argument relating political events . . . which is totally lacking in plausibility."[11] But if no hypothesis is unequivocally ruled out, none can be exclusively and unchallengably right, either. "Many are the roads," as the *priyayi* Javanese would put it, with their tolerant and relativistic approach to both morality and epistemology.

Geertz was primarily concerned, in the article cited, with the question of what significance or meaning we should attribute to the "vast internal trauma" of 1965-66 in Indonesia and the terrible killings that accompanied the destruction of the Communist Party. How do we--either outsiders or Indonesians--fit that into our patterns of explanation of events before and since? Geertz, writing before 1970, saw the upheaval as a demonstration of the depth of "dissensus, ambivalence, and disorientation" among Indonesians, asserting that whether or not this conclusion was acceptable to Indonesians, it was "the central question of Indonesian politics."[12] I doubt if many Indonesians would like to have the problem discussed in quite those terms by a foreigner; on the other hand, most are probably reluctant to engage in serious discussion of the problem at all. Yet Geertz is surely right in stressing the singular difficulty Indonesians face in either interpreting and explaining the great upheaval of 1965-66 or in attributing broader meaning to it as a major landmark in the life of their nation. Few Indonesians have addressed themselves deliberately to the task of assessing its origins and significance, except in terms of the conventional wisdom that it was a crucial episode in the life-and-death struggle for survival against the communist threat.[13] Like the people of many other countries who have terrible memories they would rather expunge, most Indonesian intellectuals tend to shy away from the awkward questions the episode poses--and who are we to blame them? But the unfortunate consequence is that most of the writings yet undertaken about the coup attempt and its consequences and significance have been the work of foreigners, with their very different viewpoints and moral values. (How would *we* react to an account of the drama couched in terms of the moral dilemmas and values conveyed in the Bratayudha?) One is reminded, incidentally, of

---

10. Clifford Geertz, "Afterword: The Politics of Meaning," in *Culture and Politics in Indonesia*, ed. Claire Holt et al. (Ithaca: Cornell University Press, 1972), p. 322.

11. Ibid.

12. Ibid., pp. 333-34.

13. The most carefully argued Indonesian account of the coup attempt is by Nugroho Notosusanto and Ismael Saleh, *The Coup Attempt of the 'September 30th Movement' in Indonesia* (Jakarta: Pembimbing Masa, 1968). Several Indonesian writers have ventured to deal with some aspects of the coup; e.g., Umar Kayam's two short stories, "Bawuk" and "Musim Gugur di Connecticut" and Usamah, "Perang dan Manusia" ("War and Humanity: Notes on Personal Experiences," *Indonesia*, 9 [October 1970], pp. 89-100). See also *Gestapu: Indonesian Short Stories on the Abortive Communist Coup of 30th September 1965*, ed. and trans. Harry Aveling (Honolulu: University of Hawaii, Southeast Asian Studies Working Paper, No. 6, 1975).

Mao Tse-tung's complaint, related by Simon Leys, that none of China's creative writers has yet dared to tackle the mighty theme of the Cultural Revolution--presumably because it would have been perilous, as well as psychologically painful, for them to do so.[14]

The coup and the killings that followed must, undoubtedly, be regarded as one of the great landmarks of Indonesia's history, but one which has left a terrible psychic scar; hence one of the greatest of the discontinuities of the last half-century, one which will be much harder to incorporate into an acceptable nationalist mythology than August 1945 or July 1959. It has had a pervasive effect on the character of the Suharto government, which has found the effort to create a new institutional basis for its power and a new source of legitimacy extremely difficult, since the PKI's former constituency has had to be relegated to the sidelines and treated as almost without continuing rights. And because we are all naturally inclined towards the view that great events must have great causes, it is not easy to square the far-reaching consequences and significance of that episode with the theory that the coup attempt itself had its origins in a rather amateurish, blundering and hastily contrived conspiracy by a handful of officers, in which the PKI itself was only peripherally involved, although all the evidence seems to point towards that conclusion.[15] How could it happen that an event so limited in itself (and shaped by so many accidental twists of fate) could spark off such a conflagration? One can only answer that question by looking deeply into the character of the Indonesian polity and society before 1965, above all at the social tensions which then burst out into such violence.

I do not pretend to have a very satisfactory explanation of that puzzle, except in terms of the *santri-abangan* rifts in Javanese rural society which had been exacerbated by the "unilateral actions" of the communists over land reform in 1964-65.[16] But if we put too much emphasis on that factor in the explanation, we have a problem later in explaining why and how rural social tensions have been damped down so easily since 1965. Clearly an explanation must be related to the ways in which those local tensions were intermeshed with the struggle for power between the PKI and anticommunist forces in Jakarta, which brings us to questions about the character of the Indonesian state itself. Geertz linked his interpretation to a set of generalizations about the nature of the polity, but his impressions (based on the situation in the late 1960s, apparently) look curiously outdated today, thus serving to warn us yet again that all explanations are rooted in a particular time and circumstances;

> if Indonesia gives any overall impression, it is of a state manqué, a country which, unable to find a political form appropriate to the temper of its people, stumbles on apprehensively from one institutional contrivance to the next. . . . The country [is] . . . as incapable of totalitarianism as it is of constitutionalism.[17]

---

14. Simon Leys, "Introduction," p. 14, to his translation of Chen Jo-Hsi, *The Execution of Mayor Lin* (Indiana University Press, 1978).

15. For a judicious summary of the problems of interpreting the coup, see Harold Crouch, *The Army and Politics in Indonesia* (Ithaca: Cornell University Press, 1978), ch. 4.

16. See Rex Mortimer, *The Indonesian Communist Party and Land Reform, 1959-1965* (Clayton, Vic.: Monash Papers on Southeast Asia, no. 1, 1973).

17. Geertz, "Afterword," p. 323.

One could hardly have anticipated from that description either the powerful centralizing tendencies of 1970-75 or the duration of Suharto's presidency. My own inclination would be to say that, while I broadly agree with Geertz's last sentence, I find the term "a state manqué" more appropriate to the late Sukarno era than Suharto's. The process of nation building has advanced remarkably over the last decade, in my judgment, although national integration cannot yet be simply taken for granted, either in regional or social terms. It is true also that the institutional basis of power (even in the Armed Forces) in Indonesia is still very far from satisfactory. The structure of government is extremely brittle—a term I find less misleading than "unstable," which Indonesia currently is not—and one cannot predict confidently that it would survive a severe economic or political crisis or shock. But in 1978 the lineaments of the state and nation seem to me to be a great deal stronger than they were when Geertz wrote those words, even though the "institutional contrivances" from which the state derives its legitimacy have not changed very much.

* * *

Earlier I suggested that we need a more historical frame of reference for explaining the key trends in recent Indonesian history, one which sheds light on both the continuities and discontinuities of the last forty years. Any search for explanations here must be able to account for the dramatic swings of the political pendulum that have occurred three or four times (at least—some might argue for more) since the collapse of Dutch rule in 1941-42. The events of 1965-66 constitute the most far-reaching of these, but the transition from "liberal" parliamentary democracy to "guided democracy" in 1959 was also a major watershed, as also the 1945 proclamation of independence and, in a lesser degree, the swing in 1948 from a leftward political trend towards the right. One can easily imagine something of a similar kind occurring at the end of the Suharto era, probably to a much lesser degree, whenever or however that might come about. Yet these dramatic changes have significance mainly at the apex of national political life, in determining the character of legitimacy and authority. At lower levels of society their effects are usually felt indirectly, in a rather muted fashion; for in most respects life goes on there much as it did before, the continuities outweighing the discontinuities.

I will conclude by listing some of the factors we need to consider if we want to get a broader perspective on the major developments since 1945 along these lines. Much more would have to be said to bring out their significance to the full, but I hope these comments will at least be sufficient to suggest some fruitful lines of approach.

One of the most remarkable continuities of post-independence Indonesian politics, to my mind, has been the general persistence of the patterns of socio-political alignment that have underlain most of the struggles for power taking place there. Basically the natural mass constituencies of the major political parties have not changed much, apart from alterations of name, or adjustments as one party or another has been eliminated by government decree. Nowhere else in Southeast Asia do we find anything like this almost "natural" basis for party politics (with the exception, perhaps, of Malaysia, although the pattern is rather different there). When we compare the election results of 1971 or 1977 with those of 1955 and 1957, the continuities are most striking, due allowance being made for the elimination of the PKI and the emergence of Golkar as a candidate for the support of the abangan constituency in Central and East Java which previously voted for PNI and PKI.[18] It is

---

18. A comparison of the 1955 and 1971 elections is given by A. van Marle, "Indonesian Electoral Geography under ORLA and ORBA," in *Indonesia after the 1971 Elec-*

noteworthy that the old PKI voters seem to have swung in behind Golkar, the government's standard-bearer (it claims not to be a political party), rather than joined the Muslim parties, their old enemy, even though the latter are now the most vocal opponents of a government which has crushed and harassed the PKI and its supporters. In other words, the basic political polarization between the devoutly Muslim (santri) elements and the syncreticly Muslim (abangan) people in Java, which constituted the basic cleavage around which the political struggle was fought out in the years 1945-65, with the Outer Islands generally tending to align with the former on most issues, has broadly persisted, although the role of the Outer Islands in relation to Golkar and the central power balance in Jakarta has changed somewhat since 1965.

It is well known that the fundamental explanation for this state of affairs lies in the communal or ethnic basis of political loyalties (in Java, the *aliran* cleavages).[19] Against the persistence of these ties, neither the class appeal of the PKI nor the potential for a military-civilian cleavage in the 1970s has been strong enough to change the basic parameters of Indonesian life. Yet we need to understand this central phenomenon of Indonesian politics also within a historical context. Is it something immutable, with roots deep in the past (something to do with the incomplete process of Islamization in Java in the 16th-17th century), or a phenomenon which itself is slowly envolving? I suspect we might find that this socio-religious polarization, while it undoubtedly has roots further back in previous centuries, has been sharpened by the intensification of mobilization politics in Java between 1945-65. There were special reasons why the struggle for power was peculiarly intense at that time--competition between party leaders to mobilize a following on the broadest basis they could find, and the ideological dispute at the heart of Indonesian politics over the question of whether the new state should be constituted on an Islamic or Marxist or Panca Sila basis. Today, however, those factors are a good deal less influential. Is it conceivable that the communal cleavage itself might gradually become less salient as a determinant of political alignments, not tomorrow or the next day, of course, but over a longer life-span? And if so, how long? These are questions of key importance to the assessment of political changes in Indonesia, but they are not easy questions to answer.

The high degree of political mobilization that occurred throughout many levels of Indonesian society in the years 1945-65, which contrasts so sharply with the process of almost complete depoliticization since 1970, constitutes one of the most striking discontinuities of recent decades.[20] The character of the pre-1965 political regime was profoundly affected by it, just as the character of the Suharto regime has been affected by the reaction against all that turbulence and disorder. One of the main reasons why the Army leaders have been so unsympathetic to the idea of revitalizing party politics since 1966 and have, on the contrary, gone to such lengths to emasculate those parties that have been permitted to survive, must be

tions, ed. Oey Hong Lee (Hull Monographs on South-East Asian Studies, no. 5, 1974). See also the excellent study by Ken Ward, *The 1971 Election in Indonesia: An East Java Case Study* (Clayton, Vic.: Monash Papers on Southeast Asia, no. 2, 1974).

19. The best analysis of this problem is given by Ruth McVey in her "Introduction" to Sukarno, *Nationalism, Islam and Marxism* (Ithaca: Cornell Modern Indonesia Project, Monograph Series, 1970).

20. For a good account of the political mobilization processes in rural Java between 1945-55, see Selosoemardjan, *Social Changes in Jogjakarta* (Ithaca: Cornell University Press, 1962), chs. 4-6.

sought in their unhappy memories of the late Sukarno years. At that time, despite many curbs on party freedoms and the fact that elections, both national and regional, had been indefinitely shelved after 1957, the political parties were far from dead and the PKI in particular managed to play a vigorous and influential role by exploiting the opportunities open to it for mass mobilization through demonstrations, slogan campaigns and exploitation of the symbols of nationalism. This was unnerving for many members of the elite who found their positions and privileges under increasing challenge, yet political intrigue became so much a part of the Indonesian way of life that it has been hard for many to change their habits. Around 1970, people in Jakarta who had for years been addicted to the constant excitements, spicy gossip and uncertainty of the capital's endless political maneuverings would often complain that life under the New Order was utterly dull and boring. Like addicts deprived of their drug, they were still subject to lingering cravings.

It would be an oversimplification to attribute the process of depoliticization since 1965 solely to the Army's heavy-handed and repressive measures in defense of its own interests. Initially, there appears to have been something of a revulsion against the all-pervasive politicization (and the exploitation of communal and ethnic sentiments) that had developed during the last years of Sukarno, when individuals in all walks of life were under tremendous pressure to take sides and declare themselves, frequently with their jobs and livelihood at risk. (The "Cultural Manifesto" controversy and intense factional conflict in the sphere of education in 1964 epitomized this trend, which became even more alarming in 1965.) Hence there was apparently a good deal of support for the proposition that political campaigning needed to be damped down to some extent, although the political parties and mass organizations supporting the New Order in 1966-67 had conflicting ideas on how this should be done and how far it should go.[21] In general, however, they were determined to curb the Old Order parties, who were otherwise likely to reemerge as the strongest, and to exclude or handicap the PKI's former supporters somehow or other. But they certainly did not anticipate that the government and Army would go as far as they have in reducing the political parties (and even Golkar itself) to mere cyphers.

The main point to be made here, however, is that the period of intense political mobilization in Indonesia between 1945-65 was a highly abnormal state of affairs. There was nothing quite like it anywhere else in Southeast Asia (not even in Vietnam). I know of no precedent for it in the earlier history of Indonesia, there was no deep commitment to the institutions or practices or values of parliamentary democracy, nor even a very long or meaningful tradition of political party activity before independence was achieved.[22] Hence Indonesians were still looking for a pattern of political institutions appropriate to their "national personality" throughout that period and they have been looking for it ever since. There were few defenders of liberal parliamentary democracy on the 1949-59 pattern, then or now. This is a dismaying thought for advocates of a more democratic form of government, but it should hardly be surprising. One may hope, of course, that just as the pendulum swung initially towards the extreme of very intense political mobilization,

---

21. See Crouch, *Army and Politics*, pp. 247-53.

22. "The Dutch had taught them that government was the wielding of power and the suppression of opposition, not the fostering of democratic practices. Indonesians had had no tradition of democratic government and the Dutch in the Indies generally informed them that democracy was unsuitable for them. . . ." Susan Abeyasekere, *One Hand Clapping: Indonesian Nationalists and the Dutch 1939-42* (Clayton, Vic.: Monash Papers on Southeast Asia, no. 5, 1976), p. 90.

then back to the opposite extreme of excessive demobilization, it may in time swing back and oscillate less violently around a more acceptable mean. It will probably be a long time before it settles down at a point of equilibrium.

Another feature of both the New Order and, in lesser degree, the previous twenty years has been the gradual transmutation of the Indonesian political system into a fully-fledged bureaucratic polity, a *beamtenstaat* or *negara pejabat*. There could be little argument against the proposition that virtually all key decisions and policies are now determined within the bureaucratic apparatus (if we use that term to embrace also the military) in the light of the bureaucracy's notions of what is best for the country and the people. (This is not quite the same as saying that the bureaucracy thinks and acts solely in its own interest.) Other sources of potential countervailing power in the political system have been curbed--and to a large extent in the society also, although Islam remains a symbol and rallying point for dissidence, while students and intellectuals have from time to time been able to assert a degree of independence.

In this respect the character of the Suharto regime has changed greatly since 1966-67, when the "New Order" was a rather motley coalition of Army (but *not* the Air Force, Navy or Police), Muslim organizations, student groups and other anticommunist elements. And the situation contrasts greatly with that of 1945-59, when the bureaucracy inherited from the Dutch was very much on the defensive against the challenges to its authority launched by Republican irregular units, civilian politicians and parliament, the armed forces, political parties, and regional assemblies in their turn. In fact, the future of the *pamong praja* looked very bleak in 1957-58, at a time when administrator types seemed to be losing all their battles with the "solidarity-makers" among the politicos. But Sukarno's inauguration of "guided democracy" restored the bureaucracy to a role of greater importance and since 1966 its position has been steadily strengthened. It is easy to identify a number of factors which have brought about the triumph of the bureaucracy--traditional notions of the state and the "Javanese conception of power," with its stress on the rightness of a concentration of authority, with power streaming down and out from the sacred center; the Dutch legacy of a tutelary rather than participant form of government; the additional strength the central government derives from foreign aid and oil revenues; the predisposition of the first generation of Indonesian nationalists towards anti-capitalist and "socialist" (or at least étatist) views about the relationship of government and society; the weakness of social classes or interest groups capable of articulating alternative ideologies; the general lack of support for notions of either individualism or pluralism. But it is again worth emphasizing that these factors are not immutable. Their influence could wax and wane, even though for the time being the forces making for continuity seem to be dominant here.

Two other trends which one can trace right through the years since 1945 but which have become particularly significant under the New Order are the processes of what I will call elite consolidation and "nation building" (if one may use that hackneyed term in an almost literal sense). About the first of these, I will simply observe that something like a "middle class" is beginning to emerge in the 1970s, particularly in Jakarta and the other big cities, in a sense in which one simply could not use that term during the 1950s. It is a middle class characterized *not* by the ownership of property for the most part, for by far the largest part of it is made up of civil servants, professional people, the salariat generally, with still relatively few businessmen (to regard it as a bourgeoisie in a classical Marxist sense, with a coherent ideology and aspirations to exercise state power in the interests of a class would be quite misleading, in my view), but united--so far as it is--by a shared lifestyle ("the metropolitan superculture") and similar aspirations for the future of their children, by a gradually emerging sense of common interests in greater security of property rights, in less arbitrary government procedures, greater regularity and predictability of administration, even "the rule of law" in some still obscurely formulated sense.[23] The members of this stratum of society do not yet constitute a class in a fully-fledged sense, either as defined by the Marxist criterion of relationship to the means of production, or in a broader sense of sharing common political interests. Most would still tend to identify politically and socially with the communal groups from which they originate (or with the armed forces, in the case of that unique "aliran") and even draw many of their basic ideas, values and attitudes from that source. But change is certainly taking place. Twenty or thirty years ago one would have been more inclined to analyze this phenomenon in terms solely of elite rivalries between the leaders of vertically segmented groups within the community, mainly engaged in a struggle for power to lay down what the character of the new state of Indonesia would be. The differences between them were then more marked than the similarities, but I doubt if one could say that today.

This brings me back to my final point, which is about "nation building" and its relevance to the analysis of recent Indonesian politics. Unless one takes into account the fact that the territorial integration of Indonesia was a matter which could still not be taken for granted throughout the first two decades of independence, one is likely to underestimate the significance of the Suharto government's achievement in this respect. During the 1950s, Indonesia's territorial integrity was directly threatened by regional dissidence on several occasions. Although the threats receded during the "guided democracy" period, the ravages of inflation and administrative breakdown gravely weakened the power of the central government in relation to the provinces and by 1965-66 the possibility of Indonesia's disintegration in the event of serious fighting between communists and anticommunists in Java could not be disregarded. Under the New Order, the situation has been utterly reversed. There has been no significant threat of regional dissidence. In a variety of ways, the processes of government and the economic life of the provinces, even of the most distant and the most neglected of them, have become increasingly bound into the cobweb of common interests, financial and communications linkages, shipping, trade and movement of people that is gradually binding Indonesia together.

Moreover, there is now a much greater sense of common identification with what "Indonesia" stands for than there was prior to 1965, when the conflict between Marxist, Muslim and Panca Sila conceptions of the proper ideological foundations for the state were still unresolved and when the political cleavage between the "Javanese-patrimonial" and "Islamic entrepreneurial" poles of political orientation constituted *the* major rift in the polity. (The resolution of the ideological conflict may have been a brutal process, and the Muslims are still far from happy about their lack of influence in the new regime; but I doubt if their leaders really aspire any longer to the hope of creating an Islamic state.) It must be admitted, of course,

---

23. In a forthcoming article on "Judicial Authority and *Rechtsstaat* in Indonesia," Daniel S. Lev shows well how and why some parts of the new Indonesia middle classes have been striving for the establishment of a *negara hukum* (*rechtsstaat*-- virtually "the rule of law") there, for the sake of "certainty, regularity, protection of personal rights, and procedural equity"--with very limited success so far, for the authority of the law and legal institutions has never been firmly grounded there, even in the colonial era, but with sufficient persistence to make it probable that the idea, because it does have support, will have some influence on the evolution of Indonesian politics. For background information on the Jakarta "middle class," I am greatly indebted to Russell Lapthorne for the opportunity to see drafts of his Monash M.A. thesis on the "metropolitan superculture."

that the centralization of power under the Suharto regime, over both the armed forces in 1969-70, the system of regional government in 1974 and the political parties after 1972, has been imposed willy nilly by sheer *force majeure*. The regional authorities have been left with very little real autonomy under the strongly centralized system of regional government, although they now receive vastly greater financial subventions from the center than ever before. Above all, the machinery of government and economic planning is now working relatively efficiently throughout the country, in a way which had not happened since colonial times. These changes have been extremely important, I believe, in giving the country time to settle down and knit itself together after all the turbulence and strains of 1945-65. Sheer time and (relative) tranquillity have perhaps been as valuable as anything else for this purpose. There is still a brittle character to Indonesia's unity, but the chances that the country will hold together through future strains and shocks are now greater than they were fifteen years ago, I believe.

* * *

In conclusion, however, I must add several qualifications and caveats. I have been trying here to sketch the outlines of an alternative way of looking at the Indonesian political system over recent decades. For that purpose, I have been more inclined (in the words of the old song) to "accentuate the positive, eliminate the negative" than common prudence would dictate. Many of my analyses and prognoses could be proved wrong tomorrow if events took a sudden turn for the worse in Indonesia (a disastrous rice harvest, for instance). The country will undoubtedly face serious economic problems, hence probably also social and political strains, in the middle or late 'eighties when (or if) its oil revenues diminish. This could bode ill for an authoritarian government which has had a serious legitimacy problem in recent years and has been steadily narrowing its political base instead of widening it (precisely the mistake made by the Shah of Iran). I prefer to be optimistic about the chances that Indonesia's leaders will foresee these dangers and avoid them. But it is difficult to deny that there seems to have developed in the 1970s an intermeshing of the structures of power, privilege, interest and repression of dissent which can only be called systemic, hence not readily amenable to piecemeal change. Yet the political system in Indonesia is never as monolithic as it seems from outside. (Nor, it should be stressed, is political repression usually as senselessly brutal in Indonesia as in other authoritarian regimes.) In the last resort, however, it is the sagacity and good sense of Indonesia's leaders themselves on which the country's future will mostly depend, not the validity of this or that theory.

CULTURE, POLITICS, AND ECONOMY IN THE POLITICAL HISTORY OF THE NEW ORDER

Richard Robison

. . .

The Critique of Cultural Politics

The "cultural politics" approach to the analysis of power and conflict in New Order Indonesia rests upon two major propositions:

a) that the nature of the New Order regime can be explained essentially in terms of the persistence of Javanese cultural perspectives which shape the political behavior of officeholders;

b) that the identity and structure of political groups and the nature of political conflict is defined by the patrimonial nature of political relationships, i.e., by vertical, personalized patron-client structures.

These propositions are inadequate in two respects: they fail to comprehend the dynamics of politics; and, more important in terms of New Order Indonesia, they fail to provide a means for explaining why power and conflict exist there in their present form.

Obsession with the cultural and behavioral works to focus the analysis upon the style of a regime rather than its substance, and it ignores the very real socio-economic dimension of the New Order. The New Order regime quite clearly constitutes one fraction of a complex alliance embracing foreign and Chinese bourgeoisie; the urban technocrat/administrative/managerial class (the so-called middle class); and the politico-bureaucrats.[1] This regime serves to integrate the alliance in two ways. First, it provides the general political, legal, and economic infrastructure for the existence of the particular form of capitalism in which the interests of the alliance are embedded. It achieves this goal by general development strategy, capital investment laws, credit, wage, labor, fiscal, and monetary policies, as well

---

1. There are several writers who have analyzed the New Order regime as one primarily shaped by domestic class structures and the form of Indonesia's integration into a global capitalist order. See Rex Mortimer, "Indonesia: Growth or Development?" in *Showcase State*, ed. Rex Mortimer (Sydney: Angus & Robertson, 1973); Herbert Feith, "Political Control, Class Formation and Legitimacy in Suharto's Indonesia," *Kabar Seberang*, 2 (1977); Herbert Feith, "Repressive-Developmentalist Regimes in Asia: Old Strength, New Vulnerabilities," Presented at the Conference on Indonesian Class Formation, Monash University, August 1979; Richard Robison, "Towards a Class Analysis of the Indonesian Military Bureaucratic State," *Indonesia*, 25 (April 1978), pp. 17-40.

as state investment in infrastructure.² The second means of integration is through extensive private political and economic alliances between specific politico-bureaucratic factions and foreign or Chinese business groups. Again, the politico-bureaucrats provide the political infrastructure for these alliances in the form of protection, contracts, licenses, concessions, and public policy.³

This dimension of the New Order regime has been largely neglected by political scientists, because it is not an inherent component of the theoretical constructs within which they work. Yet it helps elucidate a fundamental aspect of power not explained by patron-client models. It is true that the generals have a patrimonial, tribute-gathering style which constitutes the basis for a certain tension between them and the technocrats and middle classes. However, although they may be in conflict over the question of the proper use of state power, they remain in general agreement over the desirable form of the social and economic order and over the broad thrust of policy necessary to maintain and reproduce this order. To this extent, as David Levine has argued, the abangan/priyayi bureaucrats are in the same camp (albeit in uneasy alliance) with the secular modernizing technocrats.⁴

From this starting point we can detect a whole range of issues where the state has clearly been involved politically in struggles of a social and economic nature. An important issue in Indonesian politics since the 1950s has been the struggle involving the indigenous petty bourgeoisie of merchants, commodity producers, and small capitalist producers, the Chinese bourgeoisie, the foreign bourgeoisie, and the state.⁵ The central question here has been whether the state would protect and subsidize the indigenous petty bourgeoisie and bourgeoisie or pour its public and private energies into integration with foreign or Chinese capital. The struggle has been manifested in the rise and fall of the Benteng program, the introduction of PP10 (Penetapan Presiden 10--Presidential Decision #10)/1959 restricting Chinese

---

2. Here we must take account of the proposition that the social character of a regime is not defined by the class origin of those who occupy the state apparatus but by the nature of state policy. For example, a bourgeois state is not necessarily a state where the offices of power are occupied by the bourgeoisie or even a state where bourgeois political parties wield ultimate political authority. Primarily it is a state which provides the economic conditions for capital accumulation and political protection for the bourgeoisie in the process of class-conflict. This concept will be developed later in the paper. Consequently, we should be looking at the foreign and domestic capital investment laws, policy emphasis upon import-substitution industrialization and export-promotion industrialization, credit policies, and foreign exchange policy if we are to understand the socioeconomic character of the New Order state.

3. Robison, "Towards a Class Analysis."

4. David Levine, "History and Social Structure of the Study of Contemporary Indonesia," *Indonesia*, 7 (April 1969), pp. 5-19.

5. See John O. Sutter, *Indonesianisasi: Politics in a Changing Economy, 1940-1955*, 4 vols., Southeast Asia Program Data Paper (Ithaca: Cornell University, 1959); Ralph Anspach, "Indonesia," in *Underdevelopment and Economic Nationalism in Southeast Asia*, ed. F. H. Golay et al. (Ithaca: Cornell University Press, 1969), pp. 111-201; Lance Castles, "Socialism and Private Business: The Latest Phase," *Bulletin of Indonesian Economic Studies* [henceforth *BIES*], 1 (1965), pp. 13-45; Hans O. Schmitt, "Post-Colonial Politics: A Suggested Interpretation of the Indonesian Experience, 1950-1958," *Australian Journal of Politics and History*, 9, 2 (November 1963), pp. 176-83.

commercial entry into rural areas, and, more recently, in conflicts over credit policy and the scandals of military/Chinese business alliances.[6]

Similarly, the question of land has embroiled the state in rural class conflict since the 1950s. Although Mortimer, Wertheim, and others[7] have clearly indicated the importance of cultural-political structures in rural conflict, less attention has been paid to the deepening struggle between rural classes over questions of land and labor. The state apparatus and the military and civil officials who occupied offices of authority were drawn into the conflict over landownership and land reform both in the period of *aksi sefihak* [unilateral action] from 1963 to 1965 and during the massacres of PKI supporters in 1965-66.[8] In effect (I am not arguing that this was consciously intended), the state allied with the rural landowners to bring about a counterrevolution--ensuring that the process of concentration of landholdings and capitalization of farming would not be obstructed by reformist movements.

Since 1965 the concentration of landholdings and the move to wage labor have deepened class divisions, weakening old client-patron structures.[9] These developments have been assisted by the government's Bimas (Bimbingan Masal Swa Sembada Bahanan Makanan--Mass Guidance for Self-Sufficiency in Food) program and by the system of Inpres (Instruksi Presiden--Presidential Instruction) credits. Moreover, it would appear that state officials themselves, from village heads and army sergeants to bupati and high officials, are becoming prominent figures in the developing *kulak* class.

Finally, the state has constantly been involved in the struggle between foreign capital and nationalist sections of the petty bourgeoisie and middle classes, which formed an important element in the rise and fall of Guided Democracy and Guided Economy. In the last decade the debate over the role of foreign capital has been vigorous and often bitter,[10] with the New Order government being forced to move at times to placate critics by imposing controls upon foreign capital.[11] Nevertheless, the New Order must be seen as providing the conditions in Indonesia for the development of a capitalist structure in which ownership and control of the productive forces is largely vested in foreign or Chinese hands. To this extent it is

---

6. Richard Robison, "Capitalism, and the Bureaucratic State in Indonesia: 1965-1975" (Ph.D. dissertation, Sydney University, 1977), ch. 9.

7. W. F. Wertheim, "From Aliran to Class Struggle in the Countryside of Java," *Pacific Viewpoint*, 10 (1969), pp. 1-17; Rex Mortimer, "Traditional Modes and Communist Movements," in *Peasant Rebellion and Communist Revolution in Asia*, ed. John W. Lewis (Stanford: Stanford University Press, 1974), pp. 99-123.

8. Rex Mortimer, *The Indonesian Communist Party and Land Reform*, Monash Papers on Southeast Asia, No. 1, 1972.

9. Jim Hinkson, "Rural Development and Class Contradiction on Java," *Journal of Contemporary Asia* [henceforth *JCA*], 5, 3 (1975), pp. 327-36; F. Husken, "Landlords, Sharecroppers and Agricultural Labourers: Changing Labour Relations in Rural Java," ibid., 9, 2 (1979).

10. Robison, "Capitalism, and the Bureaucratic State," ch. 8.

11. For example, most foreign corporations are now excluded from certain sectors of production and are required to take indigenous joint-venture partners, while production-sharing agreements between the state and foreign resource and energy ventures gain for Indonesia a substantial share of profits by world standards.

thrown into political opposition to national economic forces, both bourgeois and socialist.

The failure of political scientists to analyze systematically these facets of power and conflict under the New Order flows partly from a very narrow conception of what constitutes politics. Their focus has tended to be upon the pursuit and the maintenance of power, and the role of such organizations as Kopkamtib (Komando Pemulihan Keamanan dan Ketertiban--Command for the Restoration of Security and Order), Bakin (Badan Intelijen Negara--State Intelligence Body), Golkar (Golongan Karya--Functional Groups), Hankam (Departemen Pertananan-Keamanan--Department of Defense and Security) and the Presidency in this process. Consequently, the state (polity) is seen as isolated from social forces merely because no social force exercises formal control of the state by means of a political party. Power appears to be generated from within rather than without the state apparatus. The state has wide autonomy of action, limited only by the capacity of political leaders and elites to build effective political organizations to exclude and repress, or coopt and integrate.

The state, however, is not exclusively concerned with its own political survival. It is also concerned with the reproduction of a specific social and economic order and, therefore, has a social and economic dimension. We must then look not only at struggles for power (which are all too often factional struggles of no fundamental consequence for any but the individuals involved), but at the question of policy. It is true that foreign and Chinese business or rural landlords have no formal control over the institutions of power. Nevertheless in the New Order state their general interests as classes coincide with the interests of the politico-bureaucrats. They are further strengthened by the fact that the New Order is limited in its capacity to interfere with the logic underlying the process of social and economic transformation at work in Indonesia.[12]

I have so far suggested that there is a socioeconomic dimension to power and conflict in New Order Indonesia which has been excluded from systematic analysis by political scientists. But serious questions also arise with regard to the value of Javanese political culture as an explanatory device. Some political scientists have been strongly influenced by perceived parallels between the structures of precolonial Javanese political authority and those of Sukarno's Guided Democracy and Suharto's New Order. The recurrence of these patrimonial forms has been attributed by some scholars to the persistence of traditional Javanese perspectives on power, which focus on individual possession of power as a concrete entity. Political activity then centers on individuals who hold power, and political structures cluster in vertical, personalized networks which compete for the patronage of these power-holders.[13]

---

12. The question of the relative autonomy of the state has been central to a debate on the postcolonial state relating largely to the South Asian and African experience. Once again the debate is one between determinists who view the state as the instrument of the ruling class and structuralists who tend to see the state as being relatively autonomous of direct control by social forces but ultimately subject to the limits imposed by the logic of the accumulation process and reflecting the class struggle in society at large. See Hamza Alavi, "The State in Post-Colonial Societies," *New Left Review*, 74 (1972); W. Zeimann and M. Lanzendorfer, "The State in Peripheral Societies," *The Socialist Register* (1977). The collection of articles in H. Goulbourne, ed., *Politics and the State in the Third World* (London: MacMillan, 1979), are most useful in looking at this debate.

13. Benedict R. O'G. Anderson, "The Idea of Power in Javanese Culture," in

Anderson provides an attractive explanation of the Indonesian style of corruption in terms of Javanese perceptions of the relationship between wealth and power.

> Millionaires (entrepreneurial or landed) usually cannot buy themselves administrative positions of power and prestige. . . . Corruption on a large scale usually takes the form of the allotting of the "surplus" of certain key sections of the economy to favored officials or cliques of officials, whether civilian or military. Rice-collection, tin mining, oil production and distribution, and tax collection are only some examples of the areas in which officially supervised venality occurs.[14]

I am not disputing the existence of Javanese political perspectives and their influence on the style of political behavior. However, there are two grounds on which an analysis focusing exclusively on this aspect is inadequate. First, there are other political cultures which may have an equally important influence on the political behavior of the New Order. Second, there is a need to explain why the Javanese political culture has survived and what are the factors which govern the historical process of transformation or petrification of ideologies and cultures in general.

A second ideological view dominant amongst the politico-bureaucrats and officials of the New Order is that the role of the political leader and administrator is as the bringer of "development." In this view, the claim to power is legitimized and the exclusion of social forces from participation in the political process justified, on the grounds that the state possesses the scientific means for determining and implementing the common good. The technocrats are ideologically important to the New Order because they constitute this scientific legitimizing factor. As Ward[15] has pointed out, such a perspective derives from North American social science, in particular the "end of ideology" thesis. This is not simply the ideology of the technocrats (the secular modernizers) as opposed to that of the generals (priyayi-abangan patrimonialism), for there is a growing integration between these groups, and, in fact, what is probably the most comprehensive exposition of this approach had been provided by General Ali Moertopo, a central figure in the military group surrounding Suharto.[16]

Finally, we must remember that states similar to that of the New Order exist throughout the Third World, states in which public power is privately appropriated, where the state holds monopoly control over key areas of economic activity, where military and civil bureaucracies monopolize power and wealth, and where popular forces are excluded. As these states are not built upon a Javanese cultural foundation, we must either conclude that Javanese culture is fundamentally similar to those of other precapitalist (traditional) ideological systems or that ideology is only one of several factors conditioning the form of the political system. It is possible

---

Culture and Politics in Indonesia, ed. Claire Holt et al. (Ithaca: Cornell University Press, 1972), pp. 1-70; Ann Ruth Willner, "The Neotraditional Accommodation to Political Independence: The Case of Indonesia," in *Southeast Asia: The Politics of National Integration*, ed. John T. McAlister (New York: Random House, 1973), pp. 517-41.

14. Anderson, "Idea of Power," p. 49.

15. Ken Ward, "Indonesia's Modernisation: Ideology and Practice," in *Showcase State*, ed. Mortimer, pp. 67-82.

16. Ali Moertopo, *The Acceleration and Modernization of 25 Years Development* (Jakarta: Yayasan Proklamasi CSIS, 1973).

that the common existence of military-bureaucratic regimes in the Third World may be fundamentally linked with the common forms of articulation between precapitalist and capitalist modes of production and the particular form in which capitalism has penetrated the Third World. . . .

Political Conflict: Patron-Client and Class

The tendency for political identity and organization in Indonesia, particularly on Java, to take the form of vertical patron-client structures and for conflict to occur between competing networks has been well documented. Both Mortimer and Wertheim have shown how the PKI was forced, to a large extent, to work through these vertical structures, because it found itself limited in its capacity to mobilize political forces on the basis of class. As we have seen, this tendency for politics to take the form of vertical, client-patron networks and allegiances has been explained by some political scientists as the consequence of cultural influences upon political behavior. To a lesser extent, these scholars argue that class politics are not prevalent because class consciousness is low and class lines are not sharply drawn. Indeed, Mortimer explains the relative absence of class politics in rural Java as the result of a rural social order where the boundaries between landlord and peasant are unclear.[17]

These discussions of the nature of Indonesian politics have focused upon rural Java, probably because it is here that a peasant-based revolutionary movement is most likely to emerge and this region provided the PKI's and Sukarno's mass support. Cultural explanations are clearly inadequate for an understanding of the tension between class and patronage politics. The specific relationship between political forms (class or patronage) and the forces and relations of production must also be investigated. I intend to argue the following:

1. That client-patron political forms do not indicate an absence of classes, but constitute one form in which classes work out relationships and seek political and economic accommodation.

2. That patron-client politics in rural societies become class politics when either the landowners secure the economic means to escape patronage relationships or when the peasants secure the political means to do so.

3. Patron-client political structures are most compatible with social formations dominated by agricultural production, where tenancy constitutes the basic form of social relations of production and landownership patterns have produced a landowning class; they tend to disintegrate with the extension of capitalist relations of production.

There are several studies which have attempted to relate the transformation from patronage politics to class politics to broader socioeconomic changes. In his study of social relationships in central Luzon from about 1890 to 1940, Kerkvliet[18] shows how patron-client relationships collapsed as the balance of power tilted in favor of the landlords. In the early years, when land was plentiful and labor in short supply, the landlords established a relationship with tenants which was based upon a fair measure of reciprocity and required them to provide a degree of welfare assistance to the peasants. As population increased and land became scarcer and

---

17. Rex Mortimer, "Class, Social Cleavage and Indonesian Communism," *Indonesia*, 8 (October 1969), pp. 1-20.

18. Benedict J. Kerkvliet, *The Huk Rebellion* (Berkeley: University of California Press, 1977), esp. ch. 1.

more valuable, the landlords found that they were able to demand a greater share of the surplus produced by tenants and to dispense with the protection and assistance they have formerly granted. Unable to secure their rights through the old patron-client networks, the peasants turned increasingly to peasant unions to confront the landlords on a class basis. In turn, the landlords increasingly moved to replace tenants with wage labor and to invest in machinery, introducing capitalist relations of production into the countryside. Patron-client relationships had flourished when there was a certain balance between landlord and peasant but these forms were rejected by landlords when it was found that their interests and position could be secured more profitably by class political action.

Alavi[19] treats a similar situation in the Punjab, where noncultivating landlords began to introduce tractors and replace tenants with machinery and wage labor. The norms and values which had previously underlain the reciprocal, patron-client relationships between peasant and landlord were cast aside now that the landlords had access to the technical means to secure a greater surplus. The decision of the landowners was also based upon the knowledge that they possessed the social and economic power to avoid or to change the existing tenancy laws and to evade legal or political repercussions. Landlord obligations ended when labor shortages ended and the possibilities for capitalist farming emerged. In seeking to survive, tenants were faced with the alternatives of continuing to work through the disintegrating patron-client networks or of severing alliances with patrons and building class alliances with other tenants to challenge the landlords on the basis of class interest.

In his analysis of political conflict in rural Java, Wertheim[20] also emphasizes the relationship between changing socioeconomic structures and the growing tension between patronage and class political forms. While he agrees that rural classes have not been sharply defined and that political organization has been forced into client-patron networks, he also argues that the spread of capitalism into the countryside in the 1950s and 1960s established a clearer definition of class identity and began to break down the protection previously afforded the poor and destitute by old village communal and patronage institutions. The passing of the 1960 Land Reform laws led peasants to expect land reform, forcing the PKI peasants' union (BTI) to take the lead in the class politics already developing, and forcing the landlords to act in political defense of their class position. The massacres of 1965-66, he argues, can only be fully understood if the class tensions in the Javanese countryside are taken into account. Further, the victory of the military under Suharto constitutes for Wertheim a counterrevolution in the countryside.

> Land reforms appear to have been put, by the Suharto regime, into the icebox. The rich landowners have regained their lands, and the military leaders are practising a sharp repression against those who tend to resurrect agrarian unrest. Non-commissioned officers appear to have been appointed on a large scale as village heads. Whereas the incipient class struggle of the poor peasantry failed, for the time being, it is the large landowners, supported by the rule of the military authorities, who are, thus, openly waging their own brand of class struggle.[21]

Since 1965, disintegrative pressures on patron-client political and social relationships have intensified with the spread of capitalist farming and wage labor.

---

19. Hamza Alavi, "Peasant Classes and Primordial Loyalties," *Journal of Peasant Studies*, 1, 1 (1973).

20. Wertheim, "From Aliran to Class Struggle."

21. Ibid., p. 15.

Collier and others have written of the emergence of new relations of production in rural Java, where landowners are dispensing with traditional use of communal village labor, and the obligation to provide such labor with a share of the crop, in favor of contract wage labor. There is also a growth in the economic importance of rice traders who purchase crops in the ground and bring in contract labor for harvesting.[22] Use of wage labor, the increasing availability of rural credit, high-yielding seed varieties, pesticides, and fertilizers are providing landowners with opportunities to become capitalist farmers rather than rent-collecting landlords. Rural society in Java appears quite clearly to be moving in the direction of concentration of landownership and the attendant polarization of landed and landless. Although detailed analysis of the process of capitalist transformation of the Javanese countryside is in its early stages, the process itself is quite clearly taking place. My point is that such a process is of crucial significance for the form of political relationships and the nature of power and conflict in Indonesia.

The emergence of a kulak class can be expected to bring fundamental changes in political relationships within villages and between village and state. Relationships between farmer and wage laborer will become primarily economic and contractual, increasingly divested of political and social ties. Client-patron networks will become more inadequate for securing political and economic accommodation between rural classes and structuring relationships between rural classes and the state. A strong agrarian bourgeoisie with an independent base of social and economic power in the ownership of capital will find their interests poorly served by existing networks of patronage, because their interests as a class can only be secured by public policy and public investment rather than personal favors from individual local officials. For example, their survival will require the provision of economic infrastructure (communications, transport systems, electricity, and public works), political infrastructures (regularization of property laws and control of the landless), and policy on marketing, pricing, credit, and subsidy.

Quite clearly the emergence of a class of rural capitalist accumulators will have important consequences for the state. First, it will mean increasing pressure, from a domestic class whose power base is outside the state apparatus, to follow specific economic and social policies. Second, it will mean increasing conflict over the marketing and distribution system which at present is controlled by the state procurement agency Bulog and the Chinese merchant bourgeoisie and petty bourgeoisie. The alliance of patrimonial bureaucrat and Chinese middleman is built largely upon various state monopolies and controls on distribution, marketing, and pricing. We may logically expect an agrarian bourgeoisie not merely to compete with the Chinese for access to monopoly positions within the existing networks of patronage but to challenge the very basis of the patrimonial state: its political control of trade.

The whole question of patron-client and class political structures is related to the question of power under the New Order. As we have seen earlier, the New Order has been characterized as a regime which generates power from within the apparatus of the state, is isolated from social forces, is repressive and exclusive, and is patrimonial in style. However, rather than looking almost exclusively to cultural and behavioral explanations I propose that a more accurate explanation of the form of such a regime can be derived from a specific historical analysis which incorporates analysis of relationships between the political and the forces and relations of production.

---

22. William L. Collier et al., "Tebasan System, High Yielding Varieties and Rural Change," *Prisma*, 1, 1 (May 1975), pp. 17-31.

Social Relations of Production, Economic Structure, and Political Forms

One characteristic of political power in postcolonial Indonesia has been that offices of authority within the political parties and the civil and military bureaucracies have generally been monopolized by relatively small groups. Consequently, much political analysis has focused upon the palace politics of Jakarta and the increasingly authoritarian and centralized style of rule. Another feature of power in Indonesia has been its patrimonial style. Bureaucratic office is commonly appropriated by a center of political power, and the authority vested in that office used to secure the political survival and personal wealth of a political faction or individual. As we have seen, this has been compared to the style of bureaucratic authority which existed in precolonial Javanese agrarian kingdoms where the ruling class were holders of appanage benefices, rather than being hereditary landowning aristocrats. This situation is, however, conditioned by a very specific historical development of forms and relations of production, and we cannot fully understand the structure of power, or the dynamics of the factors which shape it, without taking into account these economic and social influences.

From its precolonial and colonial experience Indonesia inherited a class structure which was conducive to the concentration of power within a state apparatus dominated by civil and military officials, and wherein other social forces had limited capacity to secure control of the state apparatus. The following summary indicates the major features of the class structure inherited from the colonial period.

1. There is considerable conjecture concerning the extent of private ownership of land in precolonial Java, the degree to which precolonial Javanese agricultural society was grounded upon a feudal rather than Asiatic mode of production,[23] and the impact of Dutch colonialism upon landownership patterns.[24] While it is clear that the commercialization of agriculture in the colonial period did increase private land ownership and create a class of small-holder producers of sugar, coffee, rubber, and other crops (especially in Sumatra, Sulawesi, and Kalimantan), the landowning classes in Indonesia never occupied the position of political power and influence they did in early postcolonial states in Latin America, the Philippines, Pakistan, and South Vietnam. Instead of large indigenous-owned farms, haciendas, or estates, Dutch-owned estates or, to a lesser extent, indigenous or Chinese-owned small-holdings were the predominant centers for the commercial production of crops in the Dutch Indies. Consequently, when independence was secured, the landowning class did not constitute a major social base for political power.

---

23. The literature on the Asiatic mode of production is substantial. Samir Amin provides an interesting discussion in "Modes of Production and Social Formations," *Ufahamu* (Winter 1974); and in his article, "Social Characteristics of Peripheral Formations: An Outline for an Historical Sociology," *Berkeley Journal of Sociology*, 21 (1976-77), he discusses the concept of a state class in contemporary social formations.

24. For example, Onghokham found in Madiun that the class with traditional use rights of land (*sikep*) was undermined by the system of corvée labor and state plantations established by the Dutch after 1830, and villages returned to a communally oriented form of landholding. On the other hand, in Pasuruan and Probolinggo, Elson found an increase in the number of larger landlords and villagers who relied increasingly on wage labor for income. See: Onghokham, "The Residency of Madium: Priyayi and Peasant in the Nineteenth Century" (Ph.D. dissertation, Yale University, 1975); R. E. Elson, *The Cultivation System and Agricultural Involution*, Monash University, Centre of Southeast Asian Studies Working Papers, No. 14 (Clayton, Victoria, 1978).

2. The economy of colonial Indonesia took three forms: a subsistence agricultural sector, a petty commodity production sector, and a capitalist sector which took the form of enclave commodity production and export of crops such as rubber, sugar, and coffee, and, increasingly, of oil and minerals. This form of capitalism was dominated by Dutch trading-houses and merchant banks, which controlled production on plantations and in the mines, as well as the international trade in commodities. It gave rise, in turn, to small-holder production of commercial crops and to domestic trade in commercial crops. The intermediary sector of domestic trade fell largely into the hands of the local Chinese.[25] With the coming of independence neither the Dutch bourgeoisie nor the Chinese bourgeoisie and petty bourgeoisie were able to constitute themselves as a ruling class in its full sense because both were excluded from formal participation in public political activity. They remained economically dominant, but they could not actually rule.

3. Participation of indigenous traders and manufacturers in the colonial capitalist economy was limited to a minor role in domestic trade (predominantly in Sumatra and the outer islands) and to petty commodity production of textiles, batik, foodstuffs, and kretek cigarettes on Java. In the early decades of the twentieth century the indigenous petty bourgeoisie [*pengusaha pribumi*] became engaged in a long and unsuccessful struggle with the Chinese merchants, who gradually extended their economic control into the production of textiles and batik.[26] Although the pengusaha pribumi have remained a force in postcolonial politics, their social and economic base has been too weak to enable them either to capture the state apparatus or to exert a decisive influence on the formation of state policy.

4. This socioeconomic order and economic structure was politically secured by the Dutch colonial administration, which maintained trading monopolies for the Dutch bourgeoisie, and which provided the legal basis for private ownership of estate lands, the economic infrastructure, and the political and military force to contain challenges. Within this overall colonial bureaucracy there was an extensive indigenous bureaucratic apparatus, which had been severed from its traditional tribute and incorporated as salaried officials into the colonial project of securing the conditions of existence for Dutch enclave commodity export production.

5. During the final two or three decades of Dutch rule an indigenous intelligentsia emerged both within the bureaucracy and among independent professionals such as lawyers, journalists, writers, and teachers. This intelligentsia eventually secured a position of political dominance through its leadership of nationalist political organizations.

6. Because colonial capitalism took the form of enclave commodity production rather than industrial capitalism, the development of an industrial proletariat was limited. The bulk of the urban population were, in fact, not industrial wage laborers but an indeterminate assortment of household servants, day laborers, petty traders, and state employees, such as railway workers. At the same time, the failure of capitalist relations of production to penetrate the countryside to any significant degree meant that rural society had not been transformed into a society of

---

25. An excellent picture of the class structure of late colonial Indonesia is given by George Kahin in the first chapter of his *Nationalism and Revolution in Indonesia* (Ithaca: Cornell University Press, 1952). The best general socioeconomic analysis of colonial Java is Wertheim's *Indonesian Society in Transition* (The Hague: van Hoeve, 1956).

26. Kahin, *Nationalism and Revolution*; Castles, *Religion, Politics*; Sutter, *Indonesianisasi*; and Robert Van Niel, *The Emergence of the Modern Indonesian Elite* (The Hague: van Hoeve, 1960).

landowners, capitalist farmers, and wage laborers, as we have seen, but remained a confused and overlapping patchwork of landowners, tenants, and small, independent peasant cultivators. Such a social base presented obvious problems for revolutionary political movements.

The first governments of the Indonesian Republic found themselves operating in the context of an enclave export production economy dominated by a Dutch bourgeoisie and a Chinese bourgeoisie and petty bourgeoisie. While there was no inevitability about the form assumed by the postcolonial state, the interaction between political forms and the forms and relations of production is clear. In the years following independence there was considerable debate about the most desirable form which Indonesia's political and economic structures should take, but the direction for the future had already been laid down in the first decade of independence--up to the formal declaration of guided economy by Sukarno. Because of the weakness of domestic classes and the limits upon direct political activity by the dominant Dutch and Chinese bourgeoisie, the state had a relative autonomy for action. The new leaders decided to continue to secure the general conditions of existence for the enclave commodity export economy and the dominance of the Dutch and Chinese bourgeoisie. There were two reasons for this. On the one hand, political leaders and economic planners belonging to the PSI (Partai Sosialis Indonesia), Masjumi, and the right wing of the PNI (Dr. Sumitro, Sjafruddin, and Wilopo) saw a program of very gradual disengagement from the neocolonial economy as necessary because of the inadequate development of a domestic bourgeoisie, whether state or private.[27] In effect, they argued that a domestic capacity for accumulation had to be developed before a meaningful national economy could be constructed. The Indonesian social formation had been so deeply integrated into the neocolonial economy and the class structures so specifically related to neocolonialism that extrication was an extremely difficult process, as Sukarno was later to find out. To a significant degree the new leaders were prisoners of an existing logic. Given time, of course, there is no reason why the state should be incapable of generating a national capitalist economy, although the experience of Third World capitalist economies (since Japan's emergence) is that integration with global capitalist structures intensifies.[28]

There were also more concrete reasons for maintenance of the status quo. Those who secured dominance over the state apparatus quickly discovered that they shared interests with the existing economic order. Because the economy was so heavily based upon import and export and upon exploitation of natural resources, the state occupied a strategic economic position by virtue of its control of the allocation of licenses and concessions for imports, for mining, oil drilling, and forestry exploitation. Political parties quickly secured control of bureaucratic offices in economically strategic positions, particularly in the banking system and the departments of trade, customs, and industry. These became the virtual fiefdoms of political parties and factions, as the defining lines between political power and bureaucratic authority became increasingly blurred. Licenses and concessions were commonly sold or allocated in order to secure either revenue or political advantage for par-

---

27. The views of the gradualists are summarized in Robison, "Capitalism, and the Bureaucratic State," pp. 48-53.

28. See James F. Petras, "State Capitalism and the Third World," *JCA*, 6, 4 (1976), pp. 432-43; J. Lean, "The Mexican State, 1915-1973: An Historical Interpretation," *Latin American Perspectives*, 2, 2 (1974); R. Munck, "State, Capital and Crisis in Brazil, 1929-1979," *The Insurgent Sociologist*, 9, 4 (1980). The arguments developed here suggest that industrialization invariably develops into export-oriented manufacture characterized by increasing foreign control over the forces of production with the local bourgeoisie and the national state as minor partners.

ticular political factions and individuals, as well as their families and clients. Political parties and their clients also began to form more structured economic and business alliances with foreign and Chinese bourgeoisie. In the 1950s the first business groups representing this alliance of politico-bureaucratic power and bourgeois capital emerged. They operated primarily in the area of import and distribution monopolies, particularly automobiles, and were supplemented by privileged access to state bank credit through party-controlled banks.[29]

The struggle between the state and the pengusaha pribumi must be seen in a class and economic context rather than that of a struggle between abangan and santri. Directing state power and finance towards protection and subsidy of the pengusaha pribumi contradicted the philosophy of the gradualist technocrats, because, by normal business criteria, the pengusaha pribumi were generally less able effectively to realize capital. Chinese business, with its highly developed networks of distribution was more likely to constitute the basis for a strong local bourgeoisie. Protection and subsidy of the pengusaha pribumi also contradicted the vested interests of the politico-bureaucrats because the licenses and concessions which were potential bases for capital accumulation by the pengusaha pribumi were also sources of revenue for politico-bureaucrats. This contradiction was well illustrated in the operation of the Benteng scheme from 1950 to 1955. Import licenses were supposed to be reserved for pengusaha pribumi importers but were effectively appropriated by politico-bureaucrats and their clients either for sale to, or to be used as the basis of business alliances with, foreign and Chinese business groups.[30]

Conflict between the tribute-gathering comprador state and the pengusaha pribumi has continued to be a central feature of Indonesian political history. Schmitt[31] has pointed out the influence of this contradiction upon the struggle between Jakarta and the Outer Islands in the mid- and late-1950s. He argues that the Jakarta politico-bureaucrats became committed to inflationary policies in the mid-1950s, as a means both of increasing revenue and of making more lucrative the commodity import trade to which they had become firmly attached. Inflation and an artificially high foreign exchange rate damaged the economic position of indigenous producer-exporters located mainly in Sumatra and Sulawesi. Conflict between the pengusaha pribumi and the Chinese has continued at a level of considerable intensity, resulting in occasional but short-lived victories for the pengusaha pribumi, which include the introduction of PP 10 in 1959[32] and government moves to exclude Chinese business from eligibility for state bank credit and joint venture partnership with foreign companies following the 1974 disturbances.[33] The Chinese, however, have survived and flourished, for two reasons. First, they are indispensable to the working of the Indonesian economy in its present export-enclave commodity-production form through domination of domestic distribution and credit networks. As a strong and effective business entity, they are seen by the technocrats as a major engine of economic growth. More important, the interests of Chinese business groups are commonly tied to the financial interests of politico-bureaucrat factions, such shared interests being manifested in the large number of business groups which are partnerships

---

29. Robison, "Capitalism, and the Bureaucratic State," pp. 58-62.

30. Sutter, *Indonesianisasi*, pp. 1017-35; Anspach, "Indonesia."

31. Schmitt, "Post-Colonial Politics."

32. For a general overview of anti-Chinese conflicts and movements in the post-colonial period, see J. A. C. Mackie, "Anti-Chinese Outbreaks in Indonesia, 1959-68," in *The Chinese in Indonesia*, ed. J. A. C. Mackie (Melbourne: Nelson, 1976), pp. 77-138.

33. Robison, "Capitalism, and the Bureaucratic State," pp. 437-45.

between Indonesian political power and Chinese capital, managerial, and organizational resources.[34] Consequently, neither the generals nor the technocrats are enthusiastic about either massive state protection and subsidy of the pengusaha pribumi or effective state action against the Chinese.

If the Sukarno era is to be viewed as the manifestation of a resurgence of traditional political culture this must be placed in the perspective of wider social and economic struggle. The abandonment of parliamentary and liberal democratic forms in favor of centralized authority and state cooption of the apparatus of public participation was no more a resurgence of traditional political culture than it was the quite natural collapse of a political system which had never been more than a shell. The political parties never represented the interests of powerful social forces (with the partial exception of the PKI), and there was no significant source of social and political power other than that generated within the state apparatus in alliance with foreign and Chinese bourgeoisie. Guided Democracy simply did away with the redundant paraphernalia of liberal parliamentary democracy, either encompassing social groups within state-sponsored patronage networks or excluding, ignoring, or repressing them.

Guided Democracy constituted a process of struggle between three conflicting groups: economic nationalists, modern-style appanage-holders, and the economic gradualists or pragmatists. Economic nationalists, including the PNI's left wing and the PKI, attempted, with the general sympathy of Sukarno, to create a national economy based upon state capitalist enterprise. Dutch trading-houses and plantations were nationalized and constituted as state companies. The state developed more effective means of controlling foreign exploitation of Indonesia's economic resources through such arrangements as work-contract and production-sharing agreements. Pertamina was the most notable success here. Finally, the state attempted to control imports of commodities which could be produced domestically, and to finance an industrial base in Indonesia. P.T. Krakatau steel was the most ambitious project in this category.[35]

The difficulties of accumulation in one nation are great enough, even with a highly disciplined and regularized state apparatus and party organization, as the experiences of Russia and China have demonstrated. But the Indonesian economic nationalists were forced to work with a state apparatus which was, as I have already argued, both tribute-gathering and comprador in nature. The nationalized state-trading corporations and agricultural estates were seized by the military and, to a lesser extent, by civilian politico-bureaucratic factions. These elements saw economic activity as a process whereby state power was used to extract a share of the surplus, rather than as a process of capital accumulation. As might be expected, the bulk of the state trading corporations and estates were simply plundered by the military and soon disintegrated for lack of investment, proper management, and maintenance.

In broader terms, the attempt to create a national industrial economy failed because neither the state nor the domestic bourgeoisie and petty bourgeoisie had the capacity to provide the base for national accumulation and industrialization. In

---

34. Details of business groups which manifest these alliances are to be found in ibid., Appendix B.

35. Unfortumately there is as yet no comprehensive political economy of Guided Economy. Of the existing sources the most useful are: T. K. Tan, ed., *Sukarno's Guided Indonesia* (Brisbane: Jacaranda, 1967), and K. Thomas and J. Panglaykim, *Indonesia--the Effects of Past Policies and President Suharto's Plans for the Future* (Melbourne: CEDA, 1973), ch. 3.

effect, Guided Economy proved to be a seizure and pillaging of the economic interests of the Dutch, without any fundamental alteration to the commodity-import and enclave commodity-export structure of the colonial economy. The result was a disintegration of the existing economic structures: the collapse of infrastructure; the compounding of foreign debt; the dwindling of commodity imports (notably spare parts); and the acceleration of inflation.

The New Order may be seen as a regime counterrevolutionary vis-à-vis both agrarian reform and economic nationalism. As I have indicated earlier, it halted the process of rural land reform and destroyed the political organization which represented the interests of socially revolutionary groups in the countryside. On the other hand, it provided the political base for capitalist revolution in the rural areas, establishing the political conditions for concentration of landholdings and the spread of capitalist relations of production.

The New Order also represented victory over the political alliance of economic nationalists who had seized power in the late 1950s. Immediately the military secured political control in late 1965 they began moves to renegotiate the foreign debt and to attract foreign capital investment. In effect, this was a recognition that foreign capital was an essential component of the Indonesian economy as it was then structured. Simply removing foreign capital without changing the basic structure of the economy had produced only economic disintegration. Because the generals had no desire to institute revolutionary structural changes in the society and the economy their only choice was to bring back foreign capital, and in this decision they became associated with a group of economists who believed that economic development could be achieved only through economic growth induced by the infusion of foreign capital. The New Order technocrats began the construction of a state policy designed to effect the reintegration of the Indonesian economy into global capitalist structures.[36]

One of the central thrusts of the cultural politics analysis has been to portray the conflict between the generals and the technocrats in terms of a cultural conflict between regularizers (secular modernizers) and patrimonial bureaucrats with a traditional Javanese perspective on appropriate political and economic behavior.[37] This conflict certainly exists, but it contributes little to our understanding of Indonesian politics unless we recognize that it is subordinate to a wider common interest between technocrats and generals, and that the increasing rationalization and regularization of the state apparatus and political relationships are related to fundamental changes taking place in the structure of the economy and the nature of class relationships.

The New Order is a regime operating in a social formation where the dominant economic form is in the process of transformation from enclave export-commodity production to export-promotion industrialization. In the enclave export production social formation, the demands upon the state are minimal. The bulk of the popula-

---

36. For contrasting views on the role of the technocrats in the process of economic change see David Ransom, "The Berkeley Mafia," *Ramparts*, 9 (1970), and Bruce Glassburner, "Political Economy and the Soeharto Regime," *BIES*, 14, 3 (1978).

37. Much of the emphasis has been on the way in which cultural perceptions of patrimonial politico-bureaucrats constitute an obstacle to the emergence of industrial capitalism and rational decision making and very little upon the way in which changing economic structures and class relationships influence transformations of cultural perspectives and bureaucratic structures. Even radical critiques fall into this category; see Richard W. Franke, "Limited Good and Cargo Cult in Indonesian Economic Development," *JCA*, 2, 4 (1972), pp. 366-81.

tion remain within the agricultural and petty commodity production sector, where the responsibilities of the state are primarily concerned with tax collection and perhaps maintaining buffer stocks of rice. Enclave commodity production requires limited infrastructure, apart from property guarantees and road and rail links from the plantations and mines to the seaports. Production and investment remain in the hands of foreign bourgeoisies and, in the case of Indonesia, Chinese merchants take care of domestic trade.

Within this context, the state sits astride access to trade and exploitation of resources and draws tribute for the granting of access. Pertamina, Timah, Aneka Tambang, and other state instrumentalities are essentially terminals for granting access to oil and minerals and collecting revenues from the concession holders. Therefore, the path to wealth for indigenous Indonesians lies not in investment and accumulation as a bourgeoisie but in gaining control of the strategic apparatus of the state. Since the late 1950s it has been the military which has dominated these strategic terminals and built for itself independent sources of finance.[38]

To a large extent, the state's ability to sit in apparent isolation from domestic social forces is the result of its capacity to derive finance from the foreign bourgeoisie, not only in the form of oil and mineral revenues but in the form of high levels of foreign loans directed through the state by IGGI, IMF, and the World Bank.[39] At the same time, the foreign bourgeoisie cannot directly supplant the generals of the New Order and are forced to allow them relative autonomy, which means that the state is able to apply pressure for greater shares of the surplus, both in the form of public revenue for the state and private rake-offs for individual officials and generals.[40] The relative aspect of state autonomy refers to the limits imposed by the generals' need to avoid fundamentally damaging this social and economic order.

Yet there are several contradictions within this articulation of patrimonial bureaucrats and corporate capital. The capital which returned to Indonesia in 1965 was not that of the colonial Dutch trading-houses but that of Japanese and American transnational corporations. It is increasingly being channeled into industrial production, not only in import-substitution manufacture and assembly but in export-promotion industrialization of textiles, metal engineering, plastics, car batteries, electronics, and other manufactures suited to the low labor costs in Indonesia. Sustaining this high-growth industrial capitalism involves the state in an entirely new project. It is now required to provide a much more complex economic infrastructure, including reliable supplies of electricity and water, communications and transport systems, education, health services, and public utilities for the burgeoning urban populations. Complex fiscal policies must be carefully managed to allow for debt servicing and to provide exchange rates conducive to increased export

---

38. Harold Crouch, *The Army and Politics in Indonesia* (Ithaca: Cornell University Press, 1978), ch. 11; Robison, "Capitalism, and the Bureaucratic State," chs. 6 and 7.

39. The foreign loan component of the development budget for 1979 was 42.4 percent. Oil exports account for 65 percent of public investments and 13 percent of GNP, exceeding the total development budget. Ho Kwon Ping, "Back to the Drawing Board," *Far Eastern Economic Review*, April 27, 1979.

40. Scandals over payoffs to Indonesian generals by foreign or Chinese businessmen occur quite regularly. The most recent is the case of the late Haji Thahir, a former official of Pertamina who was found to have deposited $80 million in a private bank account in Singapore. *Kompas*, February 13, 1980; *Asiaweek*, March 28 and August 8, 1980.

earnings and capital inflow.[41] Complex legal frameworks must be developed for foreign corporate investment and relationships between the state and international finance agencies. At the same time, the state can no longer allow the bulk of the population to be isolated from centralized and regularized structures of control. Wage labor must be brought under rigorous control to prevent strikes and ensure the low wage levels conducive to accumulation. The urban unemployed, rural landless, economic nationalists, and anti-Chinese Muslims all present more fundamental threats, not only because their numbers are growing but because they threaten the increasingly structured and delicate social and economic order essential for the accumulation process. Consequently, the state must maintain a highly structured and regularized apparatus of administration and political control simply because the old patrimonial tribute-gathering state cannot cope with the tasks inherent in the new state project.

The New Order is itself a microcosm of the struggle between the patrimonial forms of the old enclave production and peasant social formation and the new regularized authoritarian form of an industrializing Indonesia. While the generals have shown a willingness to regularize the apparatus of political control (Kopkamtib and Bakin), the bureaucracy in general and the military in particular,[42] there is a natural reluctance to relinquish patrimonial control of the strategic economic terminals of the state apparatus. The continuing struggle for control of Pertamina between the technocrats and the generals (who wish to operate it under more personalized control) is a major example of this type of conflict.[43]

---

41. For example, the complex implications of the 1978 devaluation of the rupiah for the Indonesian economy are treated by Peter McCawley, "The Devaluation and Structural Change in Indonesia," Paper presented to the Australian National University Research School of Pacific Studies Seminar Series, November 16, 1979.

42. Donald Emmerson, "Bureaucracy in Political Context: Weakness in Strength," in *Political Power and Communication in Indonesia*, ed. Karl D. Jackson and Lucian W. Pye (Berkeley: University of California Press, 1978), pp. 82-136; Harold Crouch, "Patrimonialism and Military Rule in Indonesia," *World Politics*, 31, 4 (1979), pp. 571-87.

43. P. McCawley, "Some Consequences of the Pertamina Crisis in Indonesia," *Journal of Southeast Asian Studies*, 9, 1 (1978); H. W. Arndt, "PT Krakatau Steel," *BIES*, 9, 2 (1975), pp. 120-26. The concept of a new form of Third World fascism or repressive technocratic authoritarianism and the relationship of these political forms to increasing industrialization has been central to recent political analyses of Third World social formations. See, for example, Philippe C. Schmitter, "The 'Portugalization' of Brazil," in *Authoritarian Brazil*, ed. Alfred Stepan (New Haven: Yale University Press, 1973), pp. 179-232; Fernando H. Cardoso, "Associated Dependent Development: Theoretical and Practical Implications," in ibid., pp. 142-76; R. Luckham, "Militarism, Class, Force and International Conflict," *Institute of Development Studies Bulletin* [Sussex University], 9, 1 (1977); Herbert Feith, "Repressive-Developmentalist Regimes in Asia: Old Strengths, New Vulnerabilities," Paper presented to Conference on Indonesian Class Formation, Monash University, August 10-13, 1979. The central thesis of these arguments is that the increasingly repressive and authoritarian nature of the regimes is related to the increasing dominance of foreign industrial bourgeoisies and the development of a growth-oriented industrial economy in which the military gain political ascendency over social classes, especially the national bourgeoisie and the popular classes--peasants and workers. Treatment of this question, however, is conspicuously absent in the analyses of the New Order proposed by North American political science.

Aside from the interaction between the forms of the state and of the economic system embodied in developing new state projects, the implications which the spread of capitalist relations of production has for both the class structure of New Order Indonesia and, in turn, for the form of the New Order state deserve our attention.

The first implication is the increasing importance of a new auxiliary class of officials: managers, technocrats, technicians, and professionals. The exclusion of this class from the strategic offices of power, and the absence of any genuinely representative political structures or rule of law have created antagonism between them and the military rulers. Nevertheless, their general attachment to the existing economic order and the relative privilege of their position have made them cautious of courting alliances with the "popular" forces. While the New Order regime has resisted demands for political participation and the rule of law, it has recognized that an educated and skilled "middle class" or intelligentsia is increasingly essential to a society engaged in industrialization. In effect, the political alliance of the urban middle-classes and the military rests upon the maintenance of increasing living standards and employment opportunities for the former. In any case, the divisions which clearly separated the military from the urban intelligentsia in the 1960s are becoming blurred as the military move into civilian administrative positions and into the culture of the urban intelligentsia. This trend of increasing integration suggests that it is likely that political relationships between the military regime and the urban intelligentsia will be characterized less by conflict over representative democracy and rule of law than by incorporation of the civilian intelligentsia into a broader technocratic authoritarian state less exclusively military in its composition, despite continuing reliance on military power for its political survival.[44]

The most powerful social force generated under the New Order has been an alliance of foreign, Chinese, and indigenous bourgeoisies. These are constituted within business groups taking the form of a complex series of joint venture partnerships in which, as a general pattern, the bulk of the capital is provided by foreign partners, while distribution, subcontracting, and often management is provided by Chinese partners, and political protection by indigenous officials. Such bourgeois alliances range from multimillion-dollar business groups with interests in a wide range of industrial, resource, property, and service industries to smaller joint ventures between local military commanders and local Chinese businessmen involving construction or transport contracts.[45]

The movement of indigenous shareholders into industrial production is important for two reasons. First, indigenous partners are incorporated into the ventures as shareholders. With forestry or trading concessions, the officials who controlled the concession often simply sold it or demanded a share of the proceeds--i.e., a share of the value of lumber existing on the lease. However, industrial production involves a process of expanded capital accumulation in which capital is invested and relative surplus product generated. As a shareholder, the indigenous partner develops a vested interest in profitability and in the provision of the social, economic,

---

44. Power clearly rests with the military and there is no immediate likelihood of any shift to effective civilian rule. However, we must distinguish between the political power-holders, i.e., the military commanders, and the state officials. The bulk of the military officers in the state apparatus are not power-holders in that they do not command military power. They are, in effect, officials drawn from the most privileged arm of the state bureaucracy. Increasing the civilian component of state officialdom would offer no fundamental threat to military political dominance.

45. Robison, "Capitalism, and the Bureaucratic State," chs. 6 and 7, and Appendix B.

and political conditions conducive to profitability. In this way, the official ceases to be a simple tribute-gatherer, even though he may provide licenses and concessions rather than capital and management, and becomes an integral, capital-owning member of the bourgeois alliance.

Second, the development of a broad bourgeois alliance is significant for the tensions and contradictions inherent within the alliance and the pressures these place upon the New Order state. At the same time that the national fraction of the bourgeoisie in Indonesia demands integration with foreign capital, there is conflict over the terms of integration and, in some cases where national business feels it is able to operate without foreign assistance, demands for the exclusion of foreign capital from some sectors.[46] While the alliance of foreign and Chinese bourgeoisies with indigenous officials or business clients is being consolidated at one level, it is being vigorously opposed by the indigenous petty bourgeoisie excluded from the alliance and consequently in decline.[47] Similarly, opposition to the alliance comes from technocrat and urban intelligentsia elements who object to the irregular and personal appropriation of state power which often underpins these bourgeois alliances and interferes with regularized and predictable economic planning and use of state resources.

The state, therefore, becomes the mediator of the conflicting interests operating within this class alliance, and its economic policies cannot be understood without an appreciation of the structure of the intraclass conflict, and of the role played by the state in general and individual officials in particular in the accumulation process. . . .

---

46. For example, the 1974 riots in Jakarta followed a prolonged critique of state economic policy and foreign economic domination by the urban intelligentsia, pengusaha pribumi, and the local Chinese bourgeoisie. See Robison, "Capitalism, and the Bureaucratic State," chs. 8 and 9, for an overview of the critique and government reactions. The line taken by the Centre for Strategic and International Studies (CSIS) clearly reflects the interests of an emerging national bourgeoisie. It calls for government action to strengthen national capital within the framework of nationally integrated economic units and refers to the Singapore, Meiji Japan, and even Guided Economy models as guides for action. See, for example, J. Panglaykim, "Struktur Domestik Dalam Interdependensi Ekonomi Dunia," *Analisa Masalah-Masalah Internasional*, 2, 12 (December 1973), pp. 37-44, and Kwik Kian Gie, "Foreign Capital and Economic Domination," *Indonesian Quarterly*, 3 (April 1975), pp. 39-72.

47. While the bulk of the indigenous petty bourgeoisie, largely through right-wing Muslim newspapers such as *Nusantara* and *Abadi*, were castigating business alliances between generals and Chinese, this traditional trading and commodity-producing bourgeoisie clearly represents a declining force. It would appear likely that real development of a national bourgeoisie will take place within the framework of the business alliances described. Expressions of the views of businessmen tied into these alliances are to be found in *Seminar Strategi Pembinaan Pengusaha Swasta Nasional 29-31 Mei* (Jakarta: Yayasan Proklamasi, 1975).

ORDERS OF MEANING: UNDERSTANDING POLITICAL CHANGE
IN A FISHING COMMUNITY IN INDONESIA*

Donald K. Emmerson

> The interviews completed, it was Mr. Biswas' duty to analyse the information he had gathered. And here he floundered. He had investigated two hundred households; but after every classification he could never, on adding, get two hundred, and then he had to go through all the questionnaires again. He was dealing with a society that had no rules and patterns, and classifications were a chaotic business.
>
> --V. S. Naipaul, *A House for Mr. Biswas*

One night in Jakarta, the national capital of Indonesia, my wife and I were coming out of a luxury hotel. As we descended the steps we could see, ahead of us, the black pavement of the exit lane used by vehicles leaving the hotel; to our left, a thin parking attendant dressed in a pale tan uniform with simple epaulettes; and, further left, a shiny black car moving over the pavement toward the exit gate to our right. In the time it took us to descend a few more steps, the driver of the car drew up to the attendant, spoke to the man through the open car window, accelerated through the gate, and was gone. In the same instant that the automobile dis-

---

* The research reported here was conducted in 1974-75 and made possible by a Southeast Asia Fellowship from the Ford Foundation, a Faculty Research Abroad award from the U.S. Office of Education, and a Graduate Research Committee grant from the University of Wisconsin, Madison. Permission to work in East Java was extended by the governments of Indonesia, East Java, Banyuwangi, and Muncar. Many officials and private individuals in Indonesia assisted me. I am very grateful to these donors, advisers, and informants, and especially to the fishermen of Muncar. My intellectual debts to Benedict Anderson, Clifford Geertz, and James Scott should be obvious to students of political change in rural Southeast Asia. However, none of these institutions and persons is in any way responsible for, nor would by any means necessarily endorse, what I have to say. Lastly, the following translations of foreign words and abbreviations may prove helpful: BUUD = Badan Usaha Unit Desa, or Village Effort Organization; *juragan darat* = owner(s) of fixed capital; *ksatriya* = Javanese noble warrior; *laep* - dearth; MPR = Majelis Permusyawaratan Rakyat, or People's Consultative Assembly; *pengambek* = owner(s) of financial capital; PPBP = Proyek Persiapan BUUD Perikanan, or Project to Prepare the Fishing BUUD; *uang ikatan* = money paid by a patron (pengambek or juragan darat) to "hold" his client; *wayang* = Javanese theater. The most important of these terms are described at greater length in the text.

appeared from sight to the right, to the left we could see the attendant undergoing a metamorphosis: moving his feet apart, bending his knees, stiffening his torso, and raising and flexing his elbows and wrists. When these rapid movements had ceased I realized with a shock of recognition that he had arranged his body in the characteristic stance of a *ksatriya*, a noble warrior from the classical Javanese past. His face was impassive; his pose motionless. Only a slight trembling of his hands and fingers showed the fact of his profound fury.

Several cab drivers and hotel employees approached the rigid attendant and spoke to him, touching his still upraised and arched dancer's arms and trying to relax his body. The attendant instead twisted free and resumed the same ksatriya posture a short distance away. This pattern of being approached, escaping, and resuming the stance was repeated several times before the man finally returned to a "normal" posture: feet together, knees straight, torso relaxed, and elbows and wrists lowered and hanging slack once more. The incident was over.

Social facts are never literally self-evident; one cannot perceive reality without also processing it according to some previously acquired criterion of interest or frame of meaning. The vaunted naked eye is in fact invariably dressed in the finery of its owner's personality and culture. But a shock such as my wife and I received on the hotel steps can at least partially strip one's vision. We had just finished a Western meal in a hotel mostly owned and inhabited by Westerners; in the cosmopolitan context, had the attendant shouted an obscenity at the departing car, his behavior would have appeared to us far more appropriate and trivial in that place. Instead he had broken through the defenses of our culture-bound perception and done something that was in our terms not comprehensible.

A performance by Western definition is premeditated and at least minimally artificial; one "plays" a role. Yet the attendant's transformation into a ksatriya warrior from the dramatis personae of Javanese *wayang* theater was a spontaneous, fiercely sincere, natural act. The pattern into which he had curved his body a Westerner would most likely call "stylized"--a term often applied to wayang puppets --in the meaning of unrealistic or surrealistic, a triumph of form over substance. Yet the emotional substance of the attendant's stance was all the more palpably real for being so smoothly contained--in the way that a bomb inspires greater fear when it ticks than when it explodes. Far from consciously subjugating his rage, he had given it instinctive, reflexive, classical expression. To have characterized the event as a traditional occurrence in a modern setting ("Indonesia, Land of Contrasts") would have missed the point that the attendant was unwittingly making with such force--or, rather, that I am wittingly making him make--namely, that adjectives like "traditional," "anachronistic," and "abnormal" are all alien definitions of his situation. To comprehend his behavior in his own terms requires some prior imagining: that historic and personal time are different; that the analytic categories of comparative social science provide less an objective understanding than a subjective domestication of reality; that without a culture we cannot see but with one are forever blind.

No approach to reality is intrinsically superior to any other because the category "superior" is itself extrinsic and imposed, but that limitation covers even the extreme solipsistic denial of the independent existence of reality. Not even on the most hostile grounds--philosophic grounds--are we intellectually warranted in declaring objectivity in social science an impossible ideal, because impossibility is itself a category of domestication: a subjective way of imagining what we cannot imagine. The epistemological paradox is not, then, a counsel of despair but a celebration of knowing as a creative act. And some approaches to understanding *are* superior to others if we define superior, as I do, to mean the degree to which they lead us to a comprehension of social reality initially in the terms of those who experience it. The word initially is important, for the generation of second-order comprehension--what we call "analytic," "comparative," or (even more devoutly) "scientific" understanding--can then proceed with less distortion and more predictive power--in second-order language, with greater "objectivity"--than if we tried straightaway to organize reality according to the abstractions of social science. Classification is a chaotic business not because society has no rules or patterns, but because Mr. Biswas' questionnaires are insufficiently related to them; he flounders because his methodology has prevented him from learning how the people in those two hundred households in Trinidad interpret their experiences every day.

What has all this to do with the study of rural political change? A lot, I think. In the novel, Mr. Biswas' households are poor; at the hotel, so is the parking attendant. Second-order language, including the language of survey research, is an elite tongue. To write a questionnaire in first-order terms is to struggle creatively against the confines of the epistemological paradox; a pretest is an objectively "hopeless"--but subjectively creative--attempt to improve the fit between external and internal frames of reference.

This line of argument points, I think, to at least three difficulties in the use of questionnaires to study rural political change. The first is that a researcher whose attention is concentrated on the survey "instrument" (itself an objectivist term) may then let the resulting "data" speak for themselves. This is something they are manifestly unable to do, for they have been written partly in one second-order mode (an operationalized hypothesis, say) and processed entirely in another (Fortran, for example). Nor can the sophisticated manipulation of data already gathered increase their inductive value. Factor analysis, another mode of the second order, is a kind of "phenomenology after the fact" that, while statistically useful, is epistemologically naive when applied to evidence, especially attitudinal evidence, obtained from populations that are peripheral to the world culture, uneducated by Western standards, and materially poor--circumstances that still describe the bulk of rural personkind.

The second difficulty is that political change usually involves interaction between elites and nonelites. Because elites are more likely to speak the second-order language of the researcher, they are better able to answer his or her questions. (Response set, for example, is inversely correlated with education.) Lacking intellectual access to nonelites, the survey researcher is likely to produce an elite-focused picture of "the way things are." No foreign scholar working in a rural area lacks one or more key informants, usually drawn from the local or regional elite. The scholar's need to be able to talk to someone in the analytic language of social science reinforces his association with these elite figures and with their versions of rural reality. Members of relatively powerless groups, on the other hand, are unlikely to represent political reality on their own terms, either for fear of retaliation after the scholar has packed up his paraphernalia and left or from general feelings of inappropriateness in the presence of second-order cultural spokesmen. The interview itself expresses a power relationship.

Lastly, rural political change is hard to study "scientifically," not only for these reasons--because it is rural and political--but because it involves change. No rural community anywhere in the world remains completely untouched by the world culture; the Tasadays in the Philippines are a "holdout" succumbing to this rule. Change is ubiquitous, and it typically involves some clash or compromise between second- and first-order experience. To attempt to understand change in purely second-order terms is to ignore the diversity and authenticity of local experience and to consign much of it to a static, residual, analytic category of the "traditional" or, teleologically, the "premodern." Structural functionalism is an example; it is no coincidence that Gabriel Almond's least structural-functional writing is about "crisis, choice, and change." Because a political crisis in a rural area typically involves elites and nonelites, it tends to lay bare the differences between the ways local officials organize experience and the ways peasants do. A time of political quiescence, on the contrary, serves the scholar who would capture first-order outlooks in second-order terms, for he lacks behavioral reminders that first-order experience has not been successfully domesticated by elites, including himself. Violence in this sense is a reality shock of the first order, one night on the steps of a Jakarta hotel, or, in the example of rural political change I want to use here to illustrate these ideas, one morning in the fishing community of Muncar on Java's easternmost coast.

The most important introductory facts about Muncar for this, an outsider's, purpose are that it is the second biggest fishing complex in the Indonesian archipelago, with a shifting population of up to ten thousand or so during the height of the sardine season; that it is located in one of the richest agricultural regions of East Java, the district of Banyuwangi, in one of the agriculturally richest subdistricts, Muncar, within that district; that Muncar subdistrict has been officially recognized as the second-best developing of all the subdistricts in East Java (itself considered by the central government to be the most successful developer of any province in the country), that one of the villages in Muncar subdistrict (Sumberberas, meaning a source of rice) has been recognized as East Java's best developing village; that during the nation's First Five-Year Plan (1969-1974) saltwater fish yields lagged behind rising per capita rice production; that the annual tonnage of sardines beached in Muncar (they are the mainstay of its catch) declined absolutely in all but two of the last ten years and fell in 1974 to a figure lower than any registered in all but one of those years; that the head of Banyuwangi district is a wealthy, forceful, Javanese lieutenant colonel determined to do something about the "fishing problem" in Muncar, which he defines not only as a case of negative growth but also of economic exploitation of poor fishermen by moneylenders and boat owners; and, finally, that, whereas the populations of Muncar subdistrict and Banyuwangi district are for the most part ethnically Javanese and nominally Muslim, the fishing community itself is mainly Madurese and thoroughly Muslim.

In February 1974 the governor of East Java, a Madurese civilian with a long record of service in territorial administration, summoned the district heads and mayors of the province to a meeting in its capital city, Surabaya; among them was the head of Banyuwangi district. One of the topics covered by the governor at that meeting was the "fishing problem," which he saw as a matter of increasing fish production (growth) while assuring the fishermen of a greater share in the value of their catch (equality). This meeting was held a few months before the nation's First Five-Year Plan was scheduled to end and the Second Five-Year Plan (1974-1979) to begin. The stress laid in Surabaya on equality was no accident, for whereas the First Plan had emphasized rehabilitation and growth to rebuild Indonesia's economy from the shambles of the Sukarno era, the nation's highest legal body (Majelis Permusyawaratan Rakyat or MPR, the People's Consultative Assembly) had already underscored the importance of narrowing the gap between rich and poor as a broad goal of state policy in its session in Jakarta the preceding year. Indeed, since the declaration of Indonesia's independence in 1945, the idea of social equity has been enshrined among the five principles (Pancasila) of the nation state.

In Banyuwangi, the upshot of the Surabaya meeting was a document (*Penjinakan Ijon Nelayan* [Banyuwangi: Kantor Pemerintah Daerah Kabupaten Banyuwangi, 9 May 1974]), signed by the district head in May 1974, in which the district government proposed a 250 million rupiah program to break the hold of moneylenders and boat owners over the fishermen of Muncar and simultaneously to boost ocean yields. A fishermen's cooperative (Badan Usaha Unit Desa or BUUD, modeled after proto-cooperatives of the same name previously introduced in the agricultural sector) would be established in order to receive bank credits that would improve the catching and marketing of fish through the purchase and repair of boats and equipment, and would capitalize the activity of *pemindangan* (the water-based cooking of fish and their packaging for wholesale in leaves and small bamboo baskets), the fish-processing mode least dominated by Chinese entrepreneurs. In the document, top priority was placed on "cutting the main channels" of the fish industry whereby *pengambek* (owners of financial capital) and *juragan darat* (owners of fixed capital, especially boats) were, in effect, able to maintain the fishermen in an economically weak position in which they continued to suffer, in the words of the report, "a most pitiful fate."

Over a period of years before 1974, Chinese businessmen had introduced three major innovations into the Muncar fishing complex: sardine-canning factories, outboard motors, and nylon purse seine nets. The factories required top-quality sardines and thus placed a premium on the speed with which the highly perishable fish could be delivered; they also sharply increased the demand for sardines. The new motors and nets arose largely in response to these incentives. The motors reduced delivery times, and the huge purse seine nets, one hundred meters deep, meant a jump in the catch by a factor of at least three and up to ten, according to some estimates, compared to existing boat fishing techniques. By 1974, however, the two innovations were not widespread. Although a number of the boats in Muncar had been equipped with motors, these still remained a fraction of the total fleet of some two thousand craft and did not alter a whole range of ongoing, small-scale means of extraction not centered on the use of boats at all. Even less widespread were the new nets; in the first half of 1974 only about twenty were operating, all but a few of these owned by Chinese and none by Madurese. (The non-Chinese owners were part of the small community of Buginese, originally from South Sulawesi, who maintain a number of stationary bamboo lift nets close to the beach.)

During the first half of 1974, the Chinese-owned canning factories bought their supply of sardines increasingly from their own motorized, purse seine-equipped boats. These boats were consistently and visibly the first to return to the beach in the morning with the most and freshest fish, which in turn fetched higher prices from the factories than the sardines other fishermen could deliver using older techniques. On 4 July 1974, over two hundred fishermen approached fishing officials on the beach to protest the use of motors and purse seine nets by the Chinese; the fishermen argued that the new methods were enabling the Chinese canners, who already dominated the fish trade on the land, to extend their control to the sea. To calm the angry mood of the crowd, local officials persuaded its members to channel their protest in the form of a petition to the government. The petition itself is a sheaf of papers showing the name and address of each (as written down by an official) and, alongside these, his mark. Of the 244 persons who joined the petition, 196 left their thumb prints; only 48, less than a fifth, were literate enough to be able to sign. The petition presented no grievance; that was done on the fishermen's behalf by the local officials in a report passed on to their superiors. In that report, the protesters were said to have requested that fishing by Chinese using motorized boats and purse seine nets be stopped and that the district head's plans to provide credit to indigenous fishermen be realized. Although the first request was undoubtedly made by the fishermen that day, and vehemently, the second one may have been suggested to them by officials anxious to make the protest seem more constructive in the government's eyes. There is inadequate evidence that on 4 July the crowd even knew about the administration's plans to help, although these had been under discussion for several months among civil servants in the district capital (Banyuwangi city) only forty kilometers away.

In any event, the district head swiftly complied with both demands. Two days later the further use of purse seine nets by anyone in Muncar was banned; some of the nets were shifted to Bali, where they were still legal, and the rest stored in factory sheds and owners' homes. The catching of fish by nonindigenous persons or enterprises in Muncar by any means was forbidden. Lastly, plans to drop credits to indigenous fishermen were speeded up. The latter program gained further momentum after a coincidental visit on 15 July 1974 by a highly placed general from Jakarta, who met in Muncar with a small number of persons, hand-picked by subdistrict and village authorities to articulate before the visitor the desires of the indigenous majority of the fishing community. At that meeting these spokesmen urged that the planned credits be dropped into Muncar as soon as possible. The general in turn spoke of the central government's intentions to promote and protect ethnically Indonesian enterprise against Chinese competition.

In August preparations went ahead to ready seven units to be turned over on easy credit terms to the fishermen. Each unit would include one nylon purse seine net, three wooden boats (two large, one small) freshly made in Madura, three ten-horsepower outboard engines, and four high-pressure kerosene lanterns to attract the fish to the surface at night when most fishing is done; kerosene, gasoline, and other items would also be supplied. Formal responsibility for the effort lay with a Project to Prepare the Fishing BUUD (Proyek Persiapan BUUD Perikanan, or PPBP), for the BUUD itself had still not been established. Effective responsibility for the project lay in the hands of three people: a Madurese resident of Muncar named Nursid, and two Indonesians of Chinese descent who lived outside the fishing complex. Mursid had been a district-wide leader of the Muslim Teachers' Party (Nahdlatul Ulama, or NU) and was well known among the fishermen; Muncar is a strongly NU community. Some of his ex-colleagues in the party had been angered, however, by his decision to leave NU and join the government's alternative, the Functional Group (Golongan Karya, or Golkar); they suspected him of having sold out to the regime in order to enjoy the perquisites of an official position. The 1971 elections, which pitted NU against Golkar in East Java amid charges of official intimidation, probably sharpened such hostility. One of the two Chinese was a businessman who had played an active role in introducing motors and purse seines into Muncar, ran one of the canneries there, and had a brother who kept equally busy in the semi-official rice trade; the brothers lived in and worked out of Banyuwangi city. The other Chinese owned and lived behind a store in a subdistrict capital between Muncar and Banyuwangi city; there he and his family sold Japanese motorbikes. All three men knew each other well and two of them were on familiar terms with the district head; the storekeeper had in fact served for a time as the district head's chauffeur.

While these three men arranged for the purchase and preparation of the seven units, the recruitment of teams to receive the equipment got under way. Each unit of outfitted boats was to be presented to a team of twelve men; only eighty-four (7 x 12) among the thousands of fishermen in Muncar would be chosen. The district head specified that only indigenous fishermen who did not already own a boat could qualify, and that the equipment was to be owned collectively by the twelve men; the point was to raise the level of living of the "have nots," not to benefit the "haves," and he feared that, were a team leader made the owner of the equipment, he would simply use it to exploit the other eleven members just as, in the district head's opinion, the juragan darat had been doing to poor fishermen for years. To make these selections, the district head relied on the territorial administrative hierarchy over which he presided: The heads of Kedungrejo and Tembokrejo villages, whose joint east-west boundary roughly bisected the fishing complex, would draw up a list and submit it to him through the Muncar subdistrict head. The two village heads were both junior army officers; one had been appointed to his post by the district head and the other elected without opposition in a coerced contest some years earlier. The district head returned the list these two men produced on grounds that some of the names on it were in fact "haves," but it was soon amended, resubmitted, and approved.

Seen from the beach, the selection process looked far less straightforward. No public announcement was made that fishermen could put themselves forward as candidates to join a team. Word of the opportunity was instead spread informally by village officials and by Mursid and his colleagues in the PPBP. Being so valuable, given the bonanza that participation in a purse seine unit could be expected to bring, the news tended to circulate among close friends and relatives. It is no coincidence that one of the teams ultimately chosen was led by the nephew of the head of a subvillage administrative unit in Kedungrejo; this uncle was a friend and subordinate of village officials and also a juragan darat, and he stood to benefit through his nephew from the government's largesse. At the risk of simplifying this word-of-mouth process somewhat, it appears that the first circle of persons made aware of the opportunity became team leaders and that each of these then proceeded to recruit the other eleven members by sharing the information with his own friends. Another important criterion, however, was prior experience in using the new technology; this consideration favored the recruitment as team members of Madurese fishermen who had worked the Chinese motorized purse seine boats while they were still legal.

As word of the impending windfall began finally to be heard beyond these circles of intimates, two kinds of money transactions began to occur and be talked about that represented dramatic breaks with long-established precedent. In order to understand these changes it is necessary briefly to portray the cones of personal obligation that customarily organize the activity of catching and marketing fish in Muncar. Breaking arbitrarily into the cycle of obligation-creation and value-sharing, let us begin with a juragan darat who has just bought an additional boat. He must now recruit men to sail it. He will not merely offer the fishermen a daily wage or share of the catch. First, he would not feel secure in that the fishermen thus recruited would be under no moral obligation to continue to take his boat out to sea; if an offer of a higher wage or a greater share came along, what would stop them from deserting his boat for another's? Second, the fishermen themselves would not agree to work for him under such insecure conditions; instead, they would expect a sum of money to be given to them by the boat owner at the start of the relationship. This sum is said to create a tie between the boat owner and the fishermen such that the latter will not desert the former. Technically, the sum constitutes a debt owed by the fisherman to the juragan darat, and the fisherman could in theory free himself from the boat owner by repaying him this amount. In the eyes of the fisherman, however, the amount appears less like a debt to be repaid than a kind of sealing of a mutual obligation between himself and the juragan darat. The money is loaned, without interest, not in the expectation that it will be repaid--on the contrary, the boat owner hopes it will not be, for that would entail the loss of his claim on the fisherman--but in the realization that it marks the beginning of an open-ended period of tenure in which the fisherman will go nightly to sea in the owner's boat and will enjoy a regular share of the catch which, though never larger than the share reserved for the owner, will enable the fisherman to maintain a subsistence living. In addition, the fisherman's moral claim on the owner can be exercised in times of sudden need--a funeral, a wedding--to extract small additional sums that are normally also not thought of as repayable debts but as expressions of the deepening relationship between the two men.

Having picked out his fishermen, the boat owner must now raise the money (*uang ikatan*) to create these ties, and also to outfit the boat and finance its initial operating costs. For this purpose, the juragan darat turns to the pengambek (freely, a moneylender, but literally, someone who "holds" the boat owner) to create a similar tie. That is, the pengambek makes an interest-free loan to the juragan darat which neither party expects to be repaid because it sanctions the new open-ended relationship between them; in return, the pengambek is entitled to five or ten percent of the value of the catch and has the right indefinitely to market that catch on behalf of the boat owner and the fishermen. The major difference in the pengambek-juragan darat dyad compared to the juragan darat-fishermen tie is that the moneylender and the boat owner are much closer to each other in socioeconomic status than are the owner and the fishermen.

Three things are worth noting about these inverted cones. First, they proliferate not through fragmentation and upward mobility but through extension and what might be called diagonal mobility. That is, a boat owner who becomes wealthy enough to repay his "debt" to the pengambek and to set himself up as a pure patron unobligated to anyone higher up is unlikely to do so, for that would mean insulting his original benefactor, the pengambek. Instead, the boat owner may choose one of three alternatives: to purchase another boat and go through the same procedure, most likely with the same pengambek, to obtain working capital for it and uang ikatan for its crew; to become a pengambek in his own right by providing uang ikatan and working capital to another boat owner in need of finance; or, if he has enough money, to buy another boat and himself provide working capital for it and uang ikatan for the fishermen he recruits to operate it. The latter two outcomes will mean that our boat owner has now also become a pengambek, and in fact the distinction between juragan darat and pengambek in Muncar has become more a matter of distinct shares than distinct individuals. However, for the fishermen, who are generally much poorer than the boat owners and moneylenders, this kind of diagonal mobility is very rare. Fishermen go to sea, while the pengambek and the boat owner (juragan darat means literally lord of the land) do not; the difference between the two groups continues to identify distinct individuals as well as functions.

Second, the important fact for the fisherman is not that he receives less of the catch than the boat owner but that the boat owner has guaranteed his subsistence. This is especially true when the boat owner, as often happens, is a senior relative of the fisherman. But even when that is not the case, the fisherman normally accepts as customary the division of the catch. The shares of fishermen, owners, and pengambek have been standardized over time for each type of boat. The cases I was able to observe indicate that on the average, across various kinds of craft, an owner obtains between twelve and fifteen percent more of each catch than a fisherman, but during my extended stay on the beach I never found a fisherman who was willing to say that he felt this unequal division to be unfair. Nor did any of my other local informants, who have lived in Muncar for many years and become during my residence there quite open with me, report such an opinion. It should also be noted that because of the steadily declining size of the average catch--which the fishermen translate into their experience with the word *laep* meaning a time of insufficiency--it has become fairly common in Muncar for boat owners to take less than their allotted share when the small yield of a night's fishing would otherwise threaten the subsistence of their fishermen. In the latter's eyes this pattern of cones and shares, far from exploiting them by confiscating the surplus value of their labor, enables them to survive; and they accept it in this spirit.

Third, pengambek, juragan darat, and fishermen are almost always indigenous Madurese (excepting the special case of the Buginese lift nets). Although the pengambek may borrow money from Chinese moneylenders or from state or private banks, this activity is far removed from the fishermen's ken. To them, the Chinese appear mainly as people who own or operate the canneries and other fish-processing establishments and who consequently buy fish from the pengambek (or, more typically, from indigenous Madurese middlemen and middlewomen called *blantik* who purchase from the pengambek and sell to the processors).

After this digression, which is in fact quite central to an understanding of what was to happen, we can better appreciate why the effects of the rumored windfall in August and September were so devastating. The first new kind of money transaction to occur was initiated by fishermen who hoped to increase their incomes drastically by somehow managing to be among the elect to be chosen to staff the seven new units. These men now sought to repay the uang ikatan their juragan darat had loaned them (in some cases many years before) and thus free themselves to join one of the new units. Part of the budget of the PPBP was in fact reserved for just such purposes, to help poor fishermen buy their way out of their existing obligations and thus break the hold of the pengambek/juragan darat upon them. But it was not that easy to join one of the seven units; there were only eighty-four places and thousands of fishermen qualified for them by the district head's criteria. The further the rumors of the impending boon spread beyond Mursid and the village heads and their circles of friends, the greater became the disparity of numbers between applicants and positions. Eventually fishermen stepped forward who were willing to buy their way into one of the new boats, and this second type of transaction, too, broke sharply with custom. At the same time it represented an attempt to coopt the new structures--still only rumored, not established--in locally meaningful terms, for at least some of these supplicants appear to have borrowed the bribe money from juragan darat or pengambek who hoped thus to gain some influence and share in the coming arrangement. Ironically, had these embryonic minicones, a clear case of corruption if judged by formally modern standards, been allowed to develop on the otherwise alien body of the new project, the events of late September might not have been so destructive to the project's modernizing goal, for a greater portion of the community's elite would have had a stake in its achievement. The fact that such furtive dyads were relatively rare is due not to any qualms the project organizers had about accepting bribes but rather to the sheer sums of money involved in the project's own budget, which already gave ample scope for the exercise of self-enrichment by its administrators. The district head's rejection of the original list submitted by the village heads may also have been read as a warning in this regard.

In any event, viewed in terms of Muncar's customary arrangements, the district head's plan to modernize the fishing industry and to channel more of its profits to the poor fishermen became illegitimate even before it could be carried out. The pengambek and juragan darat who lost fishermen to the new units were insulted, their "generosity" rejected with the help of the government; the majority of the fishermen, neither chosen by Mursid and the village heads (themselves seen by many in Muncar as, respectively, politically turncoat and alien personalities), nor qualified on grounds of prior experience operating the Chinese purse seines, nor able to purchase a share of the impending largesse, resented the good fortune of the minority who were; and both groups still associated the new technology with the Chinese who had first introduced it and had tried to use it to "control the ocean" before the successful protest of 4 July. These sentiments prompted the writing of slogans around the fishing community in the days preceding the scheduled presentation of the equipment, slogans to the effect that with the new nets "the fishermen, dying on the land, will die at sea," and that if the new nets were reintroduced, "the poor people will run wild."

On 16 September 1974, the boats, motors, nets, and accessories for the seven units, whose members had by then all been chosen, were presented to the unit teams in a formal ceremony in Muncar, attended by district, subdistrict, and village officials. From the fishing community, however, only the seven groups of twelve men each were invited; although some adults and curious children stood on the sidelines to observe the proceedings, no attempt was made to explain directly to the Muncar community as a whole the aims behind the project. In addition, the presentation was made in Indonesian, the language of the officials, not Madurese, the language of the fishermen.

A little over a week went by before any of the units could be made fully operational and the teams become sufficiently versed in the new technology to justify a first venture to sea. By the night the first unit did set out, fresh slogans had appeared on Muncar's walls; more numerous than those in the earlier wave, these voiced three imperatives, in roughly descending order of frequency: "destroy the nets," "don't be afraid," and "we must act." On the night of 28 September, the first action occurred; one of the new boats was stoned at sea by unknown persons. (How truly unknown these persons were is hard to tell, since witnesses at the subsequent trial generally avoided implicating anyone by name.) In response, the local navy commander provided an escort to ensure the safety of the boats. Intelligence officers also reportedly began to investigate the situation to prevent further incidents. In the meantime, those among the new units that were fully operational continued to bring in large catches, which were sold mainly to the Chinese-owned canneries.

On the morning of 30 September 1974, at about nine o'clock, a crowd later estimated at between two and three thousand strong began to form in the community. Shouts of "destroy the nets" were widely heard and at about nine thirty the crowd gathered in front of Mursid's home and began denouncing him. Mursid himself was in his office on the beach helping to handle the previous night's catches. Mursid's wife and children, who were at home, quietly slipped out the back door and went into hiding, but not before they had sent a messenger to Mursid to warn him of the danger. Realizing that he was not at home, the crowd, shouting loudly, moved on to his office.

Afraid, or not realizing the seriousness of his situation, or both, Mursid stayed put. But when he could hear the shouting--which included, by his subsequent report, the cry "kill Mursid"--he decided to try to escape. Unfortunately for him, his sole available route lay across the field directly between his office and the crowd. He ran, in the words of an eyewitness, "like a hunted rabbit," but the crowd soon surrounded him and began to beat him with fists and stones until he fell, bleeding from head wounds, to the ground. Mursid feels sure he would have been killed on the spot were it not for his mother, who now appeared on the scene, highly distraught. Except for some observers, she was the only woman present, and apparently out of respect for her as a mother, the crowd parted to allow her to go to the aid of her son. Cradling his bloody head, she was able to take him off to the police station in a pedicab. From there he was carried, unconscious, in a Mitsubishi Colt (minibus) to the hospital in Banyuwangi city, where his cuts were stitched and eventually he recovered.

Meanwhile the crowd began to seek out and destroy all the boats, nets, engines, lanterns, and other equipment that the district head had turned over two weeks before. The homes and storage sheds of a number of Chinese, including the businessman who with Mursid and the store-keeper had managed the project, were broken into and their contents, including the purse seine nets stored there after the July ban, looted or destroyed. Using kerosene from the lanterns and gasoline from the engines, much of the equipment was set afire. Columns of thick black smoke rose in the air at various points around the community, and with them went, for the time being at least, the district head's hopes of modernizing Muncar's fishing industry. The total damage done to property was later placed at nearly 100 million rupiah, but this figure is probably too low. No one, aside from Mursid, was injured.

In the days following, hundreds were arrested, but all save eighty-eight of these were soon released. Among the detained, eight were taken to the large city of Malang, about seven hours to the west, for political interrogation by elements of the provincial army command; and the rest were questioned by district police officers in the Banyuwangi city prison. In April, May, and June 1975, the eighty-eight prisoners were tried in the Banyuwangi district civil court by three civilian judges on charges of property damage and personal assault. The defendants were sentenced to prison terms of between eight and eleven months minus time already served, except for thirteen men against whom all charges were dropped.

The story does not end there, but it will here, for its content through July 1975 is more than sufficient to fill in concretely the ideas with which this paper began: why did the incident in Muncar happen? The answers advanced in Banyuwangi all imply the contrast between first- and second-order frames of reference. The main explanations that circulated at the time and that I want to examine here are four: subversion, premeditation, primordialism, and jealousy.

Subversion. The Muncar incident occurred on the ninth anniversary of the 30 September Movement (Gerakan 30 September), which on that day in 1965 plotted to eliminate the top army leadership. In the early hours of 1 October 1965, the plot was carried out with the help of elements from the youth and women's wings of the Indonesian Communist Party (Partai Komunis Indonesia, or PKI); seven generals and a lower-ranking officer were killed. Inheriting the army command, then-Major General Suharto quickly set out to roll back the attempted coup and, more slowly, developed his own efforts into a counter-coup against the Communist party, leftist elements in the military, and ultimately against Sukarno himself, who was forced to cede the presidency to Suharto in 1967-68. Today, 30 September connotes for most elites in Indonesia political treachery if not Communist treason; no date has more negative official associations.

Unsurprisingly in this light, one of the first interpretations of the protest in Muncar was that it might have been inspired by remnants of the PKI (the party itself having been destroyed in the transition from Sukarno to Suharto). Several police and army officers in Banyuwangi district held this suspicion, which was also reported in the press. According to this logic, out of all 365 possibilities in the year, the date of the Muncar incident could not be a coincidence.

What this explanation did not take into account--aside from the fact that, as a Madurese Muslim community, Muncar had always been hostile ground for the PKI--was the fact that the Gregorian calendar is not important in Muncar. Insofar as any system of dates organizes time in Muncar it is the lunar system of Islam. What officials knew as 30 September was much better known inside the community as 13 Ramadhan. Nor is the distinction merely religious. Civil servants in Indonesia are generally paid around the turn of the Gregorian month; its sun-established dates are an index of where they stand financially in time. The incomes of fishermen are moon-centered. The effectiveness of the kerosene lanterns used to attract fish to the surface of the water at night declines as the moon waxes; the fish become less able to distinguish the light of the lanterns from the increasingly bright moonlight that illuminates the sea's surface and are therefore harder to concentrate in one place to be caught. A full moon marks the nadir of fishing activity; at that time most fishermen do not bother going to sea at all.

This contrast between personal or first-order and historic or second-order time affords insights into the nature of the new technology as seen from the beach and of the fishermen's reaction to it. The great depth of the new nets meant that their users were no longer dependent on the relative absence of moonlight, for they could now reach down, away from a waxing moon, one hundred meters into the marine darkness. In this way, the purse seines threatened to upset the lunar rhythm of the catch. Nor is it a coincidence that on the date of the first protest, 4 July (31 Jumadilakhir), the moon over Muncar was perfectly full, or that on 1 October (14 Ramadhan), less than twenty-four hours after the smoke had cleared, it was again. Officials who interpreted the latter event in calendrical terms were not wrong to do so; they merely chose the wrong calendar, one natural to them but unnatural to the fishermen. To link the second protest to the anniversary of an attempted coup in faraway Jakarta was to make a statement as locally meaningless as to have related the first protest to American independence. I do not mean to suggest that the fishermen are in some mystical relationship of dependence on the moon--they are, in second-order language, quite rational and unsentimental about such matters--but it is clear that on these two occasions the full moon combined with widely felt laep or dearth made especially galling the contrast between the tons of high-quality fish being beached by the purse seine boats and the incapacity of the rest of the fishermen to work the illuminated sea with customary methods.

Premeditation. Although the uniquely lunar circumstances of the protests occurred, to my knowledge, to no one connected with these events, it is to the credit of explanation-seeking officials that they eventually abandoned the subversion hypothesis for lack of proof. Otherwise the detainees would have faced political charges and much harsher sentences. Yet the feeling was and still is strong among officials, especially army and police officers, that someone somehow must have been "behind" the 30 September incident. Under pretrial police interrogation, several hajis confessed to having plotted the affair and to having promised large sums of money to would-be accomplices. However, in court these supposed ringleaders denied their pretrial testimony and claimed it had been extorted from them through physical intimidation. Before the judges one of these men confronted the assurances given by a police witness that prisoners had not been intimidated by ripping open his shirt to reveal the bruises he said he had received. Although this evidence was not entertained by the court, the denials of these accused men were sufficiently convincing to lead the prosecuting attorney and later the judges to drop all charges against them and to bill the government for these prisoners' share of all court costs. The prosecution then attempted to describe the individual who had taken the most prominent part in the beating of Mursid as the man behind the whole incident, and this prisoner was ultimately given the longest sentence (eleven months); but the notion that behind the affair lay a premeditated plot was allowed to lapse. Least happy with this turn of events, and most convinced that there must have been a *dalang* (wayang puppeteer) manipulating the protest if only he could be found, was the district head.

The idea of premeditation, like the subversion theory from which it represented a tactical retreat, allowed those who believed it to preserve an image of the fishermen of Muncar as the unwitting tools of a handful of malcontents. The district administration was deeply shocked and embarrassed by what happened. Hadn't the modernization project been aimed precisely at helping the poor against those who were exploiting them? How could they have knowingly bitten the hand that had been extended to feed them? These rhetorical questions enabled officials to avoid re-examining the basic nature of the project--it was merely agreed that it had not been adequately explained to the fishermen--and also to avoid examining the nature of the Muncar fishing pattern in the latter's own terms. Instead, an official survey was conducted in Muncar in November 1974 using three different mimeographed questionnaires, one for fish processors, one for boat owners, and one for fishermen; it asked only about details of production in second-order, Indonesian language and was administered by village officials, including several Javanese who spoke little or no Madurese, who lacked either prior training in second-order survey research methods or a first-order understanding of the culture on Muncar's beach.

The validity of information obtained from the three (nonrandom) samples appears to have been highest with the boat owners and lowest among the factory managers and fishermen, which suggests that objectivist techniques work better among members of middle social strata who are neither able to see through the questions (some managers refused to answer; others prevaricated creatively) nor intimidated by them (to the limited extent that the fishermen responded honestly they appear to have done so from fear). One of the interviewers later showed me a copy of the computerized form used by the Central Bureau of Statistics in the agricultural census of 1973 and compared it unfavorably to the (unpretested) Muncar questionnaires; the categories used in the latter had not been able to capture what he saw, like Mr. Biswas, as the formlessness of his respondents' experience.

At the risk of overloading the notion of premeditation, one more comment about it should be made. Like the survey of individuals, it implied a search for individuals: who (not what) had caused the incident to happen? Officials tended to look for that handful of people who had caused a general outburst--in Indonesian, the shrimp behind the stone (*udang dibalik batu*). They did not reverse that perspective and ask what collectively felt circumstances could have encouraged mass action against the individual personality of Mursid. The latter approach would have sought an underlying structural explanation of the event and an understanding of how Mursid could have come locally to represent, as it were, an intersection of so many objectionable conditions. The trial of the eighty-eight from this perspective appears less an exercise of the law--though it was that too--than a ritual of induction meant to acculturate the fishermen's behavior into the "adult," second-order world of the official elite. On the map of that world, the cones of Muncar were unmarked; the shattering effect on them of the district head's project literally could not be seen.

Primordialism. Under this awkward heading fall explanations of the event that stress the Muslim Madureseness of its participations. But although not unhelpful, this approach too leads the observer away from structural questions and may in its extreme form reveal more about his own distance from the incident than about the motivations of the crowd. Among nominally Muslim Javanese in the district, the committed Muslim Madurese of Muncar have a reputation for fanaticism and ferocity. Officials recalled the enthusiasm of the local population for the routing and killing of leftists in 1966. (In the trial, the defense attorney tried to use this reputation to his clients' advantage as a badge of their anticommunism.) And the Chinese entrepreneurs were obvious racial and religious targets.

Several aspects of the incident, however, do not jibe with this interpretation. One of the arrested men was of partly Chinese descent; he had been prominent in the protest of 4 July. No Chinese was injured, whereas Muslim Madurese Mursid was badly hurt. And among the wall slogans that augured the two protests, unalloyed racial references to the Chinese were rare. One sign did refer to "black people," meaning the indigenous population, but the others implied discontent over the penetration by Chinese entrepreneurs of cone-making roles previously reserved for indigenes. The difference between "land" and "sea," which appeared often in these messages, is less adequately seen as a racial than as a class distinction (although neither category, I suspect, captures very much of the first-order experience involved), for the Madurese pengambek and juragan darat also operated on land. The fishermen objected not to the Chinese buying fish on the shore; the canneries had increased the demand for sardines and had allowed some pengambek to play one factory off against another for a better price, the benefits of which trickled down to the fishermen through the sharing system. What was resented was the opposite phenomenon: the blurring of their purchasing role by Chinese businessmen who began financing the new technology at sea. The Chinese appear to have become a target not because of their Chineseness, racial or religious, but because they were associated, along with Mursid and the purse seine nets, in a perceived threat to the customary structures that allowed the fishermen to subsist.

During the trial, just as officials retreated from political subversion as an explanation to mere criminal premeditation, the eighty-eight accused (partly, I suspect, on their lawyer's advice) shied away from any criticism of the modernization program (that is, of the government) and found in the anti-Chinese hypothesis an officially more tolerable explanation of their own actions. The detainees all claimed that they did not know the September nets were government property; that they had thought they were destroying Chinese nets; and that they were not against the new technology but only against its use by the Chinese. This explanation also meshed with the private experience of the district head, who years earlier had tried and failed to supply his troops from the proceeds of the Muncar fish trade by cutting out the Chinese entirely. That failure he blamed on the Chinese "fish mafia," as he put it, and although at one level he was quite willing to assign to Chinese entrepreneurs roles of responsibility in the project, at another the "anti-Chinese" sentiments of the fishermen were to him easily understood. And that was what the prisoners needed most desperately to do: to display a motivation that the official elite could, if not condone, at least sympathize with.

Jealousy. Of all the explanations of what happened, jealousy (*iri hati*) became the most widely accepted, and in some ways it is very attractive. It refers to a natural human emotion, and in that sense does not treat the fishermen's reaction as either a virulently special case of Muslim Madureseness against non-Muslim Chineseness or as a mindless rejection of modern technology. The universality of jealousy makes it compelling in both first-order and second-order frames, including those of fishermen, local officials, and myself as a foreign scholar. Everyone has felt jealousy at some point in his or her life, and it is true that in situations of shared poverty the good fortune of a minority can easily trigger the enmity of the less favored. Examples from Muncar are not hard to find. Both Mursid and his superior (an army officer) in the PPBP quickly obtained luxury goods through the access and money he enjoyed in the project, notably Japanese motorbikes and tape recorders, and this did not go unnoticed in their community at a time when some of its members were being forced to sell their furniture to survive. Mursid himself began driving his motorbike to his office. One afternoon when his boss's wife was down on the beach learning how to drive the small motorcycle her husband had just acquired, she fell off, but none of the fishermen watching made a move to help her onto her feet. The well-known revolution of rising expectations, Ted Gurr's relative deprivation, and Albert Hirschman's tunnel effect are among the many ways social scientists have interpreted political change in terms of the common phenomenon of competitive envy. Against this light, it is hard to imagine how the dropping of only seven nets into a poor community of thousands could have had any other result. Indeed, as I write, the government is trying to revive and protect the program by tripling the number of purse seines scheduled to be turned over to the fishermen.

Yet I wonder whether the roots of the incident do not lie deeper than the good fortune and conspicuous consumerism of a minority. The identity of the beneficiaries was, I think, crucial. A different set of eighty-four recipients might have made others jealous but not angry; the management of the project by persons more respected than Mursid and better known than the village heads or the Chinese suppliers might have meant envy but not violence. Had the units been turned over, not to collectivities of twelve men that had little organic meaning save for their ties to Mursid and the village heads, but to unusually respected individuals, including those juragan darat/pengambek best known for helping the fishermen who depended upon them for a livelihood, the equipment might never have been burned. (Whether such a successful project would have been a good thing or not is a separate question.) "Betting on the weak" can seem at once morally legitimate to outsiders and morally illegitimate to insiders, even weak ones, in communities where strength itself has been socialized and has a moral value. Phrasing the same point more abstractly, jealousy as an explanation assumes a horizontal plane of discrete and equal individuals, and that too ignores the interlinked cones of Muncar and the way in which they subjectively sanction objective inequalities.

Lastly, like subversion, premeditation, primordialism, irrational rejection of technology, and all of the other official understandings of Muncar circulating in Banyuwangi district in 1974 and 1975, jealousy pointed away from the most sensitive possibility of all: that the district government itself was almost completely to blame.

If these explanations are all ultimately unsatisfactory, what is left? Is there any way of approaching this case of rural protest that does not involve mistranslating local reality in higher-order terms? I think there is: through the concept of justice. Although an elaboration of such an approach exceeds my present scope, I would like to comment on it in relation to Muncar. Briefly, the great utility of the idea of justice, it seems to me, is that it has both an individual and a structural face. Behavior can be per se unjust but it can also derive its injustice from the conditions in which it occurs. A universal term, it can be made to bridge first and second orders of experience.

Economic growth on Java has brought advanced technology to the village. Previously the amount of land he controlled and the quality of the house he lived in were the surest signs of a man's economic status; they are still important, but they are being augmented by the possession of radios, tape recorders, motorcycles, even television sets. Unlike land, which has in the past provided employment for larger and larger numbers in the pattern Clifford Geertz has called agricultural involution, these consumer goods have no obvious social value to the community; they are meant to satisfy the private tastes and needs of their owners. The volume at which transistor radios are played is a good indicator of the resilience of Gemeinschaft in a rural community; it is not that radio owners enhance their private enjoyment by turning up the volume but instead that they thereby socialize second-order technology by making it sharable in first-order terms--and also, in a motivation that does not contradict the ethic of sharing, the owners advertise their own enhanced status. The point is that vertical cones and social deference constitute the structural mold in which the ethic of sharing has been cast. The great failure of the nets was that they were not socialized in this double sense of being shared in a way congruent with the structure of locally sanctioned inequality. Mursid's new motorcycle was merely a less threatening symbol of the same kind. Conditions of painfully felt dearth made these innovations and their usage all the more unjust.

The district administration assumed that justice and inequality were incompatible in local eyes. On the contrary, in Muncar justice is a characteristic of an inegalitarian moral order. By pointing to the importance of social and political structure, in which the district administration itself is implicated, yet at the same time reminding us that what is subjectively just in one culture may not be so in another, as shown by the different moral perspectives of the beach and the district, the idea of justice shows its double edge, one that, if taken seriously, would require elites, political and scientific alike, to reexamine their own perceptions before imposing them, by military force or scholarly assumption, upon others. And that reappraisal can--unless reform is no longer possible--narrow the cultural and structural gulf between different orders of experience and power that the fishermen were too weak and the officials too insensitive to cross.

More broadly, the irony of the modernization of rural life on Java, and in other comparable regions of the poor nations of the world, is that this process, partly spontaneous and partly inflicted in the name of an elite ideology of development, is undermining the structures of vertical trust and reciprocity without which it cannot be acculturated, at least not without a simultaneous revolutionary transformation of class and power relationships. Neither false consciousness nor the culture of poverty are helpful in understanding this tragedy, the one because it reifies structure, the other because it ignores it. At the interface between government and society, it seems to me, a relativistic notion of justice that interprets culture and structure and meshes different orders of experience holds far greater promise, not only of comprehending rural political change but of making it more humane.

SOUTHEAST ASIA PROGRAM DATA PAPERS

120 Uris Hall
Cornell University
Ithaca, New York 14853

In Print

Number 18   CONCEPTIONS OF STATE AND KINGSHIP IN SOUTHEAST ASIA, by Robert Heine-Geldern. 1956. (Fourth Printing 1972) 14 pages. $2.00.

Number 46   AN EXPERIMENT IN WARTIME INTERCULTURAL RELATIONS: PHILIPPINE STUDENTS IN JAPAN, 1943-1945, by Grant K. Goodman. 1962. 34 pages. $2.00.

Number 47   A BIBLIOGRAPHY OF NORTH VIETNAMESE PUBLICATIONS IN THE CORNELL UNIVERSITY LIBRARY, by Jane Godfrey Keyes. 1962. 116 pages. $3.00.

Number 49   THE TEXTILE INDUSTRY--A CASE STUDY OF INDUSTRIAL DEVELOPMENT IN THE PHILIPPINES, by Laurence David Stifel. 1963. 199 pages. $3.00.

Number 51   MATERNITY AND ITS RITUALS IN BANG CHAN, THAILAND, by Jane Richardson Hanks. Cornell Thailand Project, Interim Reports Series: Number Six. 1963. (Second Printing 1968) 116 pages. $2.50.

Number 54   CATALOGUE OF THAI LANGUAGE HOLDINGS IN THE CORNELL UNIVERSITY LIBRARIES THROUGH 1964, compiled by Frances A. Bernath, Thai Cataloguer. 1964. 236 pages. $3.00.

Number 55   STRATEGIC HAMLETS IN SOUTH VIET-NAM, A SURVEY AND A COMPARISON, by Milton E. Osborne. 1965. (Second Printing 1968) 66 pages. $2.50.

Number 57   THE SHAN STATES AND THE BRITISH ANNEXATION, by Sao Saimong Mangrai. 1965. (Second Printing 1969) 204 pages. $4.00.

Number 61   RAJAH'S SERVANT, by A. B. Ward. 1966. (Second Printing 1969) 204 pages. $2.50.

Number 68   THE BARITO ISOLECTS OF BORNEO: A CLASSIFICATION BASED ON COMPARATIVE RECONSTRUCTION AND LEXICOSTATISTICS, by Alfred Hudson. Linguistics Series I. 1967. 112 pages. $2.00.

Number 71   AMERICAN DOCTORAL DISSERTATIONS ON ASIA, 1933-JUNE 1966, INCLUDING APPENDIX OF MASTER'S THESES AT CORNELL UNIVERSITY 1933-JUNE 1968, by Curtis W. Stucki. 1968. (Second Printing 1970) 304 pages. $4.00.

Number 72   EXCAVATIONS OF THE PREHISTORIC IRON INDUSTRY IN WEST BORNEO, vol. I, RAW MATERIALS AND INDUSTRIAL WASTE, Vol. II, ASSOCIATED ARTIFACTS AND IDEAS, by Tom Harrisson and Stanley J. O'Connor. 1969. 417 pages. $5.00 each set.

Number 73   THE SEPARATION OF SINGAPORE FROM MALAYSIA, by Nancy McHenry Fletcher. 1969. (Second Printing 1971) 98 pages. $2.50.

Number 75   WHITE HMONG-ENGLISH DICTIONARY, compiled by Ernest E. Heimbach. Linguistics Series IV. 1969. (Second Printing 1979) 497 pages. $6.50.

Number 82   MAGINDANAO, 1860-1888: THE CAREER OF DATO UTO BUAYAN, by Reynald C. Ileto. 1971. 80 pages. $3.50.

Number 83   A BIBLIOGRAPHY OF PHILIPPINE LINGUISTICS AND MINOR LANGUAGES, with Annotations and Indices Based on Works in the Library of Cornell University, by Jack H. Ward. Linguistics Series V. 1971. 549 pages. $6.50.

Number 84   A CHECKLIST OF THE VIETNAMESE HOLDINGS OF THE WASON COLLECTION, CORNELL UNIVERSITY LIBRARIES, AS OF JUNE 1971, compiled by Giok Po Oey, Southeast Asia Library. 1971. 377 pages. $6.50.

Number 85   SOUTHEAST ASIA FIELD TRIP FOR THE LIBRARY OF CONGRESS, 1970-71, by Cecil Hobbs. 1971. 94 pages. $3.50.

Number 87   A DICTIONARY OF CEBUANO VISAYA, Vols. I and II, by John U. Wolff. 1972. Linguistics Series VI. 1,200 pages. $8.00.

Number 88   MIAO AND YAO LINGUISTIC STUDIES, Selected Articles in Chinese, Translated by Chang Yu-hung and Chu Kwo-ray. Edited by Herbert C. Purnell, Jr. Linguistics Series VII. 1972. 282 pages. $4.00.

Number 89   A CHECKLIST OF INDONESIAN SERIALS IN THE CORNELL UNIVERSITY LIBRARY (1945-1970), compiled by Yvonne Thung and John M. Echols. 1973. 226 pages. $7.00.

Number 90   BIBLIOGRAPHY OF VIETNAMESE LITERATURE IN THE WASON COLLECTION AT CORNELL UNIVERSITY, by Marion W. Ross. 1973. 178 pages. $4.50.

Number 91   SELECTED SHORT STORIES OF THEIN PE MYINT, Translated, with Introduction and Commentary, by Patricia M. Milne, 1973. 105 pages. $4.00.

Number 92   FEASTING AND SOCIAL OSCILLATION: A Working paper on Religion and Society in Upland Southeast Asia, by A. Thomas Kirsch. 1973. 67 pages. $3.00.

Number 95   ORIGINS OF THE PHILIPPINE REPUBLIC, Extracts from the Diaries and Records of Francis Burton Harrison, by Francis Burton Harrison. Edited and Annotated by Michael P. Onorato. 1974. 258 pages. $6.50.

Number 98   THE CRYSTAL SANDS: THE CHRONICLES OF NAGARI SRI DHARRMARAJA, translated, edited and with an introduction by David K. Wyatt. 1975. 264 pages. $6.50.

Number 100   LAO ISSARA: THE MEMOIRS OF OUN SANANIKONE, translated by John B. Murdoch and 3264, edited and with an introduction by David K. Wyatt. 1975. 60 pages. $4.50.

Number 101   AN ANNOTATED GUIDE TO PHILIPPINE SERIALS, by Frank H. Golay and Marianne H. Hauswedell. 1976. 131 pages. $5.00.

Number 103   DIRECTORY OF THE CORNELL SOUTHEAST ASIA PROGRAM 1951-1976, compiled by Frank H. Golay and Peggy Lush. 1976. 88 pages. $3.00.

Number 104   THE THAT PHANOM CHRONICLES: A SHRINE HISTORY AND ITS INTERPRETATION, edited and translated by James B. Pruess. 1976. 86 pages. $5.00.

Number 108 THE DEVARĀJA CULT, by Herman Kulke, translated and with a preface by I. W. Mabbett. 1978. 48 pages. $4.50.

Number 109 THE STATUS OF SOCIAL SCIENCE RESEARCH IN BORNEO, edited by G. N. Appell and Leigh R. Wright. 1978. 117 pages. $5.75.

Number 111 CAMBODIA'S ECONOMY AND INDUSTRIAL DEVELOPMENT, by Khieu Samphan, translated and with an introduction by Laura Summers. 1979. 122 pages. $5.75.

Number 112 DEVELOPMENT OF LABOR INSTITUTIONS IN THAILAND, by Bevars D. Maybry. 1979. 161 pages. $6.00.

Number 113 MEMOIRS OF THE FOUR-FOOT COLONEL, by General Smith Dun. 1980. 147 pages. $6.00.

Number 114 LAWYER IN THE WILDERNESS, by K. H. Digby. With a preface and notes by R. H. W. Reece. 1980. 123 pages. $5.75.

Number 115 THE MANIYADANABON OF SHIN SANDALINKA, translated by L. E. Bagshawe. 1981. 132 pages. $7.00.

Number 116 COMMUNICATIVE CODES IN CENTRAL JAVA, by John U. Wolff and Soepomo Poedjosoedarmo. 1982. 188 pages. $7.50.

STUDY AND TEACHING MATERIALS

Obtainable from Southeast Asia Program
120 Uris Hall, Cornell University, Ithaca, New York 14853

THAI CULTURAL READER, Book I, by Robert B. Jones, Ruchira C. Mendiones and Craig J. Reynolds. 1970 (Second revised edition 1976). 517 pages. $7.50.

THAI CULTURAL READER, Book II, by Robert B. Jones and Ruchira C. Mendiones. 1969. 791 pages. $8.25.

INTRODUCTION TO THAI LITERATURE, by Robert B. Jones and Ruchira C. Mendiones. 1970. 563 pages. $7.00.

A.U.A. LANGUAGE CENTER THAI COURSE, by J. Marvin Brown, Books 1, 2, 3. $4.50 each. Tape Supplements for Books 1, 2, 3, $2.00 each. SMALL TALK (Dialogue Book A), $5.00. GETTING HELP (Dialogue Book B), $5.00. BOOK R (Reading and Writing Text), $5.00. BOOK W (Reading and Writing Workbook), $5.00.

BEGINNING INDONESIAN, by John U. Wolff. 1,124 pages. Part One, revised 1977, $12.50. Part Two, reprinted 1974, $12.50. INDONESIAN READINGS, 1978, $12.50. INDONESIAN CONVERSATIONS, 1978, $12.50. FORMAL INDONESIAN, 1980, $12.50. Tapes available at extra cost.

INTERMEDIATE SPOKEN VIETNAMESE, by Franklin Huffman and Tran Trong Hai. 1980. $10.00.

Maps

Central Thailand. 7 x 10 inches; 34 km to 1 inch. Price $.25 each; $1.00 set of five.

A. 1. Jangwat Outline Map. 1955.
   2. By Amphoe. 1947.
   3. Population Density by Amphoe. 1947.
   4. Proportion of Chinese by Amphoe. 1947.

Thailand. 13 x 22 inches; scale: 50 miles to 1 inch, except B-10 as noted. Price $.25 each; $1.00 set of six.

B. 6. By Amphoe. 1927.
   7. Population Density by Amphoe. 1947.
   8. Fertility Ratios by Amphoe. 1947.
   9. Concentration of Chinese by Amphoe. 1947.
  10. Untitled (Amphoe Outline Map). 16 x 44 inches, in two parts, each 16 x 22 inches; scale: 27 miles to 1 inch.

Ethnic Settlements. Prepared by Lauriston Sharp, L. M. Hanks, William Wohnus, and K. W. Wong, Cornell Thailand Project, 1965. 27 x 35 inches; scale: 1:10,000. Price $1.00 each.

1. Ethnic Settlements, June 1, 1964, Chiengrai Province (North of the Mae Kok River).
2. Ethnic Settlements, June 1, 1964, Chiengrai Province (North of the Mae Kok River)--Akha.
3. Ethnic Settlements, June 1, 1964, Chiengrai Province (North of the Mae Kok River)--Lahu.
4. Ethnic Settlements, June 1, 1964, Chiengrai Province (North of the Mae Kok River)--Lisu.
5. Ethnic Settlements, June 1, 1964, Chiengrai Province (North of the Mae Kok River)--Yao.

Maps and Gazetteer for 1964, 1969, 1974. Maps of Ethnic Settlements of Chiengrai Province, North of the Mae Kok River, Thailand. Prepared by L. M. Hanks. 1975. 35 pages. $8.00.

INDONESIA, a semiannual journal, devoted to Indonesia's culture, history, and social and political problems.

    *No. 1, April 1966, *No. 2, Oct. 1966, *No. 3, April 1967, *No. 4, Oct. 1967
    *No. 5, April 1968, *No. 6, Oct. 1968, *No. 7, April 1969, *No. 8, Oct. 1969
    No. 9, April 1970,*No. 10, Oct. 1970, $4.50 each, $8.00 both
    No. 11, April 1971, No. 12, Oct. 1971, $4.50 each, $8.00 both
    No. 13, April 1972, No. 14, Oct. 1972, $4.50 each, $8.00 both
    No. 15, April 1973, No. 16, Oct. 1973, $4.50 each, $8.00 both
    No. 17, April 1974, No. 18, Oct. 1974, $4.50 each, $8.00 both
    *No. 19, April 1975, No. 20, Oct. 1975, $4.50 each, $8.00 both
    No. 21, April 1976, No. 22, Oct. 1976, $5.00 each, $10.00 both
    No. 23, April 1977, No. 24, Oct. 1977, $5.00 each, $10.00 both
    No. 25, April 1978, No. 26, Oct. 1978, $6.00 each, $12.00 both
    No. 27, April 1979, No. 28, Oct. 1979, $6.00 each, $12.00 both
    No. 29, April 1980, No. 30, Oct. 1980, $6.00 each, $12.00 both
    No. 31, April 1981, No. 32, Oct. 1981, $6.50 each, $12.00 both

CORNELL MODERN INDONESIA PROJECT PUBLICATIONS

102 West Avenue
Ithaca, New York 14850

*(Those preceded by an asterisk are out of print.)

*Number 1   NATIONAL STATUS OF THE CHINESE IN INDONESIA, by Donald E. Willmott. 1956. 88 pages. (Interim Report)

*Number 2   STRUCTURAL CHANGES IN JAVANESE SOCIETY: THE SUPRA-VILLAGE SPHERE, by D. H. Burger (translated by Leslie H. Palmier). 1956. 38 pages. (Translation)

*Number 3   INDONESIAN WRITING IN TRANSLATION, compiled and edited and with an introduction by John M. Echols. 1956. 178 pages. (Translation)

*Number 4   LIVING CONDITIONS OF PLANTATION WORKERS AND PEASANTS ON JAVA IN 1939-1940, by the Coolie Budget Commission. (Translated by Robert Van Niel) 1956. 131 pages.

*Number 5   DECENTRALIZATION IN INDONESIA: LEGISLATIVE ASPECTS, by Gerald S. Maryanov. 1957. 75 pages. (Interim Report)

Number 6   THE INDONESIAN ELECTIONS OF 1955, by Herbert Feith. 1957. (Second Printing 1971) 91 pages. $3.50. (Interim Report)

Number 7   THE SOVIET VIEW OF THE INDONESIAN REVOLUTION, by Ruth T. McVey. 1957. (Third Printing 1969) 90 pages. $2.50. (Interim Report)

*Number 8   SOME FACTORS RELATED TO AUTONOMY AND DEPENDENCE IN TWELVE JAVANESE VILLAGES, by Barbara S. Dohrenwend. 1957. 70 pages. (Interim Report)

*Number 9   PROBLEMS OF REGIONAL AUTONOMY IN CONTEMPORARY INDONESIA, by John D. Legge. 1957. 71 pages. (Interim Report)

*Number 10   STRUCTURAL CHANGES IN JAVANESE SOCIETY: THE VILLAGE SPHERE, by D. H. Burger. (Translated by Leslie H. Palmier) 1957. 17 pages. (Translation)

*Number 11   THE OFFICE OF PRESIDENT IN INDONESIA AS DEFINED IN THE THREE CONSTITUTIONS IN THEORY AND PRACTICE, by A. K. Pringgodigdo (Translated by Alexander Brotherton). 1957. 59 pages. (Translation)

*Number 12   DECENTRALIZATION IN INDONESIA AS A POLITICAL PROBLEM, by Gerald S. Maryanov. 1958. 118 pages. (Interim Report)

*Number 13   THE CALCUTTA CONFERENCE AND THE SOUTHEAST ASIA UPRISINGS, by Ruth T. McVey. 1958. 28 pages. (Interim Report)

*Number 14   THE BEGINNINGS OF THE INDONESIAN-DUTCH NEGOTIATIONS AND THE HOGE VELUWE TALKS, by Idrus N. Djajadiningrat. 1958. 128 pages. (Monograph)

*Number 15   THE WILOPO CABINET, 1952-53: A TURNING POINT IN POST-REVOLUTIONARY INDONESIA, by Herbert Feith. 1958. 212 pages. (Monograph)

Number 16   THE DYNAMICS OF THE WESTERN NEW GUINEA (IRIAN BARAT) PROBLEM, by Robert C. Bone, Jr. 1958. (Second Printing 1962) 182 pages. $3.00. (Interim Report)

*Number 17   ECONOMIC DEVELOPMENT AS A CULTURAL PROBLEM (Konfontasi, Sept.-Oct. 1954), by Soedjatmoko. 1958. (Second Printing 1962) 28 pages. $1.00. (Translation)

*Number 18   THE TOBA BATAK, FORMERLY AND NOW, by J. Keuning (Translated by Claire Holt). 1958. 24 pages. (Translation)

*Number 19   THE GOVERNMENT, ECONOMY AND TAXES OF A CENTRAL JAVANESE VILLAGE, by Widjojo Nitisastro and J. E. Ismael (Translated by Norbert Ward). 1959. 37 pages. (Translation)

*Number 20   THE POLITICAL CHARACTER OF THE INDONESIAN TRADE UNION MOVEMENT, by Iskandar Tedjasukmana. 1959. 130 pages. (Monograph)

*Number 21   THE SOCIO-ECONOMIC BASIS OF THE INDONESIAN STATE: ON THE INTERPRETATION OF PARAGRAPH I, ARTICLE 38, OF THE PROVISIONAL CONSTITUTION, by Wilopo and Widjojo Nitisastro. (Translated by Alexander Brotherton). 1959. 17 pages. (Translation)

*Number 22   PAST AND FUTURE, by Mohammad Hatta. 1960. 17 pages. (Translation)

*Number 23   AN APPROACH TO INDONESIAN HISTORY: TOWARDS AN OPEN FUTURE, by Soedjatmoko. 1960. 22 pages. (Translation)

*Number 24   MARHAEN AND PROLETARIAN, BY Soekarno (Translated by Claire Holt). 1960. 30 Pages. $1.00. (Translation)

Number 25   THE COMMUNIST UPRISINGS OF 1926-1927 IN INDONESIA: KEY DOCUMENTS, edited and with an introduction by Harry J. Benda and Ruth T. McVey. 1960. (Second Printing 1969) 177 pages. $5.50. (Translation)

*Number 26   ASPECTS OF LOCAL GOVERNMENT IN A SUMBAWAN VILLAGE (EASTERN INDONESIA), by Peter R. Goethals. 1961. 156 pages. (Monograph)

*Number 27   SOME SOCIAL-ANTHROPOLOGICAL OBSERVATIONS ON GOTONG-ROJONG PRACTICES IN TWO VILLAGES OF CENTRAL JAVA, by Koentjaraningrat (Translated by Claire Holt). 1961. 76 pages. (Translation)

*Number 28   THE NATIONAL STATUS OF THE CHINESE IN INDONESIA: 1900-1958, by Donald E. Willmott. Revised edition 1961. 152 pages. (Monograph)

*Number 29   SOME ASPECTS OF INDONESIAN POLITICS UNDER THE JAPANESE OCCUPATION: 1944-1954, by Benedict R. Anderson. 1961. 136 pages. (Interim Report)

*Number 30   THE DYNAMICS OF COMMUNITY DEVELOPMENT IN RURAL CENTRAL AND WEST JAVA: A COMPARATIVE REPORT, by Selosoemardjan. 1963. 40 pages. (Monograph)

*Number 31   THE CHINESE OF SUKABUMI: A STUDY OF SOCIAL AND CULTURAL ACCOMMODATION, by Giok Lan Tan. 1963. 314 pages. (Monograph)

Number 32   PRELIMINARY CHECKLIST OF INDONESIAN IMPRINTS DURING THE JAPANESE PERIOD (March 1942-August 1945), by John M. Echols. 1963. 62 pages. $1.50. (Bibliography)

*Number 33   BANDUNG IN THE EARLY REVOLUTION, 1945-46: A SURVEY IN THE SOCIAL HISTORY OF THE INDONESIAN REVOLUTION, by John R. W. Smail. 1964. 169 pages. (Monograph)

*Number 34   AMERICAN REACTIONS TO INDONESIA'S ROLE IN THE BELGRADE CONFERENCE, by Frederick P. Bunnell. 1964. 86 pages. $2.00. (Interim Report)

*Number 35   PERANAKAN CHINESE POLITICS IN INDONESIA, by Mary F. Somers. 1964. 62 pages. (Interim Report)

*Number 36   THE PROVISIONAL CONSTITUTION OF THE REPUBLIC OF INDONESIA, by Prof. Dr. R. Supomo (Translated by Garth N. Jones). 1964. 104 pages. (Translation)

Number 37   MYTHOLOGY AND THE TOLERANCE OF THE JAVANESE, by Benedict R. Anderson. 1965. (Third Printing 1979) 77 pages. $5.00. (Monograph)

*Number 38   REPUBLIC OF INDONESIA CABINETS, 1945-1965 (With Post-Coup Supplement), compiled by Susan Finch and Daniel S. Lev. 1965. 66 pages. (Interim Report)

Number 39   PRELIMINARY CHECKLIST OF INDONESIAN IMPRINTS (1945-1949): WITH CORNELL UNIVERSITY HOLDINGS, by John M. Echols. 1965. 186 pages. $3.50. (Bibliography)

*Number 40   THE TRANSITION TO GUIDED DEMOCRACY: INDONESIAN POLITICS, 1957-1959, by Daniel S. Lev. 1966. 298 pages. (Monograph)

*Number 41   A GUIDE TO INDONESIAN PERIODICALS, 1945-1965, IN THE CORNELL UNIVERSITY LIBRARY, compiled by Yvonne Thung and John M. Echols. 1966. 151 pages. $3.50. (Bibliography)

*Number 42   PROBLEMS OF THE INDONESIAN INFLATION, by J. A. C. Mackie. 1967. 101 pages. (Monograph)

Number 43   STATE AND STATECRAFT IN OLD JAVA: A STUDY OF THE LATER MATARAM PERIOD, 16th TO 19th CENTURY, by Soemarsaid Moertono. 1968. (Revised edition 1981) 180 pages. $6.50. (Monograph)

Number 44   OUR STRUGGLE, by Sutan Sjahrir. Translated with an introduction by Benedict R. Anderson. 1968. 37 pages. $2.00. (Translation)

Number 45   INDONESIA ABANDONS CONFRONTATION, by Franklin B. Weinstein. 1969. 94 pages. $3.00. (Interim Report)

Number 46   THE ORIGINS OF THE MODERN CHINESE MOVEMENT IN INDONESIA, by Kwee Tek Hoay. Translated and edited by Lea E. Williams. 1969. 64 pages. $3.00. (Translation)

Number 47   PERSATUAN ISLAM: ISLAMIC REFORM IN TWENTIETH CENTURY INDONESIA, by Howard M. Federspiel. 1970. 250 pages. $7.50. (Monograph)

Number 48   NATIONALISM, ISLAM AND MARXISM, by Soekarno. With an introduction by Ruth T. McVey. 1970. 62 pages. $3.00. (Translation)

Number 49   THE FOUNDATION OF THE PARTAI MUSLIMIN INDONESIA, by K. E. Ward. 1970. 75 pages. $3.00. (Interim Report)

Number 50   SCHOOLS AND POLITICS: THE KAUM MUDA MOVEMENT IN WEST SUMATRA (1927-1933), by Taufik Abdullah. 1971. 257 pages. $6.00. (Monograph)

Number 51   THE PUTERA REPORTS: PROBLEMS IN INDONESIAN-JAPANESE WAR-TIME COOPERATION, by Mohammad Hatta. Translated with an introduction by William H. Frederick. 1971. 114 pages. $4.00. (Translation)

Number 52   A PRELIMINARY ANALYSIS OF THE OCTOBER 1, 1965, COUP IN INDONESIA (Prepared in January 1966), by Benedict R. Anderson, Ruth T. McVey (With the assistance of Frederick P. Bunnell). 1971. 162 pages. $6.00. (Interim Report)

Number 53   THE EURASIANS OF INDONESIA: A POLITICAL-HISTORICAL BIBLIOGRAPHY. Compiled by Paul W. van der Veur. 1971. 105 pages. $3.50. (Bibliography)

*Number 54   OLD JAVANESE (KAWI), by A. S. Teselkin, Translated and edited, with a preface by John M. Echols. 1972. 107 pages. $3.50. (Translation)

Number 55   REPORT FROM BANARAN: THE STORY OF THE EXPERIENCES OF A SOLDIER DURING THE WAR OF INDEPENDENCE, by Major General T. B. Simatupang. 1972. 186 pages. $6.50. (Translation)

Number 56   GOLKAR AND THE INDONESIAN ELECTIONS OF 1971, by Masashi Nishihara. 1972. 56 pages. $3.50. (Monograph)

Number 57   PERMESTA: HALF A REBELLION, by Barbara S. Harvey. 1977. 174 pages. $5.00. (Monograph)

Number 58   ADMINISTRATION OF ISLAM IN INDONESIA, by Deliar Noer. 1978. 82 pages. $4.50. (Monograph)

Number 59   BREAKING THE CHAINS OF OPPRESSION OF THE INDONESIAN PEOPLE: DEFENSE STATEMENT AT HIS TRIAL ON CHARGES OF INSULTING THE HEAD OF STATE, Bandung, June 7-10, 1979 by Heri Akhmadi. 1981. 201 pp. $8.75. (Translation)

Number 60   THE MINANGKABAU RESPONSE TO DUTCH COLONIAL RULE IN THE NINETEENTH CENTURY, by Elizabeth E. Graves. 1981. 157 pp. $7.50. (Monograph)

Number 61   SICKLE AND CRESCENT: THE COMMUNIST REVOLT OF 1926 IN BANTEN, by Michael C. Williams. 1982. 81 pages. $6.00. (Monograph)

Number 62   INTERPRETING INDONESIAN POLITICS: THIRTEEN CONTRIBUTIONS TO THE DEBATE, 1964-1981. Edited by Benedict Anderson and Audrey Kahin, with an Introduction by Daniel S. Lev. 1982. 180 pp. $9.00. (Interim Report)